CHRISTMAS 2013
THE YEAR OF THE ICE

PAIKIN
AND THE
PREMIERS

To DAD —

From

DOUG & FAMILY

PAIKIN AND THE PREMIERS

Personal Reflections on a Half Century of Ontario Leaders

STEVE PAIKIN

DUNDURN

A J. PATRICK BOYER BOOK

TORONTO

Editor: Cheryl Hawley
Design: Jesse Hooper
Printer: Webcom

Library and Archives Canada Cataloguing in Publication

Paikin, Steve, 1960-, author
    Paikin and the premiers : personal reflections on a half century of Ontario leaders / Steve Paikin.

"A J. Patrick Boyer book".
Includes bibliographical references and index.
Issued in print and electronic formats.
ISBN 978-1-4597-0958-4 (pbk.).--ISBN 978-1-4597-0960-7 (pdf).--ISBN 978-1-4597-0959-1 (epub)

    1. Premiers (Canada)--Ontario. 2. Ontario--Politics and government--20th century. 3. Ontario--Politics and government--21st century. I. Title.

FC3077.2.P35 2013   971.3'04   C2013-903907-4
                                         C2013-903908-2

2   3   4   5   17   16   15   14   13

 Conseil des Arts du Canada   Canada Council for the Arts   Canada   ONTARIO ARTS COUNCIL CONSEIL DES ARTS DE L'ONTARIO

We acknowledge the support of the **Canada Council for the Arts** and the **Ontario Arts Council** for our publishing program. We also acknowledge the financial support of the **Government of Canada** through the **Canada Book Fund** and **Livres Canada Books**, and the **Government of Ontario** through the **Ontario Book Publishing Tax Credit** and the **Ontario Media Development Corporation.**

Care has been taken to trace the ownership of copyright material used in this book. The author and the publisher welcome any information enabling them to rectify any references or credits in subsequent editions.

                                                                       J. Kirk Howard, President

The publisher is not responsible for websites or their content unless they are owned by the publisher.

Printed and bound in Canada.

VISIT US AT
Dundurn.com | @dundurnpress | Facebook.com/dundurnpress | Pinterest.com/dundurnpress

Dundurn	Gazelle Book Services Limited	Dundurn
3 Church Street, Suite 500	White Cross Mills	2250 Military Road
Toronto, Ontario, Canada	High Town, Lancaster, England	Tonawanda, NY
M5E 1M2	L41 4XS	U.S.A. 14150

For Francesca Grosso
The premier in my home

and

William G. Davis
Still "The Premier"
to so many Ontarians

Contents

INTRODUCTION

～

B ooks often come together in strange ways.
A few years ago, the former Progressive Conservative MP, now author and publisher, Patrick Boyer and I were swapping stories about our shared love of politics. During the course of that conversation, he pointed out something that hadn't occurred to me.

Throughout my three decades in journalism, I've had the opportunity to interview all eight premiers of Ontario. And seven years ago I wrote a book about former premier John P. Robarts, who won his first election in 1963. Patrick wondered: did I realize I therefore had a connection with every Ontario premier of the past half century?

No, I hadn't. But when you put it that way, I guess it's true.

"You must have a ton of interviews with all of these premiers in the archives at TVO," Patrick continued, referring to Ontario's provincial public broadcaster, created by former premier William Davis more than forty years ago.

"Absolutely," I replied.

"And with your knowledge of Robarts from the book you wrote, there's half a century of insider knowledge about how these guys did what they did. There's a book in there somewhere, Steve," he said.

You are now holding in your hands the ultimate outcome of that conversation. The more I thought about Patrick's words, the more I realized, yes, through my privileged perch, first as a Queen's Park reporter for CBC-TV, and then over twenty years hosting five different programs at TVO, I have indeed had the opportunity to get to know the last nine premiers of Ontario a little better than the average citizen. And as I look back on the transcripts of those interviews, I can't help but think that they somewhat reflect that "first draft of history" journalists try to write. The key issues of the day are all there, providing a window into what Ontarians cared about, obsessed about, fretted about, and delighted in at the time.

So, in this book, you'll find interviews I've done with:

- a man who became premier at the tender age of just forty-one, but who held on to the job longer than anyone else in the twentieth century: **William Grenville Davis**;
- the man who replaced him and sadly (for him) presided over the end of the forty-two-year-long Tory dynasty: **Frank Stuart Miller**;
- the man who became the first Liberal premier of Ontario in more than four decades: **David Robert Peterson**;
- the man who shocked the entire country by becoming Ontario's first and so far only NDP premier: **Robert Keith Rae** (who would go on to surprise his former fellow New Democrats a decade and a half later by running for the leadership of the federal Liberals);
- the man who did what hadn't been done in more than *seven* decades, by moving his party from third place to government in just one election: **Michael Deane Harris**;
- the man who helped Harris implement his *Common Sense Revolution*, then quit politics, only to come back by popular demand and become the first Conservative premier to fail to win an election in seven decades: **Ernest Larry Eves**;
- the man who seemed hopelessly out of the race to lead his party, coming fourth on both the first and second ballots, but who somehow won on the fifth ballot and became the first Liberal premier in Ontario in 128 years to win three consecutive elections: **Dalton James Patrick McGuinty, Jr.**; and
- the woman who broke *two* demographic barriers in one fell swoop in January 2013, and, as this book goes to

press, has one of the most oppressive "to do" lists of any new premier ever: **Kathleen O'Day Wynne**.

As for the ninth premier, I was only a year old when **John Parmenter Robarts** became what was then called "prime minister of Ontario." (His successor, William Davis, changed the title to "premier of Ontario," figuring Canada only needed one prime minister at a time.) So not only did I never interview Robarts, I never even saw him.

Fortunately, a former TVO colleague of mine once hosted a remarkably eclectic program called *The Education of Mike McManus*. Mike interviewed guests as varied as author Margaret Laurence, actor/director Warren Beatty, chicken king Colonel Harlan Sanders, and 1960s revolutionary Timothy Leary. And yes, he also interviewed John Robarts, long after Robarts left the premier's office. So we'll feature some of that interview in these pages.

Half a century of Ontario premiers: What did the successful ones have in common? Why did some of them fail to achieve their potential? Do Ontarians prefer their premiers to be moderate, bland, middle-of-the-roaders such as William Davis? Or fire-breathing revolutionaries such as Mike Harris? And why has *none* of them been able to do what Leslie Frost did five-and-a-half decades ago: win three consecutive majority governments? (Dalton McGuinty missed that achievement by just one seat in 2011.)

It's a good bet that those of you reading this book have, at one time or another, cursed the names of all of the premiers in it. Particularly in an era of twenty-four-hour-a-day cable news, social media gone wild, and internet users who, shall we say, never quite graduated from finishing school, to be premier of Canada's most populous province is to invite frequent and perpetual criticism, scorn, even hatred. One viewer even called me on a few occasions promising to kill Harris.

So it's worth trying to understand more about these leaders, and to find out what makes them special — because they are special. Of the tens of millions of people who have lived in the province of Ontario since Confederation, only twenty-five have ever been able to bear the appellation, premier of Ontario.

This book is my take on the last nine, who have made Ontario's past half century, as the song says, a place to stand and a place to grow.

Portions of the interviews have been edited for length and readability, but none of the context has been in any way affected.

John Parmenter Robarts
(1961–1971)

For a man who became known as the "Chairman of the Board," suggesting his elevation to the premier's office was somehow preordained, it's remarkable how the political career of Ontario's seventeenth premier almost ended before it began.

John Robarts seemed the ideal candidate when he first ran for politics in 1950. Handsome, with rugged good looks, bright, a Second World War naval hero, a lawyer married to his university sweetheart, Robarts seemed to have it all when he ran for London city council. And yet he won that first election by just seven votes. I often wonder how the course of Ontario history might be different had four people changed their votes in that municipal election. What if Robarts had lost? Would he have washed his hands of politics? Public life is replete with examples of so-called star candidates who tried to get elected, failed on the first attempt, then never tried again. Would Robarts have been one of them?

Fortunately for Ontario, it's a question that never needed asking. Robarts won his city council seat, and just a year later parlayed that into a seat in the Ontario Legislature. Thus began one of the most impressive political careers in Ontario history, and one of the most tragic personal stories of any politician at the same time.

Robarts' move to Toronto would begin a pattern in his life that remained the same for the next quarter century. His professional development, the stuff that really animated him, was in Ontario's capital city.

But his wife, unlike the wives of many other MPPs of the day, insisted on remaining back in the home constituency. And so Norah Robarts raised the couple's two adopted children in London.

It turned out not to be a great decision. The distance between Toronto and London may be only a couple of hours, but it may as well have been a couple of light years. The Robartses increasingly spent less and less time together. The result: Norah took to the bottle and John took to Toronto's nightlife.

But we're getting ahead of ourselves here.

Robarts began to make a name for himself at Queen's Park. He won re-election in 1955, against a Liberal candidate named Clarence Peterson whose son David would become another premier from London thirty years later. And when Robarts won again in the 1959 election, Premier Leslie Frost appointed him minister of education. In those days, education was like the Ministry of Health today: it had all the money. It was a meteoric rise for the London North MPP, and placed him in an ideal position should he want to contest the Progressive Conservative Party leadership after Frost's retirement.

Indeed, Robarts wanted to be leader. Despite his wife's admonition that she never wanted to be married to a "man of destiny," that's exactly what Robarts was becoming. His chief competitor for the premier's office was Ontario's attorney-general, whose surname was almost the same.

Kelso Roberts represented a downtown Toronto riding, had a ton of support on Bay Street, much more experience than Robarts, and had already run for the party leadership against Leslie Frost back in 1949. He came third in that contest. He was rightly judged the favourite to succeed Frost at the leadership contest at Varsity Arena in Toronto on October 25, 1961. And indeed, the attorney-general led all seven candidates after the first ballot votes were counted. But he was only seven votes ahead of the minister of education. On the second ballot Robarts passed Roberts, and led on every successive ballot. Nevertheless, it took a staggering *six* ballots for Progressive Conservative delegates to decide on Robarts. The kingmaker was the third-place candidate, Robert Macaulay, who, on the advice of his campaign manager, threw his support to Robarts before the final ballot. That campaign manager's name: William Davis.

Robarts went on to become one of Ontario's most important premiers. He steered the provincial ship during what may have been its most prosperous decade ever. The 1960s saw fantastic nearly double-digit growth rates annually in Ontario. Revenue poured into the provincial treasury. And the Robarts government used that revenue to build, build, build.

We got several new universities including York in Toronto, Laurentian in Sudbury, Lakehead in Thunder Bay, Trent in Peterborough, and Brock in St. Catharines. We got an entire community college system, whose development was overseen by Robarts' minister of education William Davis. The Robarts government commissioned the building of the province's first nuclear generating station in Pickering. It anticipated the suburban growth around Toronto and thus created GO Transit to serve increasing numbers of commuters. Robarts thought science ought to be fun, so they built the Ontario Science Centre in Toronto and Science North in Sudbury. While returning to Toronto from a meeting in Niagara-on-the-Lake, he noticed the province's picturesque Niagara Escarpment, a biosphere recognized by international authorities as having global significance. And so he created the Niagara Escarpment Commission to protect our "crown jewels" as he called them.

Robarts thought kids from low-income families ought to have a place to play in the summer, so his government created Ontario Place on Toronto's lakeshore. And, as a former minister of education who understood the importance of learning to Ontario's future development, the Robarts government embarked on an unprecedented public-school building program. Frequently, he and his minister, Bill Davis, would open three new schools in a single day.

John Robarts was perhaps the first premier since Confederation to explore Quebec's relationship with the rest of Canada. First Ministers' Conferences, which would become commonplace, were unheard of in Robarts' time. But he called all the premiers together for the "Confederation of Tomorrow" conference at the top of the newly built Toronto-Dominion Centre, and had the proceedings televised. Robarts watched as bombs blew up in mailboxes in Quebec. He had a genuine thirst to better understand the changes happening in the province next door.

Some attributed that unusual characteristic (for a unilingual anglophone) to Robarts' wartime experience. His bunkmate was a francophone.

When the shells started falling, Robarts couldn't help but notice that everyone was in the same boat now.

"It was more than just metaphorical," his friend and chief economist Ian Macdonald would tell me more than half a century after the fact.

But after nearly a decade at the helm of Ontario Inc., John Robarts had had it. He had visibly aged a lot, was significantly overweight, and his knees were bothering him from all those years of university football. So with two majority governments and two decades of public life under his belt, he left the premiership and moved seamlessly into the corporate world.

Public life would beckon again. Both his successor, William Davis, and Prime Minister Pierre Trudeau would appoint him to chair task forces examining some of the most relevant issues of the day: reforming Metropolitan Toronto's municipal government, and national unity. And it looked like the next chapter of Robarts' life would follow up success with more success.

Here's TVO host Mike McManus' interview with Ontario's seventeenth premier in 1980, nearly a decade after he ceased being the last prime minister of Ontario.

MR. MCMANUS: Mr. Robarts, during the bilingual crisis in the skies, Mr. Trudeau likened it in seriousness to the conscription issue. You gave a talk in which you somehow calmed the waters by telling us that such tensions had always been a part of our history.

MR. ROBARTS: Yes, that's quite correct. I didn't agree with Mr. Trudeau's assessment. I thought he gave it much too much importance. I thought the conscription issue was much more serious than bilingualism in the skies, although the bilingualism-in-the-sky issue really was, I suppose, a polarization of a feeling; it wasn't the incident itself that was of major importance.

But, as a participant for some few years and as a student of Canadian history, we are always in a turmoil about something. Now, that doesn't mean that these turmoils aren't important and it doesn't mean that you can take them lightly or that you can disregard them. But the mere fact of a crisis, per se, is a pretty normal situation.

Q. Do you think that kind of tension has had some effect on the character of the country, the formation of the country, the identity of the country?

A. I personally think it has. I think our people, our Canadian people, are well able to deal with crises. You know, you can have screaming and yelling in one sector about something or other and you can move over someplace else and you'll find that people aren't really that concerned about it at all, so that we are, how shall I put it, crisis proof?

Q. Crisis proof. Well, we've got a new crisis to talk about, Mr. Robarts. In Quebec they're calling the election of René Lévesque and his party to power [in 1976] a new page in history. I wonder if you think of it as something very new or just more of the same?

A. No, it's not more of the same. I don't really think it is. But it's an extremely complex situation that is going to take a good deal of sorting out. For instance, this morning's *Globe and Mail* carries two statements, one by Jacques Parizeau, who probably will be minister of finance, saying that he's going to squeeze everything that he can out of Ottawa, which is really just heaping gasoline on the flames of the resentment — if there is such — in the rest of Canada to say that, before he separates he's going to get everything he can squeeze out. That's not what you'd call a tactful approach to a negotiating problem.

On the same front page is a story about Mr. Lévesque doing his best to calm everyone down, to make people feel that they really aren't going to do terrible things and so on. I suppose this is natural in the first few days until the thing gels a little bit. But it's a new situation. Mr. Parizeau has been an active player in this game for some considerable number of years. I recall when he was an adviser to Mr. [Jean] Lesage in the early sixties. And at that time, he was militant and obviously still is. You see, many people voted for René Lévesque because René Lévesque said, "Look, you're not voting for separatism when you vote for me. You're voting first to change the government. Then we'll deal with the separatist issue after that and you'll have a chance to express your opinion in another vote." Now, that's pretty clever tactics because there was a lot of resentment against Mr. [Robert] Bourassa for a host of reasons, which are not relevant to you or me at this stage of the game; they were local.

So René Lévesque did win, but now he's got this dichotomy in his own party. He's preaching downgrading separatism, but he has men like Parizeau who don't feel that way at all. Now, it's going to be very interesting to see what political skill he has in holding this thing together.

Q. And to bail Quebec out, which is Mr. Lévesque's first mandate as you said, he's going to need a lot of money, probably a lot of federal assistance. If you were in Ottawa and Lévesque was coming for money and assistance to do his first mandate, to get the province back on its feet, do you think the federal government should try to buy their loyalty?

A. Listen, you don't buy loyalty from anybody. You can try but you'll never succeed. That's number one. You don't buy loyalty. It's not for sale. You create it in some fashion. So when you use that term, "buy loyalty," my immediate reaction is you're starting a losing game before you start. You're starting out to be a loser.

On the other hand, if there are things that Canada can do to help one part of Canada, in this instance Quebec, then I think they must be given consideration and we must keep our temper, even in the light of some intemperate remarks that will come from the other side. And there will be intemperate remarks that come from all sides before this is completed — you know that — because there are intemperate men on both sides and there are men who feel so strongly that they will be intemperate to you and me when they might not be intemperate to themselves in what they will say.

We're to require a high degree of self-control and fairly critical analysis to find out where the real facts are and where the emotion disappears and so on. But I don't like the whole concept of buying anything in my own country.

Q. Would you be saying then that the federal government should, as far as financial assistance is concerned, give to Quebec the same consideration as they would give for similar problems in the Maritimes or anywhere in Canada and disregard —

A. Where the need is, quite — sure.

Q. — disregard the threat of separatism?

A. That's right.

Q. That's what you would say?

A. Mm-hmm.

Q. A political writer in the *Star* wrote we should seriously start and plan now for the possibility of Quebec separation so that, in the event that it takes place, it will take place amicably and not with hatred, which would be destructive to both sides. Do you think we should be thinking along those lines at this stage?

A. I don't think we can afford not to. I don't think Quebec will separate. I mean, it's not my belief and that belief is based on what I know about Canada from my own experience. I don't think Quebec will separate.

On the other hand, I'm a pragmatist. I'm a practical man and I would say that I accept the fact I could be wrong, and anyway, how is one to have an opinion about separation per se without looking at it and looking at the ramifications of it?

I mean, what does it mean to John Robarts sitting in Toronto? I don't know at this stage of the game, completely. I know that it's a mixture of a lot of emotional feelings. A lot of my own life, my family's life, my background, the fact I'm Canadian, it's my country and it's my country as a whole. My Canada is not Ontario.

So there's all that aspect of it which is emotional. And loyalty, as you mentioned already.

And then there's the future of myself and my children and my family and the way I like to live and the objectives I may have for Canadian citizenship.... And then there are all the economic problems. But just because it's complex doesn't mean that you don't have to look at it and try and sort out the complexities.

I think when they get down to it, when they really, really get down to it, they won't get a better deal any place anywhere than they get in the Confederation that is called Canada.

Q. And is it a fundamental belief in the reasonableness of the average French Canadian in those facts that makes you feel in the end they won't leave us?

A. Well, I don't know. Historians have said that great revolutionaries were never economists. You know, revolutionary zeal doesn't feed on the statistics of foreign trade and the balance of payments. I think what does, when you get down to that, is how much do you pay for a loaf of bread and a quart of milk and the pound of hamburger and so on? Is it available to you and at what price, and have you a society which permits you to earn enough to participate in the things you want from life?

I can remember saying about fifteen years ago that I didn't see many problems in the Province of Quebec that an increase of 15 percent in the standard of living wouldn't solve. Now that was a great big oversimplification, but there's an element of truth in it.

Q. In 1960 the Quiet Revolution began in Quebec with [Premier] Jean Lesage. You became leader of the Ontario Conservative Party in 1961. During your time, you were instrumental in forming the Confederation of Tomorrow conference. What were you trying to achieve with that conference?

A. Well, we were having some deep arguments between the province and the federal government and, as you will recall, it was Confederation [anniversary] year. And it seemed to me that every conference we had in Ottawa eventually degenerated into an argument about money. So part of the idea of the Confederation of Tomorrow conference was that there would be no discussion of finances there, at all.

It was really an attempt to let everybody in Canada understand what the rest of Canada other than themselves was looking for out of Canada and out of the Confederation. And there was no discussion of money, no discussion of sharing taxes or grants; money was banned. And some very interesting things came out of that conference in terms of what people wanted in various parts of Canada. That conference did reveal that there are differences in what interests people. I can recall going and seeing Danny Johnson, who was then the premier of Quebec, before I ever called the conference. I went to see him and I said, "Danny, I've got this idea." And the way I phrased it to him was I said, "I'll give you the biggest soapbox in Canada to tell the people of Canada what's really disturbing you and how you interpret the ferment in your own part of Canada."

Q. So, among other things, you were trying to establish more deeply the French fact in Canada?

A. Oh, quite. Certainly. And — well, establish it? More than that. I wanted others to understand it because it's quite recognizable, it's quite legitimate. And there's no reason why it can't exist and survive in our country as a Confederation.

Q. Do you think because of your efforts you achieved what you wanted to?

A. Well, now, look, in the political game in this country, I learned a long time ago there are no definitive answers to what I call the great Canadian problems. I achieved, at least partially, what I was after in that it did give us a chance to discuss and talk, and I found out afterward that wherever I went in Canada there were people in Nanaimo and there were people in Dartmouth and Yarmouth, Nova Scotia, I'd go down there fishing and people would stop me in the street. In other words, all of Canada saw that conference, all of Canada.

It's a great tribute to television, really. And in that respect, I thought it was successful. If we all try, if we don't take huge positions and hug our prejudices to our bosoms and, the other thing is too, and I feel very, very strongly about this and I recall making a speech ten or twelve years ago in which I said, "The time will come when you will have to decide —" and I was sort of speaking to Mr. Average Canadian, "— when you'll have to decide how much you really love your country, how much you are prepared to sacrifice to keep it together. You can't go on forever complaining. Sometime you've got say, 'Look, it's going to cost me something to be a Canadian, to live the way we live, to be different from our great neighbours to the south and our neighbours in Europe and in Asia and for this I must pay. How much am I prepared to pay?'"

This is the moment of truth, and these crises seem to me to bring us to this point where people have to really get down to it, stop the rhetoric and decide in your own heart, what does it mean to you? What sacrifice will you make to keep it?

Q. Why don't you come back into politics? Do you feel the urge at all to?

A. No. I left for what I considered valid reasons and I have a happy life now. I enjoy what I'm doing. I find that I have an opportunity to come on this show and express some opinions to you and, through you, to the people of Canada.

Q. No way that that love or fascination which attracted you back in, what, 1950 could get hold of you again?

A. Well, of course, you know that if you've been a practising politician it's a very complicated matter. You don't just walk in and out of politics. The whole structure of parties and choosing leaders and all that sort of thing. And timing is everything in the political world and you have opportunities at certain times that — that you have no power of control. I once told [journalist] Christina Newman in an interview that I never closed any doors completely, and I don't think anyone ever does. But that doesn't mean I'm trying to keep one open.

Q. You entered politics in 1951. Why?

A. Well, once again a variety of reasons. The game has always fascinated me. It's a highly competitive performance and I started running for little elected offices when I was in high school. So the game itself.

Q. You love the game?

A. I really enjoy the theory of government. I enjoy the art of government, which is different from politics. That's why I enjoy doing this thing I'm doing for Metropolitan Toronto [chairing a task force on governance]. Some people would find it utterly dull, I suppose, but it is an exercise in the theory and the art of government. How does our society organize itself to keep friction at a minimum and keep personal freedom at the highest level. You know, that's sort of the art of the thing. So I enjoy that. That's another reason.

Q. You hate packaging of politicians, Mr. Robarts?

A. Yes, I do.

Q. Why?

A. Well, because the minute you're packaged you're not you. You're what somebody else thinks you should be or wants you to be for their purposes.

Q. Did people put pressure on you to package you?

A. Oh, quite certainly.

Q. And you refused?

A. Yes, that's right. Well, I don't think that that's what I was elected to do.

Q. Have you noticed any change as an outsider about the style of government from the style that you — or the way government is run?

A. Yes. I can follow changes through right back to my predecessors.

Q. Are you critical of the changes?

A. No, because it's unfortunately very logical. Let me just give you one small example of how — we use this word *complex*, but it's the only word to use. For instance, when my grandfather wanted water, he went out and dug a well. I have to find a way to tie into a $25-million pipeline.

If my grandfather was ill, he went to bed in his own house and the doctor came with a little black bag and treated him. Now I go to a multimillion-dollar hospital. I get a team of technicians and doctors, eight or ten strong, with probably a million dollars tied up in their education, working on me.

Now, there's nothing you and I can do about that complex life, and our society just gets more complex and, thus, government gets a lot more complex, too.

Q. You don't think government leads the way in too much bureaucracy or overcomplicating?

A. I think there's too much bureaucracy, vastly too much. There's too much regulation. I think there's too much idea that we need government to do all kinds of things for us to make sure that the bananas are fresh. Can't I go into a fruit store and say, "That's a bad banana, I won't buy it?" Do we have to have a regulation that provides a standard of banana and an inspector to come around and see that that store has the standard of banana? This kind of bureaucracy drives me wild and all done to help me.

Q. In 1971 you left politics. Was the period immediately following your leaving difficult?

A. Yes, it was. I think I was in Europe five times in the first year, more or less to keep busy. It's a very abrupt transition. On the 28th of February of 1971 I had a personal staff of thirty-odd. One day later, on the 1st of March, I had one secretary and the phone didn't ring because I was not conducting cabinet meetings, I was not seeing delegations, and I was sort of standing, just sitting there looking at a wall. And that takes a little getting used to — but not too much.

Q. With the hindsight and the experience you have now, if you were starting all over again in politics, would you do it differently?

A. It sounds trite, it sounds Pollyanna-ish, but I would rather be a participant than a spectator. I enjoyed participating in the function of government and the life of my country. I think some of this stemmed from five-and-a-half years of war, where you were a cog and you were taking orders and you put your life on the line as a result of decisions made by men thousands of miles away who didn't even know you existed.

You kick around like that for a while and then you say, "Now, I am going to," and I think that this is a very prevalent feeling among our people today. The whole citizen participation movement is a desire on the part of people who are better educated, more knowledgeable, have more access to information, to participate in the decisions that are influencing their lives. And I think this is a very obvious thing to recognize in our society, in 1976, that wasn't there to the same extent in 1956.

Q. So the charismatic leader may be coming to an end.

A. [laughs] Never. Not as long as you have elections.

As successful as Robarts' public and corporate lives were, his private life was another story. After announcing his retirement from the premiership at the end of 1970, he asked his wife one more time to move to Toronto. After all, his career — founding partner at a new law firm, more than a dozen corporate directorships — was in Ontario's capital city, not London. But Norah refused. And so Robarts, in a move that shocked London society, split up with her. It was the sad but logical conclusion to a relationship that had become increasingly strained and remote over the years.

Robarts would marry again — a sexy American divorcee twenty-eight years his junior. He met her at a club in downtown Toronto. She didn't have a clue who he was. Despite the age gap they were a successful, loving couple. Katherine Sickafuse did all the things Norah never would — go hunting and fishing, hang out with Robarts' friends, and enjoy Toronto society life.

But on their first anniversary, Robarts' son Tim killed himself. He wrote a twelve-page, single-spaced suicide note, filled with humour, blaming no one but concluding he was only meant to live on Planet Earth for twenty-one years. His troubled life, filled with illegal drugs, was over.

A few years later, Robarts' first wife, a lonely and alcoholic Norah, choked on a piece of meat while eating a TV dinner alone at home, and died. The cause: asphyxiation.

Premier John Robarts' final resting place at St. James' Cemetery in downtown Toronto. This picture was taken on October 18, 2012, on the thirtieth anniversary of his death.

Robarts' headstone, plus the new gold-coloured marker the Ontario Heritage Trust is placing at the gravesites of all deceased premiers.

In 1981 Robarts had a massive stroke on a flight to Houston. He remained in a Texas hospital for a month, trying to recover. When he returned to Toronto, he was a shadow of his former self. He could no longer do any of the things that gave his life meaning: hunt, fish, read, belt back the scotches with the boys, or make love to his beautiful wife.

He told his daughter that was no way for the "Chairman of the Board" to live, that he'd give himself a year to recover but if he didn't ...

Robarts was good to his word. The depression, his body wasting away, it all became too much. And in the wee small hours of the morning of October 18, 1982, he walked into the shower stall on the second floor of his Rosedale home and took with him the shotgun the Ontario Progressive Conservative Party gave him as a gift for all his years of public service. And he swallowed his gun.

I never met or even saw John Robarts.

I wish I had.

WILLIAM GRENVILLE DAVIS
(1971–1985)

~

The pipe. The dull suits. The Brampton jokes. An uncanny ability to remember everyone's name. Utterly comfortable in his own skin. Scrums with reporters that would go on and on and on, and yet when they were over we'd look at each other and ask, "What did he say? Did he say anything?"

Had he wanted to, he could have waltzed to a *fifth* consecutive election victory in 1985 without breaking a sweat. Instead, at the height of his popularity, he left public life after more than a quarter of a century.

That's the Bill Davis everyone remembers.

But that's not who Bill Davis was when his premiership started in 1971. Davis found himself at Maple Leaf Gardens, in the wee hours of the morning, waiting for the fourth ballot results to be announced, at a leadership convention in which he was supposed to be the inevitable victor.

After all, the MPP for Peel North had been John Robarts' minister of education for eight and a half years, at a time when education was like health is today — that ministry had all the money. Although Robarts was careful not to tip his hand, Davis clearly appeared to be the anointed one, leading on every ballot, at the tender age of forty-one.

But most of the sharp young hotshots of the Tory backrooms were backing another contender, Allan Lawrence, who was an inferior candidate to Davis but had a much better campaign team. Legends such as Norman Atkins and Dalton Camp were with Lawrence. So it was a shock when the results were announced and Bill Davis discovered he had won by only forty-four votes out of nearly 1,600 cast. That was far too close for comfort.

Davis' first move was brilliant and would be a harbinger of how he would do business over his next fourteen years as premier, while managing to command considerable loyalty from much of the Progressive Conservative Party's stalwarts. He immediately got together with Al Lawrence's campaign team, and told the smart young bucks they were now working for him. And thus, the Big Blue Machine was born.

Frankly, Davis needed their help. Compared to the ruggedly handsome "management man" Robarts, Davis looked like the outgoing premier's son, hardly a classically strong leader (although admittedly an "old forty-one years old"), smoked a cigar (the pipe hadn't arrived yet), had a technocratic rather than warm air about himself, and was far more introverted than his predecessor. Fortunately for Davis, the PC Party had been in power for twenty-eight straight years, so its roots and organizational prowess were a huge asset. Furthermore, Davis campaigned on some very progressive ideas for a Conservative of more than four decades ago. For example, he said cities weren't just for cars but also for people and public transit too. And he promised to create North America's first ministry of the environment. And so, Davis won his first election as leader on October 21, 1971, even bettering Robarts' count by nine seats.

He would go on to win four consecutive elections, although the middle two were only minority governments. But by 1981 the Davis transformation was complete. He was finally completely comfortable in the job, and no longer felt in the shadow of his predecessor, John Robarts, whom he worshipped. He was now increasingly seen as a senior statesman in Canada, and would soon play an indispensable role in repatriating the Constitution with an accompanying Charter of Rights and Freedoms. Davis recaptured the Tories' majority government in 1981, something friends said was an important achievement for him.

No one ever accused Bill Davis of running an exciting government. Or a bold and daring government. I'm not sure he ever actually said this, but the line attributed to him, describing his governing philosophy, was: "Never put off 'til tomorrow what you can avoid doing altogether." Or there was this one: "You never get in trouble for the speeches you don't give." And, of course, the classic — when asked in a scrum at the

Legislature by the *Globe and Mail's* Hugh Winsor why he ran such a boring, bland government, Davis brilliantly summed up his governing philosophy with two words: "Bland works."

Boy, did it ever.

But for a man who prized his steady-as-she-goes image, Davis also took some wildly bold and controversial steps that, even nearly thirty years after leaving office, political observers still debate: full public funding for the Roman Catholic school system, stopping the Spadina Expressway into downtown Toronto, the creation of regional governments, rent controls, an expanded human rights code, expanded French-language services, and buying the Suncor oil company. Most of the things on that list infuriated the party's rural, small-c conservative base. But Davis did them anyway, taking the political heat but keeping the PCs relevant in urban Ontario because he also saw an increasing multiculturalism spreading across the province, and tried to warn the dinosaurs in his party to warm up to it, or else.

And so, it was with all of that on his mind that Davis found himself on the 1984 Thanksgiving holiday weekend, huddled with his family and close advisors, agonizing over the fork in the road he found himself approaching. Most observers thought he'd take advantage of his sky-high popularity and call the snap election that would keep the four-decades-long PC dynasty alive. Instead, Davis confounded everyone.

He announced his retirement.

"He'd have wiped the floor with both of us had he decided to run," recalls then-NDP leader Bob Rae, referring to himself and Liberal leader David Peterson.

I remember attending Davis' farewell news conference in the media studio at Queen's Park. The sense of occasion filled the room. Conservative Party onlookers cried. So did Davis, who had a hard time getting through his prepared remarks.

Davis had been premier since I was ten years old. He was the only premier of Ontario I had had any memory of, and it's not an exaggeration to say many of us wondered how the party would survive his departure. As it turned out, it couldn't.

I will confess to having a soft spot for Bill Davis, ever since he stepped out of the spotlight. But I'm hardly alone in that view. One day, while walking on a beach on Manitoulin Island in the late 1990s, I bumped into a former senior official with the Ontario Secondary School Teachers' Federation. We reminisced about some of the education wars that I covered, and that this official was a part of, during Davis' time in office. We then talked about the problems the teachers were currently having with the Mike Harris government.

"Little did we know," this OSSTF'er said, referring to Davis' time, "that we'd look back at those years as if they were Camelot."

After winning the premiership in 1990, Bob Rae often called Davis for advice. Despite being on the receiving end of many of Davis' barbs in the Legislature, Rae had and still has a unique affection for Davis, unlike anything I've ever seen between two men who wanted the same job and competed hard against each other for it.

The affection for the man is everywhere. When John Tory held a news conference to announce his departure from provincial politics (in the same Queen's Park media studio where Davis announced his retirement), the former PC leader managed to get through his speech and some Q&A from the media without breaking down, until the subject of Bill Davis came up.

Thirty years earlier, Tory had worked for Davis as his principal secretary, but eventually the relationship between the two men became more akin to father and son. Now Tory was leaving politics because of his failure to win a by-election designed to get him back into the Legislature after losing the 2007 election. When I asked Tory at the news conference whether he'd had a chance to talk to Davis about his departure from politics, Tory's affection for his mentor came bursting forth. He took a long pause, looked down, started to cry, and you got the sense that Tory was more upset about disappointing his mentor and hero than losing the by-election that forced him out of public life.

One should never confuse Davis' calm manner for a lack of fire. He was an intense competitor (witness his frightening shouting match with Liberal Leader Robert Nixon during the 1975 leaders' debate). He wanted desperately to win everything he participated in. But friend and adversary alike couldn't help but acknowledge his fundamental decency.

One day, several years ago, I pointed out to TVO's chief executive officer Lisa de Wilde that we had several things at the provincial broadcaster named after important people in our history, but nothing with Bill Davis' name on it. I thought it was time to rectify that, given that it was Davis who created TVO, nurtured it during his time as premier, and continued to put in a good word for the place regardless of which party occupied the premier's office.

"How about we name the studio where we do *The Agenda* after him?" I asked.

Lisa loved the idea, grabbed the ball, and, to her great credit, ran with it. She got the name change through the board of directors, then invited Davis and then-premier Dalton McGuinty to come to TVO to speak at the official renaming ceremony. McGuinty brought the house down when he admitted during his speech that when his mother hears the word *premier* she thinks of Davis, not her own son.

I had been bugging Davis for years to come to our studio and do an interview about his life. With the studio now bearing his name, and the fiftieth anniversary of his first election victory (which almost didn't happen) approaching, Davis finally relented. On June 11, 2009, he arrived at the television network he created, at the corner of Yonge and Eglinton in midtown Toronto, to talk about his remarkable run in public life.

Mr. Davis being interviewed by the author in the newly named "William G. Davis Studio" at TVO. The date was June 11, 2009, the fiftieth anniversary of Mr. Davis' first election victory as the MPP for Peel.

* * *

STEVE PAIKIN: And joining us here at TVO in the William G. Davis Studio is William G. Davis, eighteenth premier of the province of Ontario and finally in that chair, which I've been trying to get you into for months and months and months.

MR. DAVIS: Well, no, *longer* than that, but go ahead.

Q. That is true. Let's go through a bit of a resumé here of your political career and then I'm going to come back with some questions.

Mr. Davis, it was fifty years ago today that you got elected for the first time, June 11, 1959. You were elected the backbench MPP for Peel riding. In 1962 you became the minister of education for almost ten years. As the minister, you oversaw the building of an unprecedented number of new schools, new universities, the community college system.

In 1971, you became the eighteenth premier of Ontario and won four consecutive elections: in 1971, a majority, a minority in '75, a minority in '77.

A. Less of a minority in '77.

Q. Yes. And then a recaptured majority in 1981. As premier you, of course, oversaw the repatriation of the Constitution, the Charter of Rights and Freedoms, full public funding for separate schools, you stopped the Spadina Expressway, and you created this TV station in which we sit today.

You left politics in 1985, became a counsel at Torys, sitting on numerous boards, and, just to prove nobody's perfect, you love the Toronto Argonauts.

Now, let's go back to fifty years ago today. What do you remember about that night?

A. Well, listen, I remember so much it's going to take us the whole hour, and you —

Q. You haven't got the whole hour.

A. Oh, I don't have the whole hour?

Q. We have other people who want to come in, too.

A. That's too bad. I can go back to that time. It was a very difficult election for me.

Q. You almost lost.

A. I almost lost. I won the nomination in December '58. Tom Kennedy had held the riding from 1919 till '59, except for three years, and it should have been a shoo-in. But then somebody in Ottawa by the name of John George Diefenbaker decided to cancel the Avro Arrow.

Q. Which was in your riding?

A. Right in the great village of Malton. Fourteen-thousand employees, the majority of whom lived in my riding. As a result, listen, I can recall the only big meeting the Liberals ever had in that riding up to that point, who was the guest speaker? The leader of the opposition? No. A test pilot for the Arrow. That's who brought the multitudes out.

Q. So you won by about 1,200 votes that night?

A. Yes. And three and a half years later, we won by some 13,000. In the interim, John Pallett, our Tory federal member, lost, as did John Hamilton in York West and Sandy Best in Halton, all over the Arrow.

Q. I'm told that after Mr. Diefenbaker pulled the plug on the Avro Arrow, you went to see Leslie Frost, the premier, and you said to him something like, "This is going to cause me a lot of difficulty," and Mr. Frost then picked up the phone and called the prime minister in your presence. What happened on that phone call?

A. I can't use the same language as occurred when he hung up after the phone call. I'd always had Mr. Frost on a bit of a pedestal and in his call to the prime minister of this country he was not totally respectful. In other words, he sort of was semi-critical. In fact, he was quite critical of what he had done.

Q. Did he swear?

A. He used language that we didn't use in our dining room at home, yes.

Q. Now, you were twenty-nine when you won that election.

A. Yes.

Q. And, of course, the guy who you replaced had been premier [Tom Kennedy in 1949]. Did you have any thoughts at that time, at age twenty-nine, that, "Maybe I too could be premier some day"?

A. No. Except the guy who was covering it for the *Cooksville Review* had a picture at Tom Kennedy's eightieth birthday party with Frost and myself and underneath he wrote, "Past, Present and Future," but he was biased.

Q. So maybe it did occur to you then.

A. No, it occurred to him.

Q. It occurred to him. Okay. Let's move forward. You won a big majority in 1971, after you took over from John Robarts, but four years later you almost lost the government entirely. You survived with a minority and I want to know what was the biggest adjustment from going from senior cabinet minister — you know, you were education, which was like health today; they had all the money back then — senior minister to being the premier. The biggest adjustment?

A. Well, it wasn't that great an adjustment because I had been part of the cabinet for nine years. The people I asked to join me in cabinet when I became the leader of the party, a number of them had been in cabinet so I knew them all well.

I think the biggest adjustment was realizing that when the election came, I had responsibility not only for the ministers and the members of caucus but all of the other candidates who were running for us. That added a burden, no question about it.

The adjustment in terms of the operation of the government? Not too great, because I had been there.

Q. But you were forty-one when you became premier. Is that too young?

A. Yes, but I was old for my age.

Q. You were old for your age. You didn't feel too young at forty-one?

A. No, I didn't feel too young. Listen, if I felt too young — I was minister of education some nine years before that. Listen, the only thing I had taught was Sunday school. And yet we had I think probably nine of the greatest years in the history of education in this province. Not to do with me, but it was growth, enthusiasm, people wanting to participate. I mean, that's when TVO was created. I mean, that is what has given you a great career opportunity.

Q. I owe it all to you, don't I?

A. Yes, no question about that. And I had to pay you a dollar, as I recall, on a certain bet on the Argonauts.

Q. Well, like I said, nobody's perfect.

A. Nobody's perfect.

Q. I bet Ti-Cats, you bet Argos, and you lost that time.

A. Yes. I'm willing to bet again for the season, but we won't mention that on the program.

Q. We'll hold that off, for now.

A. Yes, okay.

Q. There's another anniversary of sorts tomorrow. Twenty-five years ago tomorrow, you stood up in the Legislature and announced that you were, if I may put it this way, repudiating your previously held views on separate school funding and were, in fact, going to offer full public funding to separate schools all the way to the end of Grade 13.

Can you give us any further insight today as to why you did that?

A. Yes. And repudiation is not the right word. I mean, you're very good with the English language. We're all entitled to have a change of mind, but it wasn't a repudiation.

In '71, it was very firm, no extension. I'd had the bishops' brief. John Robarts, when he left, said, "I've left you with the bishops' brief and [the] Spadina [Expressway], two simple problems." And we went through a process.

People forget something though. In the mid-sixties, I was the minister of education when the foundation tax plan was passed. You don't remember it, but that was the plan that put the separate schools on a much more equal basis up to the end of Grade 8 with respect to funding — the commercial assessment. That was a step that really, I think, entrenched the separate schools certainly at the end of Grade 8.

Then we make Grades 9 and 10, early in the '70s, and actually it left us with 11, 12, and 13.

Q. So this was more a continuation of your thinking.

A. It was, yes. And, you know, you had to really come to a decision, "Are we going to have a single school system?" which, incidentally, a lot of people would have supported, or, "Are you going to be fair and equitable with what was the public separate school system?"

Now, you've heard the story about the young people from [Cardinal] Léger [Catholic School] coming while I was cutting the lawn, et cetera?

Q. Yes. On Main Street in Brampton.

A. On Main Street in Brampton, asking me, "How come we don't have to pay a fee if we want to go to Brampton Centennial (but we do if we go to Catholic school for grade thirteen?) And I had no answer. I couldn't go to the British North America Act and the all the rest of it. For them it wasn't fair.

I had already made up my mind that the time had come; this population in the province was such that I thought it would be reasonably acceptable and I knew it was, in conscience, the right thing to do.

Q. Here's the follow-up then: Larry Grossman, one of your former ministers, once told me that you, having made this decision, that he thought you were the only person who could — *sell* is not the right word, but get it through, without society going through upheaval.

And that when you decided to retire in 1984 and Frank Miller took over, and Frank Miller obviously was not the guy to get it through, that meant trouble.

Do you ever wish you had hung on, stayed to fight that '85 election so that the kinds of upheaval that did eventually take place might not have happened?

A. Yes, the upheavals are exaggerated. The reality, there should not have been any upheaval. I mean, I saw the figures. I knew that a percentage of the people of Ontario were not enthused. That has been the case, it may be still the case today, but I think the numbers are much lower.

I could have stayed, but I was relatively comfortable that the policy was right. Every minister of the Crown voted for it — we didn't have a vote — were all supportive in cabinet except one; I won't tell you who it was.

Q. I can tell you who it was.

A. Yes. Well, you may know who it was, and I said to him —

Q. His name is Norm Sterling.

A. Yes. And I said, "Norman, if this is a fundamental matter of principle for you, I will accept your resignation." Now, listen, this is a lot of years ... I haven't had that letter yet.

Q. No, he didn't resign.

A. I'm teasing.

Q. He's still there. He celebrated his thirty-second year in the Legislature a couple of days ago.

A. Yes. He's a great member. A great member, no question about it.

Q. But he voted against it.

A. Yes, he — I'm not sure he voted against it. He may have been absent; he wasn't in favour of it, in cabinet. That much I do recall. Yes.

Q. So no regrets about not sticking around to fight that and get that through?

A. No. Because it should not have been a significant issue and, if you look at the figures, it wasn't until about the last two weeks. That is suddenly when it became an issue.

The OSSTF sent out a letter to the candidates. The candidate in our riding, a very nice young man, said, "Yes, I will review this." I think there was some question, "Would you take another look at it if you're elected?" I'm right across the road from St. Mary's, where Archbishop [Philip] Pocock spent some time.

Within twenty-four hours, I knew about how that letter had been answered. And I can tell you four days later I heard from the Jesuit community in Hamilton. Ten days later, [Gerald Emmett] Cardinal Carter called and said, "What is happening?" because the fear had been introduced that, if the Tories won again, maybe they would reassess it.

In my view, Frank had no intention of reassessing it but we didn't meet it. I'll say we didn't meet it during the election campaign head on.

Q. Do you think now that full funding has been extended to Catholics, that — and your friend John Tory suggested this in the last campaign ...

A. Yes.

Q. … do you think all faiths have to be funded now in this province?

A. I don't say they have to be funded. It's a very fundamental issue and I think John would be the first one to tell you that he understood that this was a key issue during the campaign. I can only tell you back in the late sixties, as minister of education, I had a tentative agreement with the Jewish day schools. They were all in North York. The then-director, Dr. [F.W.] Minkler, was in support. We nearly had it done and then a very able lawyer, a very fine person, came to me. He was representing the Jewish day schools. He said, "You know, I don't think we can go ahead."

I don't know whether it was because part of the agreement was they had to accept non-Jewish students but, for whatever reason, it didn't happen. But it was very close. I can't tell you where it's going to go in the future. I mean, that's up to you to speculate.

Q. We never do that here.

A. No, no. Of course not.

Q. Let's talk about one of your — I'll put it out there: The Constitution of this country would not have been repatriated without your intervention at a key moment. I'll say it and now we're going to play some tape and see if others agree.

[TVO Director] Michael [Smith], here's Bill Davis on the constitution. Roll tape, please:

> *Davis Clip from 1982: "Every citizen of Ontario shares a common right to self-advancement, to balanced and stable governments, to freedom, to justice, to equity and security as residents of a great province, a great province which has a key role to play in advancing the interests of a great nation."*

Q. You don't get to talk yet. Here's some more background, because we have a lot of younger viewers and a lot of new Canadians who will not remember 1982.

Pierre Trudeau moves to repatriate the Constitution with the Charter of Rights and Freedoms. Eight provinces are opposed. You, representing Ontario, and New Brunswick are in favour. There's this famous meeting in the kitchen where your attorney-general, Roy McMurtry, and Roy Romanow from Saskatchewan, and Jean Chrétien, representing Trudeau, hammer out a compromise. Still, Mr. Trudeau is not quite sold.

Friends, football teammates, and political colleagues since their days together at the University of Toronto: William Davis and his attorney-general, Roy McMurtry.

So you pick up the phone and you call him and Roy Romanow, who was in that chair yesterday, picks up the story. Roll tape:

> *Romanow Clip: "I'm convinced that Premier Davis at some point, either in that telephone conversation or shortly thereafter, communicated to Prime Minister Trudeau that unless he accepted the notwithstanding clause, simple majority, he had no choice but to pull out of his support for the prime minister. Now, he has never — I've tried to raise it with Premier Davis, Bill Davis. He's too discreet. He probably won't even tell you, if he was … if he is going to be on your show. I think that, in effect, amounted to an ultimatum. I don't think anybody who knows Bill Davis … this is a gentleman, a thoughtful person. I don't think he'd ever put it to him as an ultimatum, but I think the prime minister's whole card was gone because, when Ontario pulls away, you've only got New Brunswick, it's game over."*

Q. Is that right?

A. I have to tell you a little story.… But some months ago, Mr. McMurtry had a very lovely dinner at his place. The gentleman you just heard from was there. I always said to Romanow, if he had been born in Ontario, he would have been a Progressive Conservative. Jean Chrétien was there. I said, "Gentlemen, I may be writing a book. If I do, you three people have to understand, in spite of all you have said, all you have said about yourselves and have written, it will go totally down the drain, you'll understand. You were really just carrying papers for the first minister." I mean, I had some fun with them.

Chrétien said to me that night, "We heard there was a phone call." In fact, he checked with the prime minister. There was a phone call. He said, "I don't know who made that phone call." I looked him straight in the eye and I said, "Jean, you really don't know who made the phone call?" The light went on and then he realized.

But what people don't recall either is that Ontario took the position, when Trudeau thought of going to Westminster by himself —

Q. Yes.

A. — I went to see him, [Hugh] Segal was with me. We met in [24] Sussex [Drive]. I said to the prime minister, "You have to try once more." He kept saying, "It won't happen." I said, "I can't guarantee we'll go with you. I don't know what Richard will do, but I take some credit ..."

Q. That's Hatfield, Richard Hatfield of New Brunswick ...

A. Yes. I take some credit for, in fact, having that final conference and it worked. I could tell you more about it, but I shan't burden your viewers. But ...

Q. Is the word *ultimatum* an appropriate word to use?

A. I don't think *ultimatum*. It was a point of view. It was a fact. And it ... but I can take you back, and this is what a lot of people don't understand, because I was being criticized for supporting Mr. Trudeau's position.

Go back to Victoria; you don't remember because you weren't born. But we had total unanimity in Victoria. Ontario had agreed with a slight change on the social policies. Robert Bourassa was in support of it.

Q. This was in '70 or '71?

A. In '71.

Q. In '71.

A. In Victoria. And our position didn't change during those ten years' intervals.

Q. Well, okay. You don't want to call it an ultimatum, but when you have Pierre Trudeau on the other end of the phone and you say, "Look it, you've got to compromise on this notwithstanding clause or Ontario may not be able to support you," what else would you call that?

A. I'm not sure that was my exact language. All I can tell you is the tenor of the meeting was different the following day. The only thing I feel badly about that whole issue was that René Lévesque was part of those people opposing. I don't think he knew until he got to the meeting that morning that, in fact, the views of the other ministers had changed.

Q. And they hung him out to dry?

A. Well, I felt badly for him. I didn't agree with him.

Q. So do you buy into this "Night of the Long Knives," as it has come to be known in Quebec?

A. I don't think there were any knives anywhere. I think it was a mistake perhaps. People may not have thought of it. Listen, there was a lot of pressure on everybody. But I felt badly for Lévesque. I disagreed with him totally.

I have to tell you one story. I went there, the first referendum; I went down to speak at the invitation of the Montreal chamber. My speech was pretty good. My French was better than Diefenbaker's, which doesn't say much.

René called the next morning. He said, "Bill, I hear you made a great speech last night in Montreal." I said, "Well, that's good." He said, "Please come again. We went up two points in the polls last night."

I mean, that's the kind of person he was.

Q. Okay. I want to ask you about something that Brian Mulroney wrote about you in his memoirs. We all know what the Big Blue Machine was. This was this great backroom organization that somehow won four elections with you at the helm. And Brian Mulroney is said to have said in his book, "I really want your support because I want that Big Blue Machine to help me win elections, too." And he has quoted you as having said, "Brian, I am the Big Blue Machine."

Would you confirm that story for us here?

A. No, and I wouldn't disagree with Brian on his recollection of that conversation, but the reality is I said to Brian, "The word *machine* is grossly overstated. You're talking about a group of people who had a common interest, a common purpose. That was the machine." I mean, you know some of them. Some of them have passed on. I said to Brian, "I am part of the organization. I will help and, if I help, the others will help." That's a far more delicate way of saying it.

Q. You have this annoying habit of being extremely modest over the years and I'm really trying to get you to kind of just get out there a little bit and say, "You know what, Paikin? Yeah, I really am the Big Blue Machine."

A. No.

Q. That's what you said to him.

A. Yes, but no, that's what he said I said to him, and there's a difference.

Q. Okay. A couple of more minutes because otherwise your friends over on the other side of the room —

A. Listen, I warned you. I warned you at the beginning of this I might want to take the whole hour; this is my studio. Go ahead.

Q. Historians constantly re-evaluate history. Do you wonder what they will do with your time in office?

A. No. I wonder perhaps to a certain extent. I don't worry about it because I am a modest person, I really am. But I do know that in the nine years I was minister of education, they were perhaps the most exciting, where more things were done in terms of curriculum, in terms of institutions, in terms of teacher education. I feel very comfortable.

As premier, I saw patriation, I saw the Charter, I saw the ministry of the environment created, family law reform, corporations. In fact, when I joined a law firm I told them, "I can't practise law with you, but I'm here because I passed more legislation that enabled your profession to make money than any single premier in the history of Ontario." And that's factually correct.

Q. That's something you want to boast about?

A. No. No, because people will say there's far too much legislation.

But no, I am comfortable, I guess, because of the support of my family and the friends that I have that historians will do what they want to do, but I am comfortable that I did my best, I made the judgments that I thought were right. And, on occasion, I may have made a mistake; I can't think of any, but there …

Q. You can't think of any right now.…

A. No.

Q. Maybe the guys on the other side of the studio will think of a few.

A. Well …

Q. As you think about what the essence of Ontario was fifty years ago today when you got elected, is that essence, whatever it is, still existing today?

A. I think some of it is. I think people are still concerned about the quality of life. I think they're concerned about the principles, I think they're concerned about issues of violence, et cetera. But to say Ontario is the same as it was when I first entered politics is wrong. The diversity is obvious. It has been one of the great strengths, but also an important thing for our party to reach out to the new Canadians, which we haven't always done effectively and we have paid a price for that on occasion.

But fundamentals don't change. Honesty doesn't change, principle doesn't change, some degree of respect for your political opponents. I mean, what I don't understand is the sometimes degree of confrontation that takes place. I mean, you're going to have somebody on this program who is philosophically misguided, but I was with him the other night at Queen's University.

Q. That would be [former-Liberal MPP Sean] Conway, I guess.

A. Yes. He couldn't have been kinder. I mean, if Stephen Lewis were on the program and some of my right-wing friends will say, "Oh, he was a friend of yours. I thought so." I mean, we're helping him with his foundation. Bob Rae is a friend. [Former-Sudbury MPP] Elmer Sopha from the Liberals. We could battle one another in the house. We could go out and have dinner together. I mean, I think there is ...

Q. That doesn't happen anymore, does it?

A. It doesn't happen.

Q. Not to my knowledge.

A. And we used to have fun. I have to tell you one story: When Donald MacDonald got up before the orders of the day, and some will remember this ...

Q. That's the former NDP leader?

A. Yes. And he really went after me because he had received a letter from the Conservative Party of Ontario, fundraising. And he went on at some length.

I was sort of non-plussed, but I got up and said, "Mr. Speaker, I apologize to the honourable member. Very recently, we acquired the subscription list for *Playboy* magazine and that's how he got on the list." The house collapsed. He collapsed and, you know, it was the kind of fun that you could have on occasion.

Q. I want to ask you one last thing and this is a bit of a touchy-feely question, so you'll forgive me here. You're going to be eighty years old next month — more yesterdays than tomorrows. Do you think much about your mortality at this stage of the game?

A. Listen, I have twelve grandchildren. They keep you from thinking too much about your mortality.

No. And I'll go back to your other question. I don't know how long I will continue to be here. All I know is I've been involved in every single election, federal and provincial, since I retired. I am interested in what's happening in Ottawa at the moment, I am interested in what's happening at Queen's Park. I hope I continue. How long I continue is not totally in my hands, Steve.

But I don't worry about what the historians will say because, I'm being very modest, but I am not uncomfortable with what we accomplished in the twenty-five years in public life.

Q. Mr. Davis, it was a great pleasure having you in the studio that bears your name today. We are grateful that you could spare the time for us and we hope this is not your last visit to TVO. Thanks so much.

A. You're very welcome and it's because of you I'm here.

Q. You're very kind.

Because he experienced so much success in his quarter century of public life (not to mention his subsequent quarter century in private law and business), it may not occur to people that Bill Davis has seen more than his share of tragedy in his life.

Near the beginning of his political career, his first wife, Helen, died of cancer at age thirty. The couple had four young children.

Premier John Robarts had wanted to put Davis in his cabinet, but told his grieving backbencher to take the time he needed to get his personal life in order and things would take care of themselves. Robarts, who was minister of education before becoming premier in 1961, kept that portfolio for a full year, even after becoming premier. He offered the job to Davis in 1962, once Davis' personal life appeared to be more in order. Of course, it couldn't have been.

(In an awful case of coincidence, two other contemporaries of Davis' faced similar tragedy. Nova Scotia Premier Robert Stanfield lost his first wife and mother of his four children, Joyce, in a car accident, when he was forty. Saskatchewan Premier Allan Blakeney's wife and mother of his two children, Molly, died in her sleep when Blakeney was in his early thirties.)

Now that Davis is in his mid-eighties (he turned eighty-four on July 30, 2013), he has had the misfortune of watching too many of his friends and colleagues predecease him. He has buried the following former cabinet ministers from the thirty-second Parliament (Davis' last) alone: George Kerr (age eighty-three), Lorne Henderson (age eighty-two),

William Davis at his eightieth birthday party; pictured here with Bette Stephenson, his former education, and colleges and universities minister.

Leo Bernier (age eighty-one), James Snow (seventy-nine), Margaret Scrivener (seventy-five), Russell Ramsay (seventy-four), Frank Miller (seventy-three), Robert Welch (seventy-two), Thomas Wells (seventy), Frank Drea and Keith Norton (both sixty-nine), Bruce McCaffrey (sixty-three), Nick Leluk (sixty-two), and Larry Grossman (age fifty-three).

An equally lengthy list could be compiled of former first ministers he served with. Of course, no one's death from that list affected the country more than Pierre Elliott Trudeau's. When Canada's fifteenth prime minister died on September 28, 2000, at the age of eighty, we took our TVO cameras to Main Street in Brampton to interview William Davis at his home:

STEVE INTRO: Tonight, the country continues to come to grips with what we have lost. Prime Minister Jean Chrétien announced that Pierre Trudeau's body will lie in state in the Hall of Honour on Parliament Hill tomorrow, Sunday, and Monday morning to be followed by a state funeral in Montreal on Tuesday.

In the House of Commons this morning, the party leaders all offered their tributes to Canada's fifteenth prime minister. In this province, one of Trudeau's longest standing political friends and adversaries was former Premier William Davis.

Both men came together, most notably in the early 1980s, to repatriate Canada's Constitution and entrench a Charter of Rights and Freedoms. I spoke with Bill Davis this morning at his home in Brampton.

Q. Mr. Davis, I want to know where you were and how you heard the news of Mr. Trudeau's death, and what your immediate reaction was when you heard it.

MR. DAVIS: I guess it's fair to state that I was not totally surprised because I think there was some indication that Mr. Trudeau was not well, and that this sad occurrence didn't come as a surprise. But, Steve, to say I wasn't impacted by it would be a mistake. It's always difficult for people to try and explain how they feel. I was asked what I felt because I was in a similar situation when John Kennedy was shot on my way to Burlington to open a high school.

There is a certain sadness because, while we differed politically in terms of our partisan approach to public life, there was a genuine degree, I think, of mutual respect, perhaps even one might go so far as to say affection some days.

Q. I want to pick up on that —

A. Yes.

Q. — because that is interesting. He is this French, Catholic, elite, aristocratic, lots of family money. You are the small-town Methodist, very pragmatic Ontario lawyer, and yet you did, on occasions, get on very well. What was the source of your entente?

A. I guess because I was, as I was and still am and he was, and I guess the differences were such that it was kind of fun for us to share our views on some issues that didn't relate to politics. And I really think the — the respect and the affection was quite genuine.

And I never tried to match him intellectually but, coming from a small town, there is a certain degree of wisdom that we could bring to some of the discussions.

Q. But you — I think it's fair to say you're not his kind of guy.

A. No. I think that we had very little in common. I mean, he was a very disciplined person. He certainly looked after himself from a health standpoint better than I did, although I probably in my youth participated as much, if not more, than he did in certain sports.

Q. Probably more. I don't think he played football.

A. No, he didn't. In fact, we were at, I guess, two or three — certainly two — Grey Cup games together and he had his boys at one of them. It was at Olympic Stadium. And I don't say this in any critical sense, but Mr. Trudeau's knowledge of Canadian football was somewhat limited. So I explained to the boys what was happening as best I could. I remember that very well.

Q. He always said football's not a French-Canadian sport.

A. No. Although —

Q. I'll bet he would love to see what's happening with the Alouettes, now.

A. I was going to say, the Alouettes are now doing quite well.

Q. You are a Tory loyalist, as you often said, but you got on better with this Liberal prime minister than you ever did with that Tory prime minister, Joe Clark. How come?

A. Well, I — I did get along with Joe Clark. I mean, I — Joe Clark was not there for, in my view, a significant length of time to make a mark, but a man of great integrity and intelligence. I think it was partially, Steve, because I — I was involved in the public scene for a greater length of time with Mr. Trudeau, and we had certain interests in common.

I mean, a lot of people look at the 1981/1982 period. They forget that my relationship started back in '71 in Victoria, where we had actually total unanimity on the Constitution, the Charter, et cetera.

Q. Until Bourassa went home.

A. Until Robert returned to Quebec and determined — after about a week or ten days, he phoned me and said he couldn't sell it politically. But there was a relationship then because Ontario's position on it goes back to Mr. Robarts. It really didn't change all that period of time. And the great irony was, in the 1981/1982 period, were the Conservatives, who were not fond of Mr. Trudeau, if I can phrase it that delicately, couldn't understand why I was still supportive of his position, as was Dick Hatfield.

Q. I want to follow up on that because it was you, it was New Brunswick's Hatfield and that was it. You rejected, initially anyway, all of your other provincial colleagues and you stood with him.

A. No, I didn't reject them. I think it's fair to say that they did not welcome Richard and myself for a period of time.

Q. Okay.

A. I mean, at the premiers' conferences, we always left that subject to the end and we got along quite well with all of them on issues unrelated to that.

Q. But his greatest achievement was the repatriation of the Constitution and the Charter, which he wouldn't have had without you on side. Did he ever, at any time, thank you for that, express gratitude?

A. I think if you read what he has written, read between some of the lines, yes. He — he's not the kind of person that would, you know, express it in exaggerated terms. But I think he understood that the support of Hatfield and the support of Ontario and myself were really quite important to the process, and I think he was appreciative. I would be selling him short if I didn't say that. I think he was.

Q. On the other hand, at that time there was a phone call right near the end, at the eleventh hour, where you said to him, "Lookit. You've got to fish or cut bait. Otherwise, I'm going with the other side." Do you want to tell us about that phone call?

A. No, I don't think there was ever such a phone call. What there was at one point in time was the interest on his part in moving unilaterally. And that was the point where I said to him I could not support that unless we gave it one more go. And we did and the one more go was successful with the exception that the province of Quebec did not become part of it.

I always take a bit of exception to people who say we left Quebec out. I think in a factual sense Quebec decided not to come in. And I always remind people that while this was a disappointment to me, as it was to everybody else, there was some representation from Quebec at that table. The prime minister had been elected by the people of Quebec, a lot of his ministers had been elected by the people of Quebec. So to say that there was no sort of Quebec involvement, there wasn't legally. It was not the government of Quebec, no question about that, but there was some leadership — there was some leadership from Quebec at that table.

Q. You two had great — do you want to call them fights? — over the years on the issue of official bilingualism for Ontario, which he very much wanted and you thought it was not necessarily in the best interests of the province.

A. Yes.

Q. How did he try to make you change your mind?

A. Well, listen, he worked very hard at it, wanted me to entrench it in the Constitution and I told him that, from our standpoint, it was an incremental process. I was able to point out to him that we had moved in terms of the courts, in terms of the Legislature, that we had bilingual elementary schools. We moved to have bilingual secondary schools. And I recall when I was able to show the then-premier of the province of Quebec that 5.8 percent of the population of Ontario declared French as the mother tongue, that 5.6 percent of the elementary and secondary school students were in bilingual high schools and elementary schools, he was surprised. So was Mr. Trudeau.

And I think he understood that my approach was one that was working in the province of Ontario, and I think history will indicate that that was probably the right approach.

Q. But he always disagreed with you.

A. Yes.

Q. He always wanted you to take that extra step.

A. Yes. Listen, he … he was a very persistent person and very committed to this. But, at the same time, my conscience was clear because in real terms we were doing a lot of it without having it entrenched.

Q. You opposed him on the *War Measures Act*, did you not?

A. No, I didn't get too involved. Mr. Robarts was the premier at the time of the *War Measures Act*. And I don't think, I'm going back now in my memory, Steve, that there was opposition from the government of Ontario with respect to the *War Measures Act*. Now, that's just my recollection. I personally was not involved at the time. I was a minister, but Mr. Robarts was the premier at that moment.

Q. I'm thinking, though, that you were personally opposed to it at the time.

A. I may have been personally, as a matter of principle, and yet there's no question either that there was a great, I think, feeling of support for Mr. Trudeau in the way he handled what was a very difficult situation. I mean, I can recall watching it on television and so on and I think there were a lot of Canadians who didn't totally understand exactly what was happening, but who had some respect for the prime minister for what he was doing.

It was the same way — I mean, I — I don't purport to be a great scholar of history, but I do understand it a bit. And I think if you look back in terms of one of his major contributions, that single event — I don't know whether it was the Saturday night or the Sunday night before the first referendum — his speech to the people of Quebec and to the people of Canada on that occasion was, I think, one of the great political messages in the contemporary history of this country.

I can't tell you, you know, did it mean one point or ten points in terms of how people voted the next day or two days later, but certainly it had an impact in that … and I told him. I called him and I — you know, it's not always easy to call a first minister of a party which you don't support but, listen, he deserved a lot of credit for that.

Q. Do you ever feel in all of your dealings with him over the years, that you got to know the real guy?

A. I don't know that I did. I mean, I'm not going to be facetious here and say I've known you for a long time. I don't know whether I know the real

Steve Paikin. You might say, "Do you know the real Bill Davis?" and the truth of the matter, you don't. You may know more than some.

Q. Did you ever get past the façade on him though?

A. Yeah, I think so. I think there were a few occasions when our discussions related to matters totally unrelated to politics, to some of his feelings on other issues, personal issues and so on. We shared some of those experiences. He knew some of the history of my own family, et cetera.

I can't say that I knew the real Pierre Elliott Trudeau because I'm not sure how many people really did know the real Pierre Elliott Trudeau. But I did know a man who had great intellect, totally committed to Canada, one who inspired either great affection or, on occasion, less than great affection. There was no question that you either admired him or you totally disagreed with him, but I think a lot of Canadians respected him as a leader. And I think what you've seen in the last day is a clear indication that while he may not have been their first choice on some issues, he nonetheless was respected as the prime minister of this country.

Q. Premier Davis, thank you for your reminiscences on Pierre Trudeau. We appreciate it.

A. Thank you, Steve.

Strangely enough, for a man who has seen and been responsible for so much important provincial and national history, Bill Davis has never written his memoirs. Not only that, he has so far declined to cooperate with numerous authors who have no doubt asked him to do so. Even some of his closest friends and advisors have urged him to do so. Senator Hugh Segal once told him, "Premier, you must do this before you lose your marbles and can't do it." (Yes, all his former underlings still call him "Premier." No one ever calls him "Bill.")

The only biography on Davis was published the year he retired from politics. It was written by Claire Hoy, the conservative muckraking journalist who once covered Queen's Park, and simply titled *Bill Davis:*

A Biography. Davis is known to be unhappy with the book, thinks there are far too many mistakes in it, and yet, for more than a quarter of a century, seems to have been content to let Hoy have the last word on his public life. I have pointed out the oddity of that to Davis many times. The last time was a few years ago, after telling the former premier I had just finished reading a 470-page biography on Leslie Frost, who served one year less than Davis as Ontario's premier. Davis had his executive assistant send me an email with the following note:

> If I make a decision about writing a book, I will make the assumption that you would agree with me that although Mr. Frost was a great Premier, his tenure was shorter; therefore, any book I may be involved in should exceed the one on him by at least 50 pages. Bill.

Imagine having a front row seat for most of the biggest moments in Canadian and Ontario history of the past half century, but maintaining a sphinx-like silence about it all.

Come on, Mr. Davis. It's time.

William Davis and former prime minister John Turner, born one month apart in 1929, pictured here at a celebratory lunch in June 2012.

Frank Stuart Miller
(1985)

❧

Yes, history will record that it was Frank Miller, the Man from Muskoka, who was at the helm when the forty-two-year-long Progressive Conservative dynasty ended.

As much as his friends, admirers, supporters, and family didn't want to hear it, the fact was, Miller was the wrong man at the wrong time for Ontario.

Miller was, indeed, the stereotypical rural politician. He wore outrageously loud plaid and tartan jackets that made him look like a hayseed in Toronto. At a time when Ontario, and particularly its capital city, was becoming increasingly multicultural, his image screamed old Scotland. He was a successful small businessman who admired Ronald Reagan and wasn't ashamed to say so. Miller had that image and seemed to covet it.

But he was so much more than that too. For one thing, he was bilingual. He was an engineer, having earned his degree at McGill University. And he was actually born in Toronto.

He was a highly respected and successful cabinet minister in Bill Davis' government, having been appointed to all of the big portfolios: treasury, health, and industry. In some respects, he was ahead of his time. He was the original common sense revolutionary, ten years before Mike Harris would win an election with that platform. That often made him an awkward fit in Davis' government, which was far more pragmatic, centrist, and less ideological than Miller would have preferred.

When Bill Davis retired after fourteen years as premier, four senior cabinet ministers vied to replace him. Three were thought to be from the Red Tory side of the party: Larry Grossman, Dennis Timbrell, and Roy McMurtry. And then there was Miller, who had the small-c conservative vote all to himself. He led the leadership convention on every ballot, eventually winning on the fourth over Grossman on January 26, 1985.

Small-c conservatives felt great about Miller's victory. In some respects they felt they were taking the party back from the Toronto sophisticates, who in their view marginalized their participation. Even Hugh Segal, today a senator but back then a Davis confidante, acknowledged that the dynasty's end may have had its roots in his group's unwillingness or inability to make the party's right wing feel truly at home in the PC Party.

So when Miller won the convention, the right wing had its revenge. The problem was, in 1985 Ontario was not a right-wing province. Not by any stretch. The genius of the PC Party over four decades was twofold: first, having the knack of always picking the right leader for the times (and that always meant generational change); and second, picking someone who would occupy the broad middle of the political spectrum. With Frank Miller, the party picked someone who was actually two years older than the outgoing leader, and someone who wanted to tack right politically, thereby vacating the middle. Miller's two opponents — David Peterson and Bob Rae — were delighted to snap up that vacated ground.

Sadly for Miller, the election campaign he led in the spring of 1985 featured numerous errors of omission and commission. Even with the challenges I outlined, Miller still had a great reputation as a genuinely authentic and likeable person going for him. But he frittered that away with a series of bad decisions.

Miller was the last PC premier in the party's forty-two-year-long dynasty.

His brain trust told him that Ontarians wouldn't go for the loud jackets and cornpone expressions. So they put him in blue blazers and gray slacks to look more "premierial." It just didn't look authentic. That look worked for Bill Davis. But Miller wasn't Davis. Yet, somehow, his team kept trying to run him as if he were.

Then Miller said he wouldn't participate in a leaders' debate. Strangely enough, there hadn't been a leaders' debate since the 1975 campaign. But times were changing. Ronald Reagan, Miller's hero, had participated in two presidential debates in 1980 and 1984. Prime Minister Brian Mulroney participated in several debates during the 1984 federal election. Suddenly, leaders were *expected* to debate. Miller didn't want to risk blowing his twenty-point lead in the polls, so the debate was off. What made the decision particularly strange was that Miller was a good debater. He was comfortable in his own skin, and knew his brief as well as anyone in government. Conversely, David Peterson was known to have a perspiration problem during debates, and Bob Rae was only thirty-six years old but looked ten years younger. Had he debated, Miller almost certainly would have done just fine.

And there was more. At one point in the campaign, Miller wandered to the back of the campaign bus to shoot the breeze with reporters, the vast majority of whom knew him well and liked him. But that was when he was a minister. Now he was premier, and on a short leash, trying to protect a big lead.

"They won't let me talk to you," Miller said to the reporters in an almost plaintive voice. The sentence raised questions about just who was running the campaign, the advisors or the leader? Miller's reputation for openness and being himself also took a hit, since it gave further evidence to those who claimed he was running a peek-a-boo campaign.

And then there was the Catholic school funding question. On June 12, 1984, Bill Davis rose in the Legislature to announce his government would extend full public funding to the separate school system to the end of high school — a reversal of the party's position since 1971. The Ontario Legislature voted overwhelmingly in favour of the policy, with only one Tory MPP opposed. But it's also fair to say that in the Tory heartland, the policy was a major albatross around Miller's neck. Still, it wasn't a huge election issue until that fateful day when the archbishop of the Anglican

Church held a news conference and dropped a bomb in the middle of Campaign '85.

Lewis Garnsworthy was not at all happy. He saw Davis' plan to extend funding to the Catholic system as a decision taken without any consultation with him. And so, at that news conference, I asked him what, exactly, was his problem with the way the government was bringing in full funding. The answer shocked every reporter in attendance.

"This is how Hitler changed education in Germany, by exactly the same process, by decree," Garnsworthy said. The media were incredulous. Dick Chapman from the *Toronto Sun* offered the archbishop a chance to walk the quote back.

"Surely you're not comparing Adolph Hitler and Bill Davis?" he said.

Garnsworthy's reply: "I won't take that back."

Strangely enough, far from being delighted at how a juicy quote would no doubt lead to front page headlines and the lead story on the six o'clock news, reporters were offended at what was clearly an outrageous comment. They continued to offer Garnsworthy repeated chances to clarify. But he didn't.

After the news conference was over, Frank Miller called the archbishop's comments "odious." Garnsworthy went to lunch with future PC MPP Derwyn Shea shortly thereafter. His hands shaking while trying to light his cigarette, Garnsworthy said to Shea, "Derwyn, I fear I've done something terrible."

What he did was give cover to all those who disapproved of full funding, and Tory fortunes continued to fall. The problem for those voters was that they couldn't take their votes elsewhere because the other two parties supported the policy too. But it meant that much of the foundation of the Tory party would stay home in that election, depriving Miller of a chance to keep the Conservatives in power.

But to show you how deep the Tory roots went in Ontario, even though Miller ran a Murphy's Law kind of campaign, he still technically won it. When they counted the votes on May 2, 1985, the PCs still won the most seats, fifty-two. The Liberals captured forty-eight, while edging the PCs in total votes cast, 38–37 percent. Bob Rae's NDP held the balance of power with twenty-five seats.

The rest of the story unfolded in unprecedented fashion. The second-place Liberals and third-place New Democrats signed an "Accord" — a two-year road map of agreed upon agenda items they would pass through this minority Parliament — then combined forces to defeat the Miller government on the floor of the Legislature. After less than five months, Frank Miller's tenure as premier was over.

Strangely enough, when I once asked Miller's son Norm (the PC MPP for Parry Sound-Muskoka since 2001) how devastating it all was for his father, he suggested, in hindsight, it's probably a good thing his dad lost. The elder Miller had had a heart attack in the mid-1970s and a second attack was a real possibility. Norm Miller figures losing the premiership added fifteen years to his dad's life.

I've discovered that many politicians actually get a third act in political life. Frank Miller's first act was as a cabinet minister; his second was as premier. For act three, Frank Miller returned home to municipal politics, becoming chairman of the district of Muskoka. He died in 2000 at the age of seventy-three.

Ten years after presiding over the end of the Tory dynasty, Frank Miller and I talked about his time in public life in an interview on the second floor at Queen's Park:

STEVE: Well, I almost can't believe it, but as you and I sit here and tape this on Wednesday, February the 8th, 1995, it is ten years ago today that you were sworn in as the premier of Ontario, and as we sit under your portrait here, what are you thinking right now?

MR. MILLER: How lucky I am to be alive. I haven't had a lot of retrospective thought about what might have been. I only take what did happen. And as a good friend of mine said to me the other day, looking at my health history, you are probably alive because you haven't got the job.

But, really, it was very exciting. I can think of that day, particularly, being sworn in by the lieutenant-governor in the Legislature, and the feeling that somehow a kid from downtown Toronto had made it, who didn't have too many connections, really, with politics, if you stop to think of my background.

Q. Tell me the story of when David Peterson is premier. And, in front of this office, you walk in to see him?

A. Well, I was walking in, as people do, and there had never been a guard in my days. I guess no one worried about me, but there is now, as you see. So, I got to this point, and I started walking through the door, and the guard said, "Pardon me, sir, but where are you going?"

I said, "I am going to see the premier."

"Have you an appointment?"

"Yes, I do."

"What's your name?"

I said, "I'm the guy in the picture up there."

GUARD OUTSIDE PREMIER'S OFFICE: Well, that wasn't me, I can assure you.

A. No, it wasn't.

GUARD OUTSIDE PREMIER'S OFFICE: Because I have known you for a long time.

A. Then the guard stood up to attention and saluted and blushed, and I guess I was in there an hour. I came back out and he immediately popped back up again and saluted again, and said, "Sir, I am so embarrassed. I am so embarrassed. I look at that picture every day of my life, and you know, your eyes keep following me."

Q. This place was not always the friendliest place in the world for you. As you say, you weren't necessarily part of the gang.

A. No, I wasn't, but I represented, I think, a lot of people in Ontario — rural Ontario, small business throughout. I am an engineer by training, which a lot of people never knew, by the way. They know I am a used car salesman, but they don't know that I am an engineer.

I think I ran into the kinds of problems a non-professional runs into in politics, and that is because I didn't have the background and the knowledge of what it takes to survive for the first few years, when I was health minister.

Q. You ran for the leadership after Mr. Davis decided to retire, against Larry Grossman, Dennis Timbrell, and Roy McMurtry.

A. Yes. Too well, I remember.

Q. And you won that one.

A. Yes.

Q. And then shortly after you won, for a whole variety of reasons, the Tories lost power and the dynasty was over. How often do you still think about that?

A. Of course you do think about it. First, what would have happened if I had been leader? I don't know. I was asked that question the other day. I don't know whether I would have been a good leader or a bad leader. I wished I had had a couple of years before I'd had to have an election. I would like to have had a chance to be seen as Frank Miller, premier, long enough to, in effect, let the people who had to make a decision know me better and put my own imprint on things, instead of just simply get in there, call an election, and almost disappear from the scene.

Q. I don't know this for a fact, but I am going to guess. I am going to guess that when we ask Larry Grossman, would history have been different had he won on that last ballot instead of you, he would probably say, "Absolutely. I wouldn't have made Mr. Miller's mistakes. We would still be in power. We would have never heard of Premier David Peterson or Premier Bob Rae," to which you say what?

A. He may be right. I don't know that. I would say this, that we were forty-three years, I think, in power, about that time.

Q. Forty-two.

A. Forty-two? Okay. And I remember saying in my campaign, "We have given you good government for forty-two years." And people would yell, "Compared to what?" Now, I have got to tell you, they never ask, "Compared to what?" anymore.

You know, forty-two years is a long, long time for a party to be in power. You had to actually have been sixty-five in 1985 to have ever voted for a party that won, apart from the Conservatives. So, it is amazing to me we stayed in power as long as we did. There is a tremendous wave going against you, even though the polls were great, and they were great.

Q. Tell me honestly, ten years after the fact, do you still have bad feelings for those who were disloyal to you and refused to coalesce around your leadership in the Conservative Party?

A. Believe it or not, I didn't have an awful lot of bad feeling even at the time, because I think I understood the depth of dismay, perhaps, of the losers. And it is easy to focus, particularly when I got into trouble … it is easy to focus on me as the cause. That is pretty normal.

You know, I would have taken all the credit if we had won; it is only fair that I get the blame if we lose.

Q. Now the guy who leads your party today, who walks through those very doors every day this house is in session, is Mike Harris. And something tells me that you would fall right into line with the way Mike Harris has taken the Conservative Party. This is probably your kind of party today, isn't it?

A. Yes, it is.

Q. That is kind of ironic, isn't it?

A. Well, it is also true that when a party is not in power, you don't have a lot of people attracted to it who don't believe in it. The people who are Conservatives today have survived ten tough years. They are Conservatives because they believe the party is right, not because there are some rewards for being a Conservative.

* * *

I had one more interview with Frank Miller after this one. We took our TVO camera crew to Bala, Ontario, a town of just a few hundred souls in the heart of cottage country in Muskoka Lakes Township, where he'd retired. TVO was in the news quite a bit during this time, as the Harris government was considering privatizing it. Miller let slip during our visit that he himself tried to sell TVO twenty years earlier, but Premier Davis wouldn't let him.

"In hindsight, I'm glad we didn't," he said. "Up here in Bala, we don't have cable, and TVO is pretty much the only channel we get. If we'd have sold it, I'd have nothing to watch right now!"

But one of my fondest memories of Miller came the day his government fell in 1985. On what must have been the worst day of his political life, what was Frank Miller doing after he lost the vote that would end the forty-two-year-long Tory dynasty? Selling raffle tickets to other MPPs and members of the press gallery. Just because the Conservatives' world as they knew it was coming to an end didn't mean some charity in Muskoka couldn't benefit from Miller's involvement.

That was Frank Miller: the original common sense revolutionary.

Miller's family thought it a blessing in disguise that he lost power. Given his bad heart, he probably lived much longer than he otherwise would have.

DAVID ROBERT PETERSON
(1985–1990)

David Peterson was born in very conservative London, Ontario, in December 1943. That fact, politically speaking, wouldn't be terribly interesting, except it meant that for all but four-and-a-half months of Peterson's life, his home province was governed by the juggernaut that was the Progressive Conservative Party of Ontario.

And until the results started coming in from the election on May 2, 1985, it seemed as if David Peterson would continue to live in Tory Ontario.

But then something quite shocking happened that election night. For the first time since the Ontario general election in 1937 — nearly half a century earlier — the Liberals got more votes than the Conservatives. Led by Peterson, the Grits won 38 percent of the total votes cast, compared to 37 percent for the PCs. But because of the way the votes split, the Tories actually captured more seats: fifty-two to forty-eight.

The Conservatives described it as an illegitimate coup. How dare the party with the most seats *not* have the right to govern? But the Liberals and New Democrats saw it differently. They saw a forty-two-year-old dynasty that seemed tired. They saw a mere four-seat difference between first and second place. They saw the second place party actually get more votes. Even if the Tories didn't like it, they also knew that Ontarians don't elect governments, they elect Parliaments. Whichever party can maintain the confidence of Parliament gets to govern. And for the first time since David Peterson was four months old, that party would be the Liberals.

Technically, it was Lieutenant-Governor John Black Aird who made Peterson the premier. Once Frank Miller's PCs lost a vote of confidence on the floor of the Legislature, the last Tory premier in the forty-two-year dynasty went to visit the lieutenant-governor, and had to confess he couldn't command the confidence of the House. Theoretically, he could have asked Aird to dissolve the House and call a new election. That would have put Ontario into a full-blown constitutional crisis. Could the queen's representative really deny a request from the sitting premier of the day?

But that hypothetical situation never arose. Miller knew it would be intolerable to send people back to the polls after just six weeks, particularly since the Liberals and New Democrats had a signed an "Accord" guaranteeing two years of governing stability. Furthermore, fully 63 percent of the electorate had backed the opposition parties on election night. There was a government in waiting. It had a mandate. David Peterson would lead it. And Bob Rae would support it.

To be at Queen's Park at this time was to see a kind of giddiness in the hallways. Most folks thought the Tory dynasty was so entrenched that even a leader with as many shortcomings as Frank Miller could keep it alive.

But this was 1985. Ontario was changing as never before. Economically, we were emerging from the recession of the early 1980s and things were looking up. And David Peterson seemed to embody so much of what so many Ontarians were looking for.

First and foremost, he was the picture of youth and health, a significant contrast to Miller, who was two weeks away from fifty-eight years of age on election day and looked every bit of it after two heart attacks. Peterson, meanwhile, was only forty-one and always seemed to be photographed jogging with his beautiful, blond actress wife, Shelley. They also had three photogenic kids.

By the election campaign of 1985, Peterson also looked as if he'd held a starring role in *Extreme Makeover*. When he won the Liberal leadership in February 1982, Peterson looked nothing like the man who was about to be sworn in as premier just three years later. But image guru Gabor Apor was brought in to give Peterson the once-over. He got rid of Peterson's coke-bottle eyeglasses and put him in contact lenses. The nerdy, professorial jackets with patches on the elbows also bit the dust, in favour of sharp business-like suits. And Apor went back half a century for the finishing touch. He remembered that Liberal legend Mitchell Hepburn wore a red tie, so he appropriated that idea and made it Peterson's trademark.

It became such an iconic look for Peterson that on election night CBC-TV's Stu Paterson, manning the Niagara region desk and seeing several new Liberal seats, proclaimed, "They'll be handing out red ties across the Niagara Frontier tonight!"

Suddenly the Tories became your parents' or grandparents' party. Peterson's Liberals were the cool party. And nothing reflected that new, modern approach to life and politics more than the Liberals' promise to bust up the LCBO and Brewers' Retail monopoly, and allow corner stories to sell beer and wine.

(Just to show you what a funny business politics is, that promise never saw the light of day in 1985. It sounded great on the campaign trail but actually putting it into effect proved to be much more complicated than anticipated. Twenty-seven years later, we still don't have beer and wine in the corner stories, but one thing has changed: the Liberals under Dalton McGuinty opposed the idea, whereas the Progressive Conservatives under Tim Hudak are campaigning in favour of it. That's politics.)

David Peterson, seen here with CBC-TV reporter Stu Paterson in the late 1980s.

On the day the Miller government fell, Peterson gave a tough, one might even say overly nasty, speech on the floor of the House. He accused the Tories of having been judged by the people of Ontario, and the verdict was in: the PCs were found to be sadly and miserably wanting. It was a pretty over-the-top conclusion given that the Tories had actually won more seats than the Grits, and only received 35,000 fewer votes than the Liberals out of nearly 3.6 million cast. The truth was, the public wasn't crushing the life out of Miller's party at all. The election was basically a tie, with Bob Rae's NDP having the tie-breaking vote.

The iconic red tie made an appearance on the floor of the Legislature on the day the Miller government fell. Literally. On the floor. After the votes were counted and the Liberals and New Democrats had successfully combined forces to oust the Conservatives, one Tory MPP crossed the floor and plunked a red tie on Bob Rae's desk. Rae tried to look calm by chucking it on the floor. But the message had been sent. It wasn't a coalition government. Rae was no junior partner in this enterprise. This was David Peterson's show.

In fact, most Conservative politicians I talked to at the time figured this entente of Peterson and Rae's wouldn't last. Almost no one in the Liberal cabinet had any governing experience at all. For example, Elinor Caplan became chair of the management board of cabinet, responsible for approving tens of billions of dollars of government expenditures. She had seven years as a North York city councillor to draw upon. So the Tories figured they'd sit back and watch the freak show unleash itself. The Liberals, they assumed, would be completely incompetent. The Accord, they reasoned, would fall apart because Peterson would break his commitment to implement it. Or Rae would back out. Either way, there wasn't a snowball's chance in hell that this peace treaty would last for two years as both sides promised.

Except a funny thing happened on the way to the Legislature. The Liberals weren't incompetent. They actually looked like they knew what they were doing. Expectations were low for this merry band of rookies, so when they did mess up the public seemed to forgive them. The Accord held. There were no protests at Queen's Park demanding an end to this "illicit, unconstitutional arrangement," as Tories branded it. In fact, the public quite liked it.

Peterson, with Rae's support, actually implemented former premier William Davis' pledge to provide full public funding for Roman Catholic schools. (The Conservatives voted against it, perhaps demonstrating their true feelings about the issue.) But the Peterson government's activism didn't stop there. Ontario got its first freedom-of-information legislation. It embarked on social housing projects as never before with plans to build ten thousand new co-op or non-profit housing units. It took an unprecedented approach to environmental activism, essentially threatening the worst polluters in the province to stop spewing the sulphur dioxide emissions that cause acid rain into our air, or risk being shut down. (Remarkably, their compliance was also unprecedented.) Legislative committees were given more teeth to give proposed legislation the once-over. Campaign finance reform; television in the Legislature; a ban on extra billing by doctors; pay equity; full coverage of medically necessary services for Northern Ontarians if they had to travel south for treatment; the right for workers to know about toxic substances in their workplaces; pension reform; workers' compensation reform. And on and on it went.

Senator Hugh Segal once told me he thought Ontarians wanted their government to act like the cleaning lady. In other words, do a good job, but don't get in our faces and, for heaven's sakes, don't break anything.

David Peterson was rejecting that analogy in a big way. He was in our faces every day. He'd "scrum" with reporters daily, sometimes two or three times a day. And he'd stay for every last question. The beast needed feeding? No sweat. The Liberals were running a popular activist government, and they didn't mind telling everyone.

So when the Accord's two-year cycle was over, Peterson called an election, telling the public he'd kept his promises, provided good government, and now wanted a majority. The NDP tried to make the case that Peterson only looked good because he had the NDP looking over his shoulder. Without that oversight, Rae said, the Liberals couldn't be trusted. And the poor Conservatives seemed totally lost in the wilderness. They'd chosen Larry Grossman to replace Frank Miller. Grossman was Miller's opposite in every way, despite the fact that the two had both been treasurers, both been health ministers, both been industry ministers, were both diminutive in stature, and both wanted to replace Bill Davis.

But where Miller was rural, Grossman was very urban, representing a downtown Toronto riding. Where Miller gave off an unthreatening, folksy demeanour in public, Grossman looked like a sharpie from Bay Street. And where Miller was a white Anglo-Saxon Protestant (the foundation of the PC Party), Grossman was Jewish (still a hard sell with some delegates), which probably accounted for some of the reason why Grossman lost to Miller by just seventy-seven votes on the third ballot of the January 1985 leadership convention to replace Davis.

The 1987 election was simply a dream come true for the Liberals, and a nightmare for the Tories. It was a summertime campaign and Peterson spent most of it on the barbeque circuit. The economy was heating up, and so was the Liberals' popularity. On September 10, it was a landslide for Peterson, winning 95 out of 130 seats. The electorate decided the Liberals didn't need the NDP looking over their shoulder. Rae moved up to leader of the opposition, but it was a pyrrhic victory since he lost six seats as well. But the election was an unmitigated disaster for the Conservatives, who fell to third place for the first time since 1919. And Larry Grossman lost his seat. (Tragically, ten years later, he'd lose his life to brain cancer at just fifty-three.)

What followed was one of the most astonishing stories in Canadian political history. In just three short years, David Peterson went from being perhaps the most popular politician in the entire country, to losing the government and even his own London Centre seat.

In June 2010, a quarter of a century after David Peterson became the first Liberal premier of Ontario in forty-two years, we invited him to TVO to reminisce about his premiership: how he so unexpectedly came to power, what he did while he was there, and how it all ended so prematurely.

STEVE: And joining us now, the man who was the twentieth premier of the province of Ontario, David Peterson. Welcome back to TVO.

MR. PETERSON: Nice to be back, Steven.

Q. I want to take you, twenty-five years ago tomorrow you became the first Liberal premier of the province of Ontario in forty-two years. And I want to know now, twenty-five years later, you can tell us honestly, when that 1985 election campaign was called did you believe you had a hope in hell of winning?

A. No.

Q. Okay. Good. Now we're getting somewhere.

A. Well, in a sort of way I thought we had a shot at it. Now, we were twenty points behind in the polls and, you know, you just ... there are certain times in opposition which was pretty desperate and some pretty lean times, as you'll recall. But I kind of had this sense that we could maybe do it. And so you're going to ask me why.

Q. Where did that come from?

A. I'll tell you where it started. When Brian Mulroney won in 1984, there were no Liberal governments left in Canada in 1984.

Q. Federally or provincially, nothing left?

A. Federally or provincially, which is an interesting observation because most people ... that would be contrary to most people's instincts. And I knew things were changing. There was just a mood to change things. I didn't know what the circumstances would be, I didn't know who I'd be facing. It could have been Bill Davis, who is a very wily and successful politician. It would have been a different campaign.

But Frank Miller came out of the Conservative mill and it presented us with certain opportunities to present a fresh face and a different face.

The other reality is that there's nothing to lose when you're campaigning, like I was, for the first time. I had nothing to protect and so you let it all out there and it kind of worked, it kind of came together.

Q. Well, I want to remind everybody what the times were like, because the year before Brian Mulroney had won the largest majority in Canadian history; Liberals were in trouble everywhere. You had, I think, three or four of your MPPs quit your caucus.

A. Four.

Q. Four. Okay.

A. I remember this.

Q. Sheila Copps, Albert Roy.

A. Don Boudria …

Q. And Cunningham.

A. And Eric Cunningham.

Q. Eric Cunningham. Okay.

A. Four key members.

Q. Right. Who all quit because they didn't see you going anywhere, frankly.

A. Exactly.

Q. How bad was that previous year?

A. It was terrible. I remember when this happened. [My wife] Shelley and I had sort of a deal. And she would do one play … she was an actress. She would do one play a year and we rented a cottage and I would look after the children. So here we were at Grand Bend. She was rehearsing all day. I was looking after these three kids, two were in diapers.

I remember getting the phone call. Then I remember there was — don't ask me why — chicken stew on the stove that was burning over. I was making this. One kid in dirty diapers, the other one about to get dirty. I was responsible for all this and a phone call coming to say these four people had quit. Now, this was the low point of my entire life and I couldn't abandon my kids.

But you have the sense, if the ship is going to go down the captain should at least be on the prow. But there, I wasn't even there and it really was a desperately conflicted out, emotionally, intellectually and every other way.

But you know what saves me is I am an eternal optimist about life, always have been.

Q. Well, and here's what happened a year later. Let's put these numbers up because election night, May 2nd, 1985, this is what the numbers said: fifty-two Conservative seats, forty-eight Liberal seats, twenty-five New Democrat seats. The Tories got more seats, but you actually got more votes.

So, I mean, it's ... you know, they say a week is a lifetime in politics so, in the course of a year, suddenly, you're a bit in the driver's seat. What did you think would happen when you saw those numbers?

A. I think ... and the big thing there, Steven, was I think the momentum. There was a sense in the last week that we were really coming on. And if it had gone another week, we could have had possibly a majority because things change so quickly in politics.

So when we came out of that election, there was a sense we had won even though we really hadn't on the numbers, and that the Conservatives had lost and the NDP had not performed to their own expectations.

Q. But they were kingmakers.

A. Well, they were kingmakers. And it was a very curious set of numbers. They had roughly half the number of seats of the two of us, so ... and they were concerned. At that point, everybody was concerned about survival.

The NDP did not want another election, knowing that we had momentum. The Tories were shell-shocked and they were starting to turn on each other, as these parties do. And we were sitting there — and I'm not saying smugly, but saying, "Look, you want to go back to the people? We're ready to go." And we were feeling very good and confident and we had a very strong caucus in that forty-eight members. I think that out of that we probably put together, let me say, the strongest cabinet probably ever assembled in this province. People with no experience governing but moved into governing without hardly putting a foot wrong — brilliant people that really executed well.

Q. You may not like me putting it this way, but the fact is Bob Rae made you premier. You guys sat down, you had negotiations with him or your team, the Conservatives did too, and ultimately he decided to back you guys.

A. That's right.

Q. Now, why did you —

A. Well, it was very easy. He could have backed the other guys and lost everything. He could have played the game and sort of gone back and forth, but we held the cards at that point, in my opinion. And if they didn't want to support us, that's fine. I'll go back in the House, we would be the official opposition, and he would have to deal with his own conscience.

Well, they came at this that it was in their best interests, not our best interests because everybody was negotiating their own best interests at that point. They decided their best interest was to not have an election — that was the key to the NDP — and to support us because we had campaigned on a number of things in common. Not everything. They certainly put demands on the system we could not live with, but there were the things — we were very pragmatic and found the things that we had in common.

Q. When you see what happened in Britain now where they actually have a coalition government, they gave up cabinet seats, was that ever under discussion at this time, twenty-five years ago?

A. At one point, it sort of bubbled up and somebody said, "Well, maybe we should have a coalition," and I said, "Absolutely not."

Q. How come?

A. I was not prepared to share the executive power because I thought it would go nowhere. They could support us in the House. Don't forget, I had witnessed two minority governments, Steven, that Bill Davis had run and we were ... and the NDP and the Liberals would alternately prop up the Conservatives, deciding on, you know, what was in their best interests at various times, and the issues and the policy at hand, until Bill Davis decided to pull the plug. You'll recall that.

So I had seen minority government work and I had been part of that, so I wasn't fearful of that, and didn't think we had to do anything sort of dramatic in terms of a coalition.

I also didn't think there was enough energy to put a coalition together. There was no national emergency.

And it's going to be interesting to see if the one in England works. It certainly looks good at the moment, two people adapting to the circumstances, but we didn't need that.

Q. You didn't need that. So you signed a two-year "Accord" with the NDP led by Bob Rae, an Accord of agenda items to get through. And then let's put this picture up; and this is what happened then as a result. On the 26th of June, 1985, twenty-five years ago tomorrow, you're the first Liberal premier sworn in, in forty-two years. The Tory dynasty is over. What do you remember about that moment as you were being sworn in as premier?

A. Well, that was the moment on the lawn.

Q. Yes, out front.

A. Well, we did something that was totally different than anybody else and we thought about this. There was a stage already set up for July 1st for the big [Canada Day] celebrations at Queen's Park and we said, "We are a new government." We had nothing to protect. We represented a different wave of thinking. I think we understood feminism. I think we understood the desire of new communities to become involved in governing.

You know, the Tories had been kind of a whole bunch of old white guys sitting behind closed doors, smoking cigars and running the place out of the Albany Club.

Q. That's a very fair, generous —

A. No, I am overstating. I am overstating a little bit …

Q. Yes.

A. … but not that much. There was a sense of an exclusive right to power among certain kinds of people. We represented something totally different than them. I think we understood that in our bones, I think we understood it in our hearts and in our brains.

And when we threw the doors open, and I … and we had thousands of people on the lawn. Fortunately, the weather cooperated. And we invited all the civil servants. And there was just a sense of the dust being blown out of the place, that a whole new sense of energy and optimism … and it really was a glorious day. So I remember that with great fondness.

And I had allergies at the time. My nose was running, but that's just a small by and by.

Q. Did you know that when you invited everybody to come into the Legislature that you were almost responsible for the building falling down?

A. I did not know that.

Q. I don't think that many people had been in before.

A. There were thousands of people that came in. And we opened it up; it was their house. And you'll remember that we spoke about creating a government without walls or barriers.

Q. Yes.

A. We were very sensitive to who we represented. It was not an exclusive group; it was every single Ontarian.

Q. The Tories had governed Ontario for forty-two straight years before you got there. And I wonder if you could share with our viewers what you think was the single biggest way in which your government changed Ontario during those first two years that you were in power?

A. First of all, the Tories gave us pretty good government, you know, and they changed when they had to and they were pretty good people and they are moderate people; they weren't polemical, they weren't ideological. And they were pretty practical and good people. Bill Davis is a good man, John Robarts, a good man.

So what was the big thing? We had, I think, one of the most active periods of legislation in the history of the province. There was hardly anything we didn't sort of reform, whether it was the court system. We brought in even, I don't know, television into the Legislature, whether that's a good thing or a bad thing....

We invented the Blue Box. The Blue Box was invented here in Ontario by our government and it's now being adopted all around the world. We had environmental policies that were second to none, French language, minority thing ... language things.

And I'm very, very proud of the activist agenda that we had and the people that were able to put it together.

So if you ask me if there was any one thing, I don't know if there's any one thing that trumps everything else, except I think, for the first time, there was a sense that the government belonged to the people; it wasn't the exclusive domain of the governors.

Q. You lasted the two years obviously with the NDP and the Accord. You ran for re-election. You won 95 out of 130 seats in 1987 to win re-election. And I remember Fraser Kelly, the television anchor at the time, saying, "Boy, this guy's good. He can be premier as long as he wants to be, as long as he plays his cards right."

A. It just shows Fraser's not that good, eh? So many times, you guys get it wrong.

Q. Three years later, as we know, it was all over and Bob Rae beat you in that 1990 election. At what point do you stop asking yourself, "How did this all end so quickly?"

A. First of all, I don't beat myself up with recriminations about this. Just as I didn't feel smug about winning, I didn't feel depressed about losing. I mean, the only bigger surprise to losing in 1990 was winning in 1985. That's the nature of the business. And you put it out, you do the best you can and you don't — so, my life has always been moving on forward and finding the next opportunity.

I could discuss with you why I think we lost. Everybody has got interpretations of this and whether it was a premature election, my bad campaigning, arrogance on our part, Meech Lake, you know, a recession that was coming. There's a lot of things all adding together.

And I really do believe, Steven, and this is my belief and I may be naïve, that people didn't really want to kick us out. They wanted to chasten us, they wanted to slap our wrists. But if we could have done that election again the next day, they would have said, "Holy smoke, do we really want to go there?" Because we actually — the government was actually fairly popular. I think maybe I wasn't, but there's a difference.

Q. When you think back, what's the one thing you might have done differently presuming you wanted to stay in office a lot longer?

A. Do you know, I don't think I campaigned with the same edge. Remember, I told you earlier that in the first campaign we campaigned without an edge, without recrimination. I don't think there was a clear enough defining issue. I don't think I articulated well enough. Reality is one of the — I probably spent too much time worrying about national unity. Now I care about it and I don't second-guess myself, but other people would second-guess that.

I was very worried in the wake of the death of Meech Lake that we would go into a terribly difficult period. I needed a strong hand to deal with Ontario. I had strong views on the future of our country. You will recall that separatist sentiment was then running up to 75 percent in Quebec. It was a very volatile time and I needed a strong hand to deal with that, I felt.

Now, it didn't work out that way but I also know how explosive these issues are in politics and how terribly destructive they can be. And don't forget, we came within a hair of losing the country after that, so ...

Q. But Ontarians, I think — you know, we've both lived in this province a long time and, you know, you either do or you don't have a sense about where you think the people are. They want Ontario premiers to play a role on the national scene.

On the other hand, they also want you to stick to your knitting a bit, too. Do you think you got too much on one side and not enough on the other?

A. I probably did. I don't think that was the only issue. I think it was a factor and it spoke, I think, to perhaps being a little too unilateral, being a little too arrogant, sort of doing some things that other people think we shouldn't have given away to try to keep the Meech Lake Accord together. And maybe I spent too much time with it. Perhaps I didn't get that balance quite right.

So, yes, I think, and a lot of people would say I didn't get that quite right. I was too much there. I was there spending too much of my own personal political capital in that debate.

Q. In our last minute here, I want you to take a look at the monitor. I'm going to show you one last picture. And maybe you could tell me what's going on here? *[Peterson is covering his wife's mouth with his hand.]*

A. You know, that was my wonderful wife. I don't know. We were just having fun. Oh, you know what that was? I do remember that. She was talking to some reporter and said, "We're going to win all the seats," or something like that and so I just grabbed her and I said, "Don't talk like that, because you can't go out and say you're going to win everything."

But, you know, when I look back at that, I could not have done that without Shelley and she is the world's best friend and very, very smart, great instincts about politics. She was there every bit of the day in success and in failure.

And when you have a wife like her and a family like I have, other successes and failures don't matter that much, because the real stuff is at home.

Q. That's a wonderful place to leave it. We have five people who can't wait to have a bit of a discussion about the Peterson legacy at Queen's Park, so we're going to get to that now.

A. It's now going over to the hands of the experts. I'm going to be very interested in hearing what they have to say.

Q. Me, too. And we're very grateful you came in today to share some memories of twenty-five years ago tomorrow. Thanks so much, David Peterson.

A. Thank you, for letting me share this.

David Peterson's political career came to an end when he was just forty-six years old. He didn't leave on his own terms as every premier wishes he could. And worst of all, he was defeated by Bob Rae, whom he neither liked nor respected much. The two both won the leadership of their respective parties in February 1982, and for the next eight-and-a-half years were intense rivals.

Peterson with his former-environment minister Jim Bradley, at the Shaw Festival.

But while Peterson did suffer one of the worst defeats in Canadian electoral history, he also sowed the seeds of a personal comeback on election night, September 6, 1990. As he spoke to his troops in the wake of losing fifty-nine seats (including his own), he reminded everyone that it was no sin to get knocked down. The sin was in not getting back up.

And so, after licking his wounds for awhile, Peterson began the difficult process of putting his professional life back together. He's now senior partner and chairman of Cassels Brock & Blackwell LLP (where another former premier, Mike Harris, is senior business advisor), was founding chairman of the Toronto Raptors basketball team, served as chancellor at the University of Toronto for six years, and led Toronto's successful effort to win the Pan-American Games in 2015.

Unlike in 1990, when many Liberals wanted him off their Rolodex for unnecessarily losing the election, Peterson today is probably the most popular Liberal in Ontario. Candidates want him at their fundraisers. When he makes an entrance at a political or cultural event, people gravitate toward him. He's always impeccably dressed and doesn't look anything close to the seventy years of age he will turn in December 2013.

The Peterson Clan: David (centre) flanked by his brothers Jim (left) and Tim (right), and their mother, Marie, now age ninety-nine, photographed at a farewell dinner for David Peterson, after he completed his chancellorship at the University of Toronto.

The pendulum has swung back. His premiership should have been longer. History will record that his last campaign was a failure. But David Peterson sure looks like a winner these days.

ROBERT KEITH RAE
(1990–1995)

~

I've had the privilege of covering the 1984, 1988, 1993, 1997, 2000, 2004, 2006, 2008, and 2011 federal elections, and the 1985, 1987, 1990, 1995, 1999, 2003, 2007, and 2011 Ontario provincial elections. That's seventeen in all.

The results more often than not were predictable. But none was as astonishing as the 1990 Ontario provincial campaign.

I was the anchor of the CBC Television News election-night coverage in 1990. The election was held on September 6th. Five days before E-Day, the executive producer of our coverage approached me late one afternoon, just before I was to go on the air to anchor the six o'clock news.

"Steve, come here for a sec," said Elly Alboim. Elly was the most experienced political producer in the country, bar none. He'd produced every CBC federal and provincial election-night broadcast for years — probably two dozen by the time he'd come to CBLT-TV in Toronto in 1990. When Elly talked, people listened, particularly if you were about to anchor your first election-night broadcast ever, as I would be in a few days.

I followed Elly into an empty edit suite. He shut the door and told me to sit down. "I'm going to tell you something now, and I want you to start processing this information," he said. "You're going to need a few days to get your head around this so listen up."

He had my undivided attention. What he said next was the craziest thing I'd ever heard come out of the mouth of one of my superiors. Ever.

"Steve, next week, Bob Rae is going to win a majority government, and David Peterson is going to lose his seat."

That was it. Just like that.

I have to confess my initial reaction was to burst out laughing. I had been covering Queen's Park intensely for a few years, covering it on and off for almost a decade, and had lived in Ontario for all but one of my thirty years. Elly knew national politics like nobody else, but, I thought to myself, he doesn't know Ontario politics as well as I do, and there's just no way he's right about this.

But I couldn't say that. So I stifled the guffaw and simply asked, "How do you know?"

His answer didn't fill me with confidence. "I just know," he said.

"Can you show me some polls?" I followed up. "Can you tell me who's telling you this?"

"Nope," he replied. "But that is what will happen next week. And I'm telling you now because I want you to get used to the idea, and I don't want you doing what the anchor in Alberta recently did."

Apparently, during the CBC's election-night coverage of the 1989 campaign in Alberta, the anchor was so shocked to see the Liberals double their seats on election night that she said something to the effect of, "Holy shit, can you believe they won that riding?"

"We don't want you doing that," Elly told me.

While I sympathized with his desire not to see his broadcast sullied by an impertinent comment, I did have to push back on the information he was giving me.

"Elly, what you're telling me is impossible," I said. "Yes, people are pissed off at Peterson, but they're going to reduce him to a minority government. They're not going to defeat him. There's just no way."

We went back and forth a few more times, but, truth be told, I left that edit suite unconvinced. With the exception of one year going to university in Boston, I'd lived in Ontario my whole life. I followed politics carefully. I had a "feel" for what was possible in this province we called "a place to stand and a place to grow." Ontarians simply did not elect NDP majority governments. And they hadn't defeated a sitting premier in his own riding since George Drew lost High Park in 1948, and even then it wasn't because they were trying to get rid of his government. In fact,

Drew's Progressive Conservatives won a majority in that election. But the premier suffered personal defeat because an anti-booze movement, led by William "Temperance Willie" Temple, targeted Drew, accusing him of not being strict enough on liquor sales and consumption.

But those unique circumstances were not at play in 1990. Yes, David Peterson's poll numbers would drop significantly. But in the dying days of the campaign, they rebounded somewhat. With a week to go, Rae's New Democrats actually hit 44 percent in one public-opinion survey — a surefire majority government. Rae's advisors warned him to be careful of his rhetoric because (unlike me) they saw an NDP victory in the offing and didn't want the leader to commit his future government to promises that would prove impossible to fulfill.

The Liberals went on a rampage in the last week, mercilessly attacking the NDP as completely unfit to govern. At one point, referring to the oncoming recession and the NDP's inability to manage it, Peterson even suggested "children would starve in the streets" if Bob Rae became premier.

The tactics worked. Rae's numbers started dropping. A seed of doubt was sown in some of the electorate, but not quite enough for the Liberals.

As I took my place on the set on election night, Elly's words were still in the back of my head. But I just couldn't envision it. Someone asked me before the polls closed how I saw the night unfolding. I stuck to my story. "Peterson loses thirty seats, but hangs on with a minority government," I said. Peterson went into that election with more than 90 of the Legislature's 130 seats. He could "afford" to lose a few dozen and still retain power. Or so I thought.

That was the night I stopped making predictions.

Yes, the Liberal carpet bombing in the dying days depressed the NDP vote by about seven points. So New Democrats had to be satisfied with just 37.6 percent of the total votes cast. But the votes split in a miraculous way for them. And that's how Bob Rae became Ontario's twenty-first premier, winning 74 out of 130 seats. Peterson's Liberals lost *fifty-nine seats*, not the thirty I anticipated. Even though they were only five percentage points behind the NDP in total votes cast, they ended the night with just thirty-six seats. (Lost in the astonishment of the NDP win was a slightly improved performance by the new leader of the PCs, a mostly unknown fellow named Mike Harris, whose party actually dropped one percentage point in support compared to the 1987 election, but gained four seats. We would hear more from him in the years to come.)

How does one win a majority government with just 37.6 percent of the votes? Well, of course, absolutely everything had to fall into place, including some much better-than-expected performances from Ontario's so-called fringe parties. The Family Coalition Party went from 48,000 votes province-wide in 1987 to 111,000 in 1990. The Confederation of Regions Party, running on a platform of opposing multiculturalism and increased French language services, went from non-existence in 1987 to 76,000 votes in 1990. The Green Party went from 3,400 votes to 30,000. The Libertarians went from 13,000 to 24,000, and so on. Take that phenomenon and sprinkle it over enough ridings, and those parties bled votes from the Liberals and contributed to the NDP's improbable win.

Oh yeah. That damned Elly Alboim was right. Bob Rae did win a majority. And David Peterson did lose his London Centre seat, which he'd held for fifteen years. The good news from the CBC's point of view was that I did not go on the air that night and proclaim, "Holy shit, can you believe the NDP won!" However, the bad news was, I was so incredulous at

Ontario's twenty-first premier with Canada's seventeenth prime minister: Bob Rae and John Turner.

the turn of events and so amazed at the history I was observing, that after being the first CBC anchor in Ontario history to proclaim "it's an NDP majority government," I went on to say to everyone that was watching our broadcast that night: "It's the story of the century!"

Just for the record, I didn't *really* think the NDP victory was a bigger story than, say, the First and Second World Wars, the assassination of John F. Kennedy, or the fall of the Berlin Wall, etc. In my excitement, I just neglected to say three rather important words: "At Queen's Park." Had I said that, everything would have been fine because, frankly, it was the biggest story ever in Ontario political history. It was just the second time Ontarians elected a government that wasn't Liberal or Conservative. The last time was in 1919 when they gave the United Farmers of Ontario a minority government.

But this was a majority. And at the beginning of the campaign, no one saw it coming.

Having declared the NDP win the story of the century, my next job while anchoring the broadcast was to start jotting down some questions I could ask the incoming premier, assuming we could get some head-phones on him after his victory speech. And to my delight, we did.

We went through the typical newsy items: Would he call an inquiry into the development industry's potentially too-close ties to politicians? Would he follow up on the "Patti Starr Affair?" When would he begin to implement his promise to develop a public auto-insurance scheme? And so on. Having got all the basic business out of the way (or as much as one can reasonably do in the two to three minutes one has), I knew I wanted to end on something personal, emotional, and memorable. And so I asked about something that cut very close to Bob Rae's core:

"Finally, Mr. Rae, you have had your share of tragedy recently. Your brother David died of leukemia last year. Your in-laws were killed by a drunk driver in a car accident. Do you see tonight's victory as somehow payback for all that tragedy?"

It was one of those questions that could have gone either way. Rae could have been angered at being reminded of all this tragedy during his moment of triumph. He could have simply taken the headset off and walked away. Or he could have blown me off with a pat answer. Instead, he gave us a little insight into his day.

"Well," he said, "I was just saying to my mother this morning that I thought the Rae family was due for a party."

Nice.

Elly Alboim, to whom I owed an apology after I got off the air (I'd never doubt him again), said after the broadcast it was the best moment of any post-victory election interview he'd ever seen. I was humbled by the compliment, but still ticked at myself for neglecting to say, "It's the story of the century *at Queen's Park.*"

Bob Rae's first act in politics began with a by-election victory in the old Toronto riding of Broadview in 1978. He beat a fellow named Gerry Caplan for the NDP nomination. Caplan would go on to make a significant contribution in the backrooms of the New Democratic Party. Bob Rae would go on to win personal election nine more times, both federally and provincially.

So Rae became a member of Parliament at age thirty, became the NDP's boy wonder and finance critic, and moved the motion to defeat Joe Clark's government in 1979. Not a bad first act.

His second act began in 1982, as Ontario New Democrats begged him to bring his talents to the provincial Legislature and lead the third-place party. Three years later he moved the motion to defeat Frank Miller's PC government, thereby ending the forty-two-year-long Tory dynasty. Two years after that, he was leader of the opposition. Three years after that, he was premier. Not a bad second act.

Of course, the timing of his second act couldn't have been worse. Rae was sworn into office on October 1, 1990, at the University of Toronto's Convocation Hall. As guests took their seats, they couldn't have helped but notice the ironic music playing in the background. It was "Side by Side," whose opening stanza would prove to be sadly prophetic ("No we ain't got a barrel of money, maybe we're ragged and funny ..."). Economists were already predicting the worst recession since the Great Depression, and as soon as Rae's cabinet got a look at the books and the projections for plummeting tax revenues, they knew this governing thing wasn't going to be a walk in the park.

The conventional wisdom at the time was that Rae and his team demonstrated a complete lack of ability and skill in running the government. The party's most high-profile promise — to nationalize the auto-insurance system — was officially shelved on the first anniversary of the election. As revenues continued to tank, the deficit exploded to almost $10 billion — three times bigger than anything Ontario had ever seen before. Drastic times called for drastic measures and Rae decided not to fight the deficit but rather to fight the recession. He ramped up spending in hopes of protecting people from the worst ravages of the economic downturn, and, in doing so, brought unprecedented opprobrium down on his government's head.

Two-thirds of the way through his term, Rae determined the worst of the recession was over and now it was time to get the books back in shape. That made people even more furious. His "three-legged stool" approach included major tax increases, tough spending cuts, and a unique Social Contract, which saved thousands of public sector jobs by forcing government employees to take several days off work, unpaid.

Politically, it was an impossible predicament. The public sector unions, protected from much of the recession in a way private sector employees hadn't been, screamed bloody murder that their collectively bargained agreements were being unilaterally abrogated, and by a pro-labour government no less.

In hindsight, Rae's finance minister, Floyd Laughren, said the politically wiser thing to do would have been simply to fire 20,000 people and find the savings that way. But the NDP wanted to find a more creative way to save money, and in doing so angered the general public for going soft on public sector unions, and angered the public sector unions for daring to ask their members to give a little and share in some of the sacrifices that countless others had already made.

With a week to go before the 1995 election, Rae's prospects for staying in power seemed hopeless. Still, he visited our studios at TVO to make his case for a second term:

STEVE PAIKIN: Well, exactly one week from right this minute, the polls will close all over the province, the votes will be counted, and we will find out who gets to form the next government of Ontario. The man who has had the job for the past four and a half years, of course, wants it again.

This is an interesting time for Bob Rae. Pundits are working over-time considering his future. Will this be Bob Rae's last week as premier of Ontario? Will he be opposition leader again? Or is there a stunning comeback in the offing? After all, a week is a very long time in politics.

And let me more formally welcome you, Bob Rae, to Studio 2, once again. Good of you to take the time.

PREMIER RAE: Nice to be back. I appreciate the chance to be with you, Steve, as always.

Q. Thank you, so much. What has been the most difficult thing for you to try to get across to the public in this election campaign?

A. I think it has been a great campaign. Well, I think it has been the most fascinating campaign both to be in and, see, it has really been almost two or three campaigns in one. The first one, I think the public's view of Lyn McLeod changed quite substantially, and I think the Liberals fell very rapidly as a result of that; Mr. Harris went up.

And I think in the last week or so, we are beginning to see some other changes taking place. And my sense is that voters do not want the right-wing revolution that Mr. Harris is proposing, and I think our message has been very consistent. It is to say that the promises that are being made by the others are completely unrealistic, completely irresponsible, don't add up, don't make sense, that they will damage health care. And I am delighted now, in the last five, six days of the campaign, to have Lyn McLeod's full support.

Q. I am not sure she said that, but let me persevere.

A. Well, she has borrowed every single phrase, word, and argument that I have been making since the beginning of the election. Having spent a year and a half being a quasi-Tory, she is now hoping to go out in the last week as a New Democrat. I don't think people liked her as a Tory; I don't think they like her very much as a New Democrat.

Q. Well, some have suggested that you have finally turned into a real New Democrat in the last week of the campaign, and let me tell you what I think they mean: You spent the first four and a half weeks of the campaign quoting frequently from Abraham Lincoln's second inaugural address, appealing to the angels in all of us. And you wanted to tap into that generosity in society.

And I guess in the last week and a half of the campaign you have found out that it isn't there to be had, and you have gone aggressive. Isn't that fair to say?

A. No, I don't think so. I think we have been very consistent. I think it has been an appeal to people's generosity. It is also an appeal to people's self-interest. I think you would see from the beginning what Mr. Harris and Lyn McLeod are proposing is not in people's self-interest. Most people won't get the full benefit of the tax cuts that are being offered by Mr. Harris or by Lyn McLeod. Two-thirds of the tax cuts that Mike Harris is proposing will go to the top 10 percent. If you make over $200,000 a year, you will get a bundle from Mr. Harris. You will get thousands and thousands and thousands of dollars.

Q. Regardless of how much you make, you will get something from Mr. Harris?

A. Oh, no, no, because you've got a … no, no. Steve, you've got to … you haven't been doing your homework.

Q. Well, hang on. If you make $30,000 a year, you get a tax cut as well.

A. Yes, but just a second.

Q. If you make $20,000 a year, you get a tax cut.

A. No, I am sorry, Steve, you are not doing your homework. You have got to then add up what is the cut going to be in the transfers to municipalities, what's the increase going to be in the property tax of the person who is on fixed income? The person who is watching this program who lives in East York or in the west end of Toronto or lives anywhere across the province and lives on a fixed income, he might get a little trickle-down from Mr. Harris. But they will get whacked by their local municipality. If their son or their grandson is going to university, his tuition fees will go up $500, $1,000, $1,500.

So, you know, the Harris deal is a benefit for the rich, and it is going to provide real threats to services for most of [the] people in the province. Most people in the province rely on a good health care system, they rely on good public support for services, they rely on good public support for education. And the kind of right-wing revolution that Mr. Harris is proposing is a revolution for the rich. That is what it is. It is a revolution for the rich by the rich, and it is time we called it for what it is. It is not going to help out ordinary people. It is going to threaten the services that ordinary people rely on, and I think people have got to start looking again.

I think, frankly, the media — everybody — has got to have a hard look at Mr. Harris' numbers, what Mr. Harris is proposing. It is the most reactionary … is it revolutionary? Yes, it is. But I don't think people came to this province, I don't think people moved to this province, whether they came in 1780 or whether they came in 1990, they didn't come here for a revolution. They came here for jobs, fairness, decent public services. They came here, if I may coin a phrase, for peace, order, and good government, not for the kind of revolutionary nonsense they are getting from Mike Harris.

Q. Let's hear from them. Blair, you are on line nine calling from Toronto. The premier of Ontario is waiting for you here.

BLAIR: I guess what I am thinking is if we make people on welfare work for their cheque, if you work out the numbers, they are only making something like four bucks an hour. And I have got a friend who works in a warehouse who makes $8 an hour, and I guess I am thinking if tomorrow we start out making someone on welfare work for $4 an hour to do the same kind of work, how long is my friend going to be making $8 an hour?

The second thing that I am really worried about is where is Mr. Harris going to get all of the work to make all of the people on welfare do? And I actually heard him on the radio this morning saying that he might actually charge corporations for sending people on welfare to their workplaces to find work for them to do. And it just seems to me that what this is really all about is sort of creating a mass supply of cheap labour, and I am wondering if you have got any views on that?

A. I don't think Mr. Harris has begun to work this thing out. I think it is a bumper sticker, it is not a policy. It is not thought through. If you take all the people that are unemployed, that are on unemployment insurance, or the people that are unemployed that are on social assistance, you have got a few hundred thousand people. So, Mr. Harris is talking about an army of 300,000 people going off somewhere to rake leaves or babysit or monitor halls or do whatever practical jobs he has in mind. There is no training involved. It seems … he doesn't seem to have any clue about the training involved, doesn't seem to have any clue about the organizing involved, doesn't seem to have any clue about the costs involved.

Can you imagine organizing 300,000 people, getting to work in some reasonable fashion all in one go, some sort of workfare program, the bureaucracy that it would require, the —

Q. Well, premier, in fairness —

A. — intrusiveness of the whole effort? It is a hugely unpractical …

Q. But he hasn't said everybody would get it. He hasn't said … what he has said is single employables would be forced to work.

A. And how many … how many hundred thousand of those are there?

Q. There are 400,000 people, 490,000 people, I think, in the province, who are depending on social assistance, and presumably single employables doesn't make up all of them.

A. Yes. If you add … Steve, I repeat: if you add up the number, you look at the proposals that he is making for the people who are now receiving social assistance, who are covered, you are looking at hundreds of thousands of people. It is not a practical proposal.

I would suggest to the caller, and I would suggest to anyone listening, go beyond the bumper stickers. This is not a doable idea. What is workable is what we are doing. Jobs Ontario training is working — 65,000 people at work in the corporate sector, full-time jobs for which they are being paid by the corporation, not by the government. The government is giving the corporations money for their overall training efforts.

We are saving $420 million in social assistance by virtue of that program. We have people in JobLink where we are getting people who have been out of the workforce for a long time, giving them the help. The people of this province want work, they don't want punishment, they don't want bizarre, wacko ideas that are suddenly thrown on to a bumper sticker, and then said, "Here is an idea. Let's blame people who are poor."

BENNETT: I am wondering, why haven't you pointed out the fact that Mr. Harris' platforms, each and every one of them, are totally identical to the platforms that Newt Gingrich put out during the congressional campaign...?

Q. He has said that.

BENNETT: ... and subsequently?

Q. Bennett, hang on, he has said that. In fact, maybe to your regret, you called the Tory ... a lot of the Tory platform, you know, "adolescent Republican freaks" was how you described a lot of the policymakers.

A. No, I said that there were some Ayn Rand enthusiasts that were hanging around Mr. Harris, but I think the caller is making a very good point. I think some more work should be done, perhaps, by some enterprising journalist who is looking at the rise of Mr. Harris and analyze the similarity between Mr. Harris' proposals and not only Mr. Gingrich's, but actually look at the gubernatorial ... the campaigns for governor carried on by a lot of Republicans in 1992 and 1994. The language is exactly the same, talking about a revolution, talking about ... using that word. Talking about workfare, talking about blaming the poor, talking about tax cuts for the rich and for the wealthy.

Q. Those governors all won ...

A. That is fine, but Steve, if I can say directly to you, Ontario is not the fifty-first state. That is Mr. Harris' mistake, and that is where I think he is wrong, that is where I think he has miscalculated terribly.

I don't think the people of Ontario want a revolution, and I don't think they want to turn this province into the fifty-first state, and that is Mr. Harris' fundamental mistake.

MARK: I have to say right now, you are going to win. There is no question, because you are the only one who is talking any, if I may say, common sense at all.

A. That's all right. That is one phrase we can recapture for the —

MARK: Well, it is not such a bad phrase.

A. — for the English language.

MARK: It is just that some people have taken it over.

Q. It is a great phrase. No one has taken it over.

A. Can I ask you a question, Mark?

MARK: Yes.

Q. What poll have you seen that the rest of us haven't seen that indicates that Bob Rae is going to continue to be premier after next week's election?

MARK: Well, I used to be a Liberal, and I know that people — the Liberals are running from Lyn McLeod in droves, and they want to stop Harris, and I think that is what I want to ask the premier about. How do you plan to move the Liberals, who are uncomfortable with McLeod and the undecided, over to you so you can beat Harris?

A. By doing exactly what we are doing, and that is by not just appealing to Liberals, though I think it is very important to people who voted

Liberal in the past. I am also appealing to a lot of people who voted Conservative in the past.

I listen to Mr. Harris, and I don't hear the voice of Bill Davis, I don't hear the voice of reason, I don't hear the voice of moderation and of balance. I hear a voice that is extreme, that frankly becomes almost more extreme every day.

Q. Davis wasn't $98 billion in debt.

A. Oh, no, I am sorry. Look, Steve —

Q. Davis wasn't —

A. — if you want to apologize for Mr. Harris tonight, that is your business, but I think it is important for people to know that there really is a major, major difference between what Mr. Harris is proposing and what has been proposed before. And besides, if you think a $6-billion tax cut, which is the real value of what he is proposing, is the way to get the province out of debt, then you have got a slide rule that nobody else in the world has ever seen.

PAT: I wish you the best of luck in the election, but I have a question to you with regard to you … something that you mentioned earlier. You said the people of Ontario are not ready for a revolution. I would like to challenge you on that. I think that the people of Ontario are ready for a lot of changes, drastic changes, some of the changes that Mr. Harris has suggested, such as the workfare program. Working people in Ontario are tired of watching people sit at home, collect more money than they get when they are working.

They are in the workforce, and I think it is time that those people, whatever ideas he comes up with, it is time for those people to begin to work for their benefits.

A. Well, let's analyze what you are saying. Like, I mean, I think that, first of all, if you look at the benefits, for example, for a single employable person, those benefits would be somewhere in the area of between $500 and $650, depending on the person's rent, a month. I don't know too many people out there who are looking at living on much less than that. It is well below the poverty line.

I think, again, if you look at the facts with respect to what people are living on, on social assistance, there aren't too many employable people who are there because that is where they want to be. I think the fact of the matter is we have gone through a recession and we have to create work.

Our approach is to create work, is to create opportunity, is to create opportunities for training and to create opportunities for people to get their skill levels back up. But I think that is a much better approach than the one that Mr. Harris is putting forward.

And look, we will see what happens on election day, whether the kind of stuff that Mr. Harris is talking about, where he is promising tax cuts worth somewhere between $5 billion and $6 billion, whether those are the kinds of proposals that make sense to people. I don't happen to think they make sense. I don't think his proposals add up, but if you feel that they do, that is your right.

All I can say to you is, your health care will suffer, brother, and you will have a rougher, much rougher time getting the services, and your children will have a much rougher time getting the services and the education, the quality services that they need, because Mr. Harris is cutting out all the underpinnings, all the foundation for the services that you need.

Q. Pat, when you talk to your friends about this, does the workfare issue come up frequently?

PAT: Sure it does. I am a university graduate. I am finishing this year, and just the job prospects are poor, as university graduates in general. I myself have a position. I start in September but, in general, prospects for graduates are poor. And it frustrates many of us that people can just stay at home and they have no incentive to work because they can collect benefits. Why work when I can sit at home and collect the same amount of money?

A. But you are not ... again, you are a university student. Let's go back ... let's have a look at the facts. It is like unemployment insurance. People collect unemployment insurance and then at the same time they are training to get a job. There are lots of people who are on social assistance who are in university. There are 100,000 people who are on social assistance who are out there getting work and doing work and supplementing their income.

So, I mean, again, I don't quite see how punishing people who don't have a job helps us very much or helps the economy very much.

I would have thought that a more practical approach would be to say, "Let's create more opportunities for work. Let's create new opportunities for jobs," rather than punishing people who don't have work right now.

ERIC: I work in the auto-insurance industry, as well as owning two businesses of my own, which I did not have much help from [MPP] Marilyn Churley's office in setting up. How are you any different? What are you doing that is going to make me believe your promises any more than anyone else's? Because you certainly didn't follow through with your promises in auto insurance. All you did was transfer the burden from the health care system to the insurance industry.

A. Well, again, let's look at some of the things that you are saying — and how am I any different? Well, I think ultimately people will have to reach that conclusion themselves, but I think that we have demonstrated it. If you look, for example, you talk about transfers to municipalities and what we have had to do.

We faced a recession, Eric. I think everyone understands that, a recession in which the transfers coming to the province from people, the revenues coming into the province were cut dramatically. We had to make many difficult decisions. One of them was the Social Contract, through which we saved 40,000 jobs. The approaches that have been taken by other governments is to slash and cut far more dramatically, and to reduce transfers and reduce the supports for people much more dramatically than that.

And if you compare the campaign that I am running this time to the one that is being run by my opponents, they are out there making all sorts of promises. Lyn McLeod is out there with hundreds and hundreds of promises, and Mr. Harris has got his billions and billions of dollars in tax cuts that he is offering people, none of which, I think, is very realistic.

So, I think what we are proposing is much more realistic and much more practical. And I think those words, to me, have a lot of meaning, because I know what it takes to have to make some of the decisions in the premier's office, and I would listen to what the others are saying, and I just don't think it is doable.

HANK: The thing that I would like to know from the premier is: what is it you want to do? I have heard so much talk now about welfare and all this type of stuff. The real issue, as far as I can see, is the big businesses' attitudes toward the workers. Fifteen years of service or more, you are a liability to the company. That is where the biggest problem is in our country.

What is the premier willing to do in order to change that attitude with the big business?

A. We are the only province that has the most extensive wage insurance, for example, that protects people's wages no matter what happens to a company. We have the most extensive and worker-friendly approach to severance pay and to making sure that people are protected and making sure that people have rights with respect to companies' decisions to make decisions to lay off and do those sorts of things.

I think what is happening out there is that all of us have to realize that the solution, for example, to unemployment, or the solution to the number of people who are on social assistance or are collecting unemployment insurance is not so much to blame those people, but it is to create the work, the virtuous circle between companies and the economy and government and workers that will create more jobs.

And we must have been doing something right recently. In the last year, we have seen the creation of a lot of work in the province. We have seen productivity improve, we have seen the overall ability of the province to export improve. Job creation has gotten better. These things are all heading in the right direction.

I think the key for the next term, for the next five years, is to make sure that we are working more effectively together, that we don't see confrontation between workers and management, that we encourage workers to organize, we don't punish people for organizing, for being in a union and having certain rights. And we also recognize that companies have got costs to meet, and that we have got to work with them to make sure that the cost of doing business that they have are comparable with that found in other places. I think if we succeed in doing that — well, I think in many cases we are succeeding already — we are going to see employment expand steadily, rather than the kind of ... taking the kind of action that Mr. Harris or Lyn McLeod are proposing.

KEN: My question is concerning the Bob Rae Days. I am involved in the transit in Toronto. And I have asked questions through the union about these next Bob Rae Days, if we are going to have to take any more. The extra money is coming out of our paycheques. My question is if the NDP gets back in, do we have to take more Bob Rae Days?

A. Until April the 1st, the law is in effect — April the 1st of '96. Look, we faced a tough choice, and the reality is that if we hadn't had the Rae Days, a lot of people who were driving transit would have had to have been laid off. We would have had somewhere around 40,000 layoffs. Across the broader public service of the province, a million people, we would have lost 40,000 jobs. It would have been the largest mass layoff in the history of the province.

I didn't want that to happen. I wanted to create a climate in which work would be created, and in which we would continue to be positive about providing services. So everybody working in the public service, me included, you included, we all took a pay cut, and the Rae Days is one way of managing that.

Q. What happens after April 1, though, when the law expires?

A. Your union will have to negotiate regular collective bargaining, how we are going to allocate, work through the fact that there isn't going to be a ton of extra money coming down, and people are going to have to recognize that whatever happens, that money can't simply be injected back in. We don't have another $2 billion to give to the broader public service in transfers; we just don't have it.

Q. I am just wondering, and maybe you can help us with this, Premier. The NDP leaked a poll today saying that in Metropolitan Toronto, they are now second, and the Liberals are now third, The Tories, of course, still number one. And I am obviously curious as to how this is actually going to play out in terms of seats.

A. I think what is interesting is that again, a poll is like a picture of a horse race taken at a certain point in the horse race. The one thing you don't know, Steve, is which horse is tired, which horse is picking up, which horse has got steam, which horse is coming in from behind. I have a sense of that because I am out there every day, but I think that the Harris thing has peaked. I think it is coming off. I think callers are in the focus that people have. I think the more people focus on what it is he is suggesting and the more people start to analyze it, and the costs, and the more people start crunching some of the numbers, which don't add up at all, they just don't add up, I think that is going to start to have an impact. And I do believe that people are then going to say, "Well, what have we got here?"

And I think what you have got is a leader, me, who has been working hard for the last four and a half years, with a steady approach, going into the election saying, "Folks, I am sorry. I am not going to go into this election making you a ton of promises about what tax cuts are going to be, and what all the freebies that you are going to get." I am just not going to do that.

We are going to have to pay our way. We are going to have to keep coming down and getting the deficit down. We are going to have to do it in a practical way, but we are going to do it in a caring way. We are not going to sacrifice the poorest and the most vulnerable as we continue to make sure that we work well together. And we are going to make sure the economy becomes more productive, that we get health care strong, that we keep it strong, that we make sure that it stays there for people.

We are not going to punish people who are living on fixed incomes. We are not going to engage in radical or strange ideas, such as the ones that Mr. Harris is proposing or the 350 promises that Lyn McLeod was making that people have now forgotten about.

And I think what we are seeing, and certainly in our polling the last three nights — we polled in Toronto, we polled up north, and we polled in Southwestern Ontario each night, and it shows that we are doing extremely well. And I think that is going to continue to be the case.

Q. Are there rolling trends here that you can tell?

A. Yes. In each case we are up and support is growing quite substantially, so I … I mean, I …

Q. Tories are still first in all three of those areas, though, are they not?

A. No. No, sir, they are not.

Q. Well, the Tories are first in Metro, they are first in southwestern.

A. No, they are not first in Southwestern Ontario.

Q. Who is first in southwestern, now?

A. We are, according to our poll — 34–33–33.

Q. Up north?

A. 37–32–31 for us.

Q. For you guys?

A. Yes.

Q. Eastern Ontario, different story, right?

A. We haven't polled there yet.

Q. You are not going to waste any money there, either, are you?

A. I am just saying to you, you know, the fascination with the horse races are out there. Everybody is entitled to those fascinations, but the point is that things move during an election. People make up their minds. Polls don't vote, people vote. Let the people have their chance. Don't say so-and-so doesn't have a chance, or so-and-so isn't in it, or they are in it, they are out of it, he is going to win, they are going —

Q. You haven't heard me say that tonight, have you?

A. The people will make up their minds, and I think that there is a tremendous tendency on the part of the media to say, "This is what is going to happen, that is what is going to happen."

We went through the beginning of the election, everybody said Lyn McLeod was going to win. Everybody said you are way back in the pack, you haven't got a prayer. We kept punching along, going along, saying this is what is going to happen. Then people said, "Oh, Harris. It's Harris, Harris, Harris, right-wing surge, da-da-da." I don't think that is what is going to happen. I honestly don't believe it.

I think, at the end of the day, people are going to say, "We don't want this province to become a kind of right-wing U.S. state. That is not what we want. We want this province to have the sense of balance and the sense of compassion that has been at the heart of Ontario life for 125 years."

JOHN: My question is about the auto insurance. Last time, when you were running here you said it was going to go down. In our area of town, anyways, it has done nothing but go up, 21 percent.

Q. John, are you upset that the premier didn't nationalize the auto insurance as he promised to do in 1990?

JOHN: Yes, I am very upset about that.

Q. Is that issue significant enough for you to make you not ... I don't know how you voted last time, but to make you not consider him this time?

JOHN: Well, yes, because that is one thing that a person pays a lot for. I mean, your income tax and stuff like that, that is just something you have to deal with.

A. The difficult choice we faced, John, on car insurance and you will have to make up your own mind about the election, but the choice that we faced on car insurance was that when we came into office the recession was becoming more and more serious, and it became clear to us that if we had moved to a public plan, we would end up with tremendous problems in terms of unemployment for literally thousands and thousands and thousands of people who work in the insurance industry.

And it was my call, I guess, and the cabinet's call but certainly my recommendation to people that we not move ahead with the plan because of the disruption that it would cause in terms of people's employment.

I think if you compare the rate increases in Ontario with the rate increases in other places, our rate increases over the last five years have been lower than they have been in the rest of the country. That is not great comfort to you, I know, but it does, I think, give you some sense that, you know, the rates have gone up in a lot of other places far more rapidly than they have gone up in Ontario. And that's just —

Q. Would you revisit this if you win again?

A. I don't think, overall, across the province, it is a huge preoccupation and priority for people. I think the priority still remains health care and jobs. And I have made it clear that as far as I am concerned, I am going to pick and choose my priorities pretty carefully in terms of health care and jobs.

Q. If you had a nickel, though, for every time somebody came up to you and said, "You know, I voted for you because of that car insurance thing."

A. Well, you know, it is interesting. I think in some parts of the province, that was a big factor, but in other parts of the province I don't think it was. And I think it varies tremendously in terms of people for whom it is an issue of top or primary importance. There is certainly no question that I feel the need … I don't feel defensive, but I certainly feel that I have got to explain why I said I would do something and then I decided not to.

I think my explanation is quite a logical one. I think when you explain it to people, they say, "Well, yes, I guess if I was in your shoes, I wouldn't have laid off 10,000 people either," which is really the reason we made the decision.

Q. Let's go to the hometown of Premier Rae's favourite caucus mate, Welland, Peter Kormos' hometown. James, in Welland, let's hear from you now.

JAMES: Mr. Rae, it is common knowledge that you are an advocate of the French. And I don't know what the rationale is, but our hospital has deteriorated in care, and I am a victim of that. How can you, in good faith, fund a million-dollar complex for the French in Welland for their own health care centre? Secondly, the news media has reported that you are adamant on making Ontario officially bilingual. That means two of everything, double the cost. Now where is the rationale in such a move? Could you please tell me that?

A. Well, James, look, I think it is important that we provide services to people across the province. I think it is important for us to recognize the rights of the francophone minority in this province with respect to services in health care and in education.

French-speaking people have been part of our life as a province for hundreds of years. French is one of the official languages of the country, of Canada, and it is a language which has a recognized status in Ontario, which is to say we have French-language services which are provided, we have French translation in the Legislature. We have assurances that people can get trials in the French language, we have French-language schooling.

And I will tell you, for the life of me, I can't really understand why people would object to that. I don't think we can build a great country or a great province on the basis of people resenting someone getting something.

If you have a complaint about services that are provided to you through the health care system, then I think that is something that you have a right to complain about. If you feel that you haven't gotten a service that you need, and that you want us to do a better job, that is fine. But don't take it out on your French-speaking neighbours. They have a right to services in their own language, as well. They have a right to be able to bring up their families and their children in French. So …

Q. He also suggested you were planning to make Ontario officially bilingual, which —

A. I have no such —

Q. Maybe this is a case of my not having done my homework again, but I didn't know that.

A. I have no such plans.

Q. Can I just gently suss you out a little bit here on tax cuts? Because in your last budget, in your last official budget, you offered a holiday for those who wanted to employ people this year on paying the employer health tax. It is a tax cut. I appreciate that you are going to say the difference between that and the *Common Sense Revolution* is one of great scope, but do you, by doing that, recognize that tax cuts are a good thing; they can be beneficial.

A. If they are tied to a specific target and they are tied to a specific objective and if, over time, you understand that you can't undermine the revenue base of the province. And I think what Mr. Harris is proposing, and indeed what Lyn McLeod is proposing are tax cuts of such a size and such a dimension, and they are so unfocused, and frankly so thoughtless in how they are being constructed that they are not tied to the creation of work, they are not tied to a particular problem or a particular challenge.

You know, we don't have any particular plans to raise taxes across the board or to decrease taxes across the board, as a government.

In a budget, one is going to make certain changes from time to time, and I will be quite blunt about it. I think that one of the goofiest ideas that Mr. Harris has come up with this week is the idea that signing the petition — I am not sure he knew what he was signing when he signed it; it probably sounded like a good idea that he saw on a bumper sticker somewhere, he went off and did it in a scrum — was to say that every time I change the tax system even a jot …

Q. That is not what he meant, though.

A. That is not what he says he meant. That is what he signed. His signature is there. So, I mean, you can … as I say, you can defend him vigorously …

Q. I am not defending him, I am telling you what he said was. What he said was, "Any time I …"

A. I know what he said.

Q. "Any time I make a net increase in taxes …"

A. I know what he said. I also know what he signed.

Q. Yes.

A. And what he signed was, maybe he hadn't thought it through. Maybe he didn't know what he was signing. I mean, it is great; a terrific advertisement for what you have to do when you are premier, but there you are. The idea that every time you touch the tax system, you have to have a referendum. Well, excuse me, I mean, you can't run a railroad this way. This is nuts.

ANDREW: I wanted to know: if Mike Harris' tax cuts are not practical, are you basing this on the fact that the NDP are the only ones that know the true financial picture, seeing how you did not bring down a budget this year?

A. No, I am basing it on the fact that first of all, there is a budget statement by the minister of finance, which makes the financial picture of the province perfectly clear. In fact, the famous Moody's rating agency from New York said that on the basis of what they saw in that document that they were satisfied the province was clearly on track for 1995/1996.

So I am basing it on my understanding of what a $5-billion to $6-billion tax cut, which is what a 30 percent income tax cut really means, would mean for a province of our size and with the obligations that we have. It costs us, Andrew; it costs us a lot of money to run the health care system. That is exactly what Ronald Reagan told Americans in 1980, as a result of which the United States has a multi-trillion-dollar debt problem. I do not want to put this province in the same position. It is voodoo economics and I say, with great respect, there are ways of doing things and there are ways of not doing things, and Mr. Harris is a classic example of ways of not doing things.

Q. And, on that note, thanks for being here.

A. Thank you very much.

A decade and a half after Bob Rae's premiership, the public seems not only more prepared to sign on to Rae's policies, but they have also rewarded governments for taking that approach. Stephen Harper, Dalton McGuinty, and Alison Redford, not to mention Barack Obama, all have won re-election in the midst of the Great Recession by saying, in effect, let's save jobs today and worry about balancing budgets tomorrow.

But the public wasn't in that mindset in 1995. The result for Rae's NDP was electoral defeat at the hands of Mike Harris' Progressive Conservatives. But it was not a crushing Kim Campbell-style defeat (two seats in 1993). The NDP still won seventeen seats, including Rae's own. They earned 21 percent of the total votes cast as well. Both those numbers are down only slightly from the NDP's traditional base of support. And on February 7, 1996 — fourteen years to the day after becoming NDP leader — Rae ended his second act in public life, telling supporters who begged him to stay, "It's better to leave when they want you to stay, rather than hang on too long when they want you to go."

Here's his exit interview on TVO as Ontario's twenty-first premier:

STEVE: Bob Rae officially steps down as NDP leader on February 7th, fourteen years to the day since he won the NDP leadership. He will resign his seat before the Legislature reconvenes in March and, for the first time since 1977, Bob Rae will be out of elective politics. How does that sit? Has that yet registered with you?

MR. RAE: Not totally. I'm sort of living this as it goes along, you know. I made the decision over Christmas that this is what I wanted to do and to try something new and try something different and to make a break with elected office. I don't know how it will feel. It's going to be different.

Q. What do you and did you love about politics and being in the arena, as they say?

A. People. Meeting people, helping people, being part of the community in every way. Politics is a lot more fun, I think, than people sometimes give it credit for. I mean, you should probably have a program where you do nothing but get politicians to tell you stories about canvassing — canvassing stories.

I mean, whenever politicians get together you can tell amazing stories about meeting the public, what they say, how people react, the challenge of office. You are, in a sense, in the arena, as [Theodore] Roosevelt said. I mean, you really are making decisions and the people are judging you and they're saying you did this wrong and you did that wrong.

I remember once when I had a function when [Blue Jays' manager] Cito Gaston was there and I said to him, "You know, the interesting thing about being manager of a baseball team and premier of the province is these are two of the only jobs where everybody else thinks they can do a better job than you can." Everybody — I mean, everybody's — got an opinion. Everybody's got a point of view.

Q. What did you hate the most about politics?

A. I didn't hate anything about it and I still — you know, I don't. I don't hate anything about anything. But what I think I found trying at times is having to make some really difficult decisions and I think having to recognize that it's become more intangible, or the swings are greater. And I think the way in which it gets personal.

Now, I can't complain about that because I've dished out as much as I've taken. But it is a tough — it is a blood sport. It's a tough business in many respects. And it's not particularly fair and neither is life, but politics certainly reflects the highs and lows of that.

Q. Did you, during this period of time where you thought about whether you were going to stay or whether you were going to go, did you hear from people who said, "Bob, the going is tough now. It's no time for the tough to get going. We need you now more?"

A. Mm-hmm.

Q. Why did you disregard their advice?

A. Because, as someone else said to me, "You could be eighty-five on the side of the road and there'd be somebody come along and say, 'You've got to stick to it, pal.'" Because, I mean, when I say it's a cruel and tough business, I mean when Bill Davis left in 1984 and I had chatted with him a bit this fall about that and I said, you know, "Did you have resistance from your…?" He said, "Resistance." He said, "Nobody wanted me to go." I mean, and …

Q. They all thought he was going to go out and win another election?

A. Yes. And I remember sitting around, waiting for that press conference [Thanksgiving, 1984] not knowing whether he was calling an election or whether he was doing something else.

And I think it's much better to go when people want you to stay than to stay when everybody wants you to go. I mean, Diefenbaker I am not. I don't want to hang around while people say, you know, the bell has rung, the cat is in.

And I think you're going to find already today it's good, it's healthy. People are saying, "I'm thinking about running. I may run." Lots of people who are entitled to run, entitled to be the leader of the party and to aspire to that are now coming forward. And being in a job for fourteen years, I don't have a monopoly on this thing. There's other very talented people who will come forward. The good thing about TV is it can very quickly establish you as a credible figure across the province. It's not going to be impossible for others to be established. And I —

Q. But many of those people, Premier … Premier? I keep calling you "premier."

A. Well, whatever you like.

Q. Okay. Many of your caucus colleagues told me, in confidence, "I know how we can get him to stay." And these are people who even want your job. "I know how we can get him to stay. We get him to stay by convincing him that we can win again. If we can convince him that he can become premier again and that our party can return to government, he'll stay."

A. That's wrong. That was … I mean, that would —

Q. Well, I infer from your leaving that you don't think you can win again.

A. No. You see, that's because you're basing it on a misconception. I made this decision for very personal reasons, as partly for political reasons in terms of what I think is best for the party. I don't think it's healthy for one person to be the leader of a party for twenty years. I think that's nuts. I mean, there's too many other talented people, there's too many other creative people.

For one person to be in one job at the top, being there means nobody else has a chance to do it and to take it in the direction that they want to go. And I think I was a good leader, but I don't think I'm indispensable.

But the thing that's wrong about it from a personal standpoint is, think about it. Let's say I do become premier in three or four years, back again at age fifty/fifty-one. I'm then at fifty-five saying, "Now I don't want to stay until I'm sixty." But this isn't a life profession. I have to think about — I hope people will understand, I have to think about my family.

I have three daughters who are teenagers, two of them. One of them is eleven; she's going to be a teenager. These are very critical years in the life of the girls and Arlene and I, and if I don't focus on the family and focus on what I want to do with my private life now, you know, they'll be gone to university. They'll be off and away and that will be it.

And so this is a very precious time for me and I — sure there was pressure from the party, but at some point I have to say, "Thank you, very much, and I appreciate your wanting me to stay," and I know there will be people who will criticize me, saying, you know, "You're bailing out." But, like I say, I could stay until I'm seventy and leave then and people would say, "Oh, you're bailing out at a tough time."

I mean, sometimes you've just got to go and you've got to make up your own mind.

Q. Let's talk about the unbearable lightness of being a social democrat nowadays. In 1990, when you won, I remember you talking about the NDP not as a party but as a movement, as a social movement, as a force. And there will be many nowadays who say that's not the case anymore. It's not a movement, it's a party like any other. They had to get in. They had to deal with the realities of governing and the practicalities of balancing budgets and all that stuff.

A. Yes.

Q. And now your party is going to have a hell of a debate as to whether or not it wants to move back to the left and be the social conscience or be a more pragmatic leftish but not leftist, necessarily, kind of party. Talk about that a bit if you would.

A. I think it's a good debate. I think if you have a sense of perspective, every single industrial country in the world has had it. I think the media and everybody else should open up their eyes to what's happened in Australia, what's happened in England, what's happened in France, what's happened in Sweden, what's happening around the world. I think Canadians generally need to understand that the changes we're undergoing are not unique to us. They're very widespread. They've caused a discussion in every movement.

When the Labour Party first formed a government in 1924 and they did it again in 1929, in England, tremendous problems. They came back in '45. They showed they could do it. They came back in '64 and they're going to come back again in England.

But the parties in each party —

Q. A big, different party, though.

A. Yes.

Q. Tony Blair's Labour Party, this is not.

A. Exactly. Exactly. And Bob Rae's New Democratic Party is not the same as the CCF in 1935. Why should it be? What else is the same as it was in 1935?

Q. But the critics say you sold your soul for power, in a nutshell.

A. Well, they're wrong. Let's just put it that way. I mean, I've been arguing with those folks for a long time. I suspect that discussion will continue. I disagree as profoundly as anything with people who think that it's immoral to seek political responsibility.

I think the higher immorality and the higher irresponsibility is to say, "We're going to stay here, pure, on the margins of politics, and let the right-wing jerks control things for the next fifty years." I think that's the worst thing you could possibly do.

And the other theory which I've heard expressed, even in the last couple of days, that somehow the answer for the party is to become once more in some golden age a radical socialist party, as if in knocking on doors, what we find is what people really crave in Ontario is a party that's more left-wing than the NDP. Excuse me? Not on any doors I've knocked on.

Q. So go the whole way. Make a formal — if not a coalition, a merger with the Liberal Party and be a centre-left force to take on, strongly, the Conservative Party.

A. Well, I mean, who knows what the future will bring?

Q. Do you like that idea?

A. I'm not saying I do. What I like is a party that's prepared to take responsibility and prepared to do what needs to be done. But again, I think I can speak with some candour and as well as with some experience, if the Reform and the Conservatives form a coalition or if the Reform and coalition forces do things as the economies change and as our whole province and society changes, the key thing is to make sure that those people who believe in community and those people who believe in some sense of common values and those people who believe in solidarity and those people who believe in an efficient economy get together and work from a common perspective. I don't think there's anything wrong with that.

Q. The premier of the day, Mike Harris, when asked what the Bob Rae legacy will be for Ontario — I'm sure you've seen the quote — he said, "I can sum it up in one word. Deficits." Now, while that may not be charitable, how accurate is it?

A. Well, first of all, it's not a question of being charitable. I don't think it's very classy but, you know, people say whatever they want to say. I don't think it's particularly accurate either. We had a recession. If Mr. Harris didn't have this peculiar sort of obsession that he has, I think he'd understand that Mr. [William] Davis' government, Mr. [Frank] Miller's budgets all reflected the fact that, in the late '70s and early '80s, we had a recession. Not as severe as the one we faced and not as deep as the one we faced, but they had it and they ran serious deficits. The Davis government never ran a balanced budget. They had a deficit every budget for thirteen years. So to sort of single me out and say, "This is all your fault," frankly, I just think it's silly and superficial. But you know, naturally I'm sorry that the premier would have chosen this occasion on which to say this is a particular legacy. I'm sure that on balance he would take a somewhat more — not charitable view, but a little more generous-spirited view of what — what my time in office has represented.

Q. Do you, seven months after the election date, understand why people voted for him, why 45 percent of the people voted for him anyway, which was a large plurality.

A. Sure. They partly wanted a tax cut. They wanted to express their frustration with the recession, with the fact that life wasn't the way it had been, and the fact that in this day and age it's easier to be against something and to blame somebody for the difficulties, and the fact that we haven't grown that much as an economy for the last fifteen, twenty years. And that incomes are stagnant and, for a lot of people, are down. They haven't seen a tremendous increase in the amount of opportunity for them and people are clutching at solutions, whether they're here on the spectrum or there.

And I think, frankly, the same kind of volatility, which produced our election in 1990, also produced our defeat in 1995.

Q. And yet Roy Romanow in Saskatchewan figured out a way around it.

A. Yes.

Q. What did he know that you didn't know?

A. I don't know. I'm going to have a drink with him tonight, so maybe I'll find out.

Q. Is he in town?

A. I think, yes, he is. But I think — it's hard to have a drink with somebody who's not in town.

Q. I figured you were leaving here and hopping a plane to Saskatoon. Sorry.

A. First, I think he had a way of getting it done that we didn't have. I think he set out at the beginning to do the things that needed to be done. It took us a year and a half, I think, to realize that that's what we needed to do and that was a lot of valuable time, in a sense, that we took to get there.

Secondly, I think within Saskatchewan there is a much stronger tradition of people accepting the need for solidarity and accepting the fact that it's going to be a period of sacrifice. And he succeeded, frankly, in berating and belittling the solutions that were coming at him from the right for a tax cut and for this and that which, in the case of our own province, proved to be very, very enticing.

And I think our provinces are different. But I think it says a lot about Roy Romanow's abilities, frankly.

Q. I remember in this studio having a chat with Larry Grossman once and saying to him, "God, Larry, don't you feel bad for Bob? I mean, he finally gets to be premier and it's in the middle of the worst recession in sixty years." And Larry, without missing a beat, said, "Are you kidding? Feel sorry for him? At least he got to become premier."

Here's a guy who obviously thought he should have been and never got the chance. Do you think about it that way, sometimes?

A. I think that it's a moment for me of enormous pride, pride to have been the premier. A lot of people who are critical of what we did or what we didn't do, they didn't get it. They didn't do it. They didn't make it.

So, from a personal standpoint, if you're sort of elbows up and saying, "What do you think?" sure I do a little bit. But looking at it more dispassionately, I think for the party and for the movement of which you speak, I think, importantly it has been a very, very necessary experience.

It was a necessary time for us and I think it's something which has changed the party forever, for the better. I believe profoundly that the test of power, the test of political responsibility is one that we met with compassion, it's one we met with graciousness and I think that ultimately that's going to stand the test of time.

I believe that it won't take very long. Already now, I was on the subway yesterday with [daughter] Lisa, going down to see *Phantom of the Opera* and people coming in and saying, you know, "Sorry you're leaving," and I figure, "Gosh, this is great." I mean, I should resign every day. It's amazing the things that people say and feel.

And I think there is going to be a different perspective on our government and on what we were trying to do and the sense of solidarity we were trying to create within the context of tremendous change in our economy. That's going to do the party a world of good for the future.

Q. I hate to throw this at you with just a minute left, but I asked you this at the news conference on Saturday and I've thought about it some more and I want to ask it of you again.

A. You want a better answer.

Q. No. Your answer was fine last time, but maybe my question will be a little better.

You spent a year of your life on the Charlottetown Accord. It failed. Much of the legislation that you brought in, in your five years of office, is being overturned right now and, by the time the Harris Tories are finished, maybe all of it will be gone. Yes, there is a casino in Windsor. How will we know Bob Rae was ever premier?

A. Well, I think there are — if I just try to sum up what I said before and say it again as emphatically as I can: There are values as well as institutions, I think, that have profoundly been affected by the fact that we've been in government. There's a sense, I think, of solidarity and of caring in this province that we helped to sustain during our time in office.

We went through a tremendously difficult time. I think in terms of the legislation that we passed, much of it will stand the test of time. Much of it will be seen to be necessary, perhaps in some other form, perhaps in some other way but, you know, equity doesn't go out of fashion, compassion doesn't go out of fashion. The need for decent housing doesn't go out of fashion. The need for fairness in employment doesn't go out of fashion. The need for effective partnerships between business and management and business and labour, these things don't go out of fashion.

Q. And that will outlive your time in office?

A. That will outlive our time in office. It will outlive — most importantly, I think it will outlive whoever's in office. And some of these things are more permanent even than governments, whether they're governments of our stripe or governments of Mr. Harris' stripe.

Mr. Harris shouldn't believe that he's building a way of life that's going to last for a thousand years either because, believe me, it ain't, and these things will return.

Q. We thank you for your time.

A. Thank you, sir.

Q. And we wish you well in private life —

A. Thank you.

Q. — practising law. Robert Keith Rae, the twenty-first premier of Ontario, private citizen in a couple of weeks.

Shortly after his resignation as Ontario NDP leader, I interviewed Rae at his new office at Goodmans law firm. Yes, there was a certain irony in his working for a firm named after one of the Tory party's most legendary back-room advisors. This time we talked about the race to succeed him. Four candidates vied for the job, all former cabinet ministers: Howard Hampton, Frances Lankin, Tony Silipo, and Peter Kormos.

Q. Well, in a way, it is 1982 again. The next leader of the NDP will come in as the leader of the third party, as you came in —

A. That's right, yes.

Q. — in 1982, as a leader of the third party. So, give him or give her some advice; what do they need to know?

A. I think the key is to start building for the next election. I think you have got to keep your eye focused clearly on that campaign. You have got to build a team for that campaign. You have got to get the best available candidates. You have got to build a party platform that is going to make sense for the election in 1999 or in 2000 or in whenever it comes. And I think, in that campaign, go for government.

Remember that that is how I campaigned every time. People laughed at me in '85 and '87 and '90, when I did it, but I really believed that that was an important message for the party, as well as for the public. And I think the last fifteen years in politics have proven that any one of the three parties can win, and that should be the strategy and objective of the next campaign.

Political preparation for the campaign is all very important. I would keep the policies as simple as possible. The party probably has too much policy, but this is a personal bugbear of mine. But getting the right people on the team, getting the right candidates. You know, we are going to have a smaller number of ridings, 103 ridings. We are going to have to really focus on where we can win and get the campaigns going on the ground that can build the momentum before the election.

Q. Who do you hope wins?

A. I really don't have a preference. I mean, I have encouraged a number of the people to run, and some didn't need encouragement — some did. I think it is important for the party to have a wide range. I think that the people that are running are very capable of being the leader.

Q. Any four of them?

A. Well, I am not going to pretend that I have equal views about all four, but I certainly think that, you know, there is a capability there in that team to become the next government and to build the team for government. I think that is the key point.

Q. You know, [former premier] John Robarts pretty clearly signalled who he hoped succeeded him; he kind of wanted [Bill] Davis. And Davis, even though he never said it, but he was pretty clear that he didn't want Frank Miller to win.

A. Yes, but who did he want?

Q. Well … he wanted Larry Grossman to win. At least, that is what Larry tells me all the time.

A. I am sure they all … I am sure they all tell you …

Q. So, who did Bob Rae … you gave Frances Lankin, basically, the most responsibility when you had the power to decide these things. Do I assume from that that you'd like her to win?

A. Well, if you look at … well, no, you look at the three, the three ministers that stayed in cabinet and that were in cabinet. They all had major responsibilities, they all took on a range of responsibilities. And when I made the major shuffle, sort of the key shuffle in January of 1993, I switched both Howard and Frances and gave them new responsibilities, not because they weren't doing well — they were doing a great job. Both of them were doing well, and Tony Silipo took on a major responsibility in ComSoc [Community and Social Services].

So, you would find it pretty hard to detect in what I have done that I have got a preference.

Q. Should the next NDP leader continue to move the party closer to what … I don't know, do you want to call it the pragmatic middle or closer to that sense of where Ontario is? Is that a good idea?

A. I think you have to have an understanding of the need to appeal to the broad middle of the public. You have got to remember that the middle is where most of the public is at.

At the same time, in order to mobilize support and to mobilize our people, you have got to be raising issues, and you have got to be taking issues on that are going to cause a debate in the province, you can't be wishy-washy, and you can't have nothing to say. You've got to stand for things, you've got to have something to say if you are going to be able to mobilize support.

But you have also got to remember that if you want to succeed, to get beyond the 20 or 25 percent, which is sort of the base of the party — you want to move up to the 30s and 40s where you have to be in order to win — you have got to appeal to a broad group of people who aren't very political, who probably don't think about politics more than a few times in a year, and who don't have a strong ideological attachment to anything.

And if you lose the support of those people, then you can't ever, ever, ever form a government.

Q. There is a certain losing of one's virginity, though, once you get in, don't you think?

A. Yes, but I think even getting elected involves that. I mean, as soon as you knock on your first door, you start to make compromises, because you are knocking on the door, and you are dealing with somebody who doesn't think the way you do and has a different perspective, and you are trying to win their vote. And any elected politician, as soon as he enters into that realm of the day to day and the realm of meeting constituents, and the realm of talking to people, as soon as you do that, you start making compromises. Life is about making compromises in many respects, in order to get along.

Q. It has been a year since you became the un-premier.

A. Yes.

Q. Do you still miss being premier?

A. I don't miss being premier. In fact, I have made the adjustment remarkably quickly, I think partly because I could see the train coming in the other direction, perhaps as could a number of other people.

But there are times and places when I regret the fact that I am not premier, and when … not to say it too grandiosely, when I think I could make a contribution that I now can't make because I am not there.

Q. Just finally, you have been in China for the last two and a half weeks. You were in Hong Kong before that. You seem to be not at home as much as when you were premier, and I thought private life was going to give you time at home.

A. The way Arlene puts it is, she says, "You are not home any more often than you were before, but when you are home, you are in a better mood."

Q. Thanks so much for your time.

A. Thank you.

* * *

His third act, back in federal politics, was still a decade away when Rae visited us at TVO later in 1996 to discuss his first two acts, which he described in a new book.

STEVE: Bob Rae always said he wanted to be premier of Ontario in the worst way and he is just self-deprecating enough to admit in his new book that, a year after he took office it was clear his wish had been granted.

In the 129-year history of Ontario, there have been only twenty-three premiers of this province. Bob Rae had the good fortune to be one of them. He had the misfortune to get just the job he wanted as Ontario was heading into the worst recession since the Great Depression, but he learned a lot during the NDP's five years in power and he shares some of his thoughts in his new book. It is called, *From Protest to Power: Personal Reflections on a Life in Politics*. And we welcome Bob Rae back to *Studio 2*.

How are you?

MR. RAE: I am extremely well. Thank you, very much.

Q. You know, you never would have answered that question that way if you were still in politics today. You know that, eh? Because I hear you are extremely well.

A. I'm doing fine, thank you.

Q. Making a nice living.

A. I have a good life and I do some teaching, I practise law. And I've just obviously finished this project, which is now underway, and I'm a happy man.

Q. If I may offer an opinion here, and since you didn't ask, I'm going to give it to you anyway: One of the things that frustrated me about your book is that I was hoping to hear the whole story from you and I don't think I did on a lot of things. And let me give you some for instances.

You tell a pretty interesting story in this book about how David Peterson used to come up to you on occasion, slap you on the back, and say, "Bob, you're a nice guy but you'll never be premier." And you never, at any point in this book, tell me about your true relationship with David Peterson, which I know is not a good one. Why didn't you?

A. I wouldn't say it's not a good one. I'd say — I mean, I'd say it's one where we were rivals in Queen's Park. We both started out as leaders of the opposition parties and that rivalry, I think, put a distance between us. We've known each other for a very long time and we certainly got along well enough that we were able to defeat the Tories, and Mr. Peterson formed a government.

So, I mean, there's no particular hard feelings on my side.

Q. He wouldn't go fight for the Olympics for you. You asked him to. I mean, there are a number of opportunities where he could have made a transition easier for you; he didn't.

A. Yes, that's probably true. But on the other hand …

Q. You don't take a shot at him in the book for it.

A. Well …

Q. I thought you might.

A. I haven't gone through life taking a whole lot of shots. I take some. I took some in this book where I felt the air needed to be cleared or people needed to know where I was on an issue or what I felt about something or somebody.

Q. Well, let me give you another one. Shelley Martel. I mean, the Shelley Martel episode was big in the life of your government. Maybe not the substance of it, but it turned into one of those "things." And you don't share with us much of your deliberations or your contacts with her at the time. I wanted to know the real story behind the scenes of the

Shelley Martel thing. I don't think I know that much more having read your book.

A. One of the things about writing a book is you get to write about what you want to write about. And you want to write a book, you write ...

Q. I wanted you to write what *I* wanted to know about.

A. You write your book and I'll write mine. And I think that's —there's 300 pages. There's a lot of stuff that you end up cutting out. The first draft was longer than the last draft and I wanted to focus on some subjects and some problems.

I mean, my own view of the Shelley situation was that it was completely overblown by the media and by the opposition and that it wasn't — frankly, for me it wasn't something that I was totally preoccupied by or felt was a huge preoccupation. Maybe I should have.

Somebody might say, "Well, you know, if you'd paid more attention to that at the beginning it might not have gone on to kind of ..." It was certainly — it lasted longer than I wanted it to from a political standpoint.

Q. The media loved you when you were the boy wonder in opposition, and then, when you got into power, I mean, people jumped. The ankles were breaking off members of the media, they jumped off that bandwagon so quickly.

Now, Mike Harcourt, when he did his book — we talked about this just before we went on, really gave it to the media for the way they had a kind of a shark-like feeding frenzy at his head. You didn't. I don't know why you didn't.

A. Well, I don't own a television station and I don't own a printing press.

Q. I hear one TV station is for sale in this province, if you're interested.

A. Yes. I know. I'm not sure how much money is required. No, but seriously, I mean, I think I have views about the media, which I express in the book, and I think there's ...

Q. Gently. You express them gently.

A. Yes, well — I would, yes.

Q. Look at how Harcourt went after the guys in B.C.

A. No, but Mike had his own things he wanted to say, his own things he wanted to do. That may be the subject of another book. I'm not sure when a politician says the media are subject to a feeding frenzy and they whip things up and then they get whipped up and — which is true, which is what happens. You can see it. Physically you can see it happening, you can watch it happen. You can see how they go on.

I've watched a couple of news items the last little while and, certainly, that's how it works. And it's a cruel business when you see it happen, when you see one person being singled out and then suddenly everybody goes after that person, and everybody relentlessly feeds and builds on each story. And then one quote is taken out of context and wham, there you are. But that's also the seas in which we sail.

One of the reasons that I would find it a little difficult is I have to remember that I took advantage of that as leader of the opposition. I participated in that culture for a long period of time. For me to stand back and say, "Well, now that I've been premier I can say it's all been terribly unfair," — life isn't fair and neither is the media, so you just get used to it.

Q. Bill Clinton: I know if I'd asked you two years ago, in 1994, when everybody said Bill Clinton was an irrelevant president after the Republicans took over that sweep of Congress, I mean, even you would have probably said he's done for. And here he is, he has repositioned himself as a "new democrat."

A. Right.

Q. You're both "new democrats." You didn't know that, eh? He's a "new democrat" and he's going to win again.

A. Yeah.

Q. Do you ever think, "God, what did he figure out that I didn't figure out?"

A. Sure. Of course I do.

Q. What answers do you come up with?

A. First of all, I mean, I think there's a couple of things. One, I think his party is different, in terms of his political base — and he's had, I think, a different instinct as to how to handle that and certainly he moved into the centre in a big, big way. I tried and I think we did from many, many points of view. But my own party was not as prepared to accept that as his party was prepared to accept it. So that's one difference.

The other difference is, I think, he's a better politician than I am. He's a better politician than most people and he's got a much better personality. I think he's got a capacity to kind of take hits and then come back. I don't think it's any secret that I kind of grew a little tired of the combat in the sense I became less enamoured of the game. I became a little more removed from the game at a lot of moments and a lot of times and I didn't run the kind of campaign and didn't lead up to the kind of campaign with the way in which I think we should have.

We ran a kind of a minimalist campaign, minimalist in the sense of saying, "We're not going to make a whole lot of promises. We're simply going to tell you that the other guys are full of it. They're not being honest. We're being honest," and we were. But it's not good enough to do that. I think that Clinton's offering a program and I think we failed to offer people a clear enough program. I think we paid a heavy price for it.

Q. I'd like to gently pursue … gently …

A. Don't be so gentle. I mean, no need to be gentle.

Q. … not in a feeding frenzy kind of a way. Talk a bit about the price of power. There are people with whom you had longstanding — and, forgive me, this is going to get a little personal. There are people with whom you had longstanding relationships before you became premier.

A. Yes.

Q. You don't speak to them anymore. It's a pretty impressive list of people with whom you just aren't friends anymore. Mel Swart is on that list. Here's a guy who nominated you to be leader. You broke the promise on auto insurance or you changed your mind on it and he doesn't talk to you anymore. There's a few others. You know, Stephen Lewis is not your biggest pal anymore either.

A. Yes, there are some people with whom I am certainly less close and who are less close to me. I mean, certainly Mel isn't going to call me up and say "How are you doing today?" And that is, I think, a function of politics and a decision of his in a sense more than of mine. I haven't written anybody off out of my book and said, you know, "I'm not going to talk to you anymore."

Q. My point is there's a price to be paid for being premier and one of them is you lose a lot of friends along the way.

A. I don't think it's a function of being premier. I think that is what happens as you go through changes in life. I think if you talk to anybody in their forties and fifties and say, "Do you have every single one of the people that you were friendly with when you were twenty-five or thirty, are you friendly with them today?" No. I think you develop new friendships along the way. I don't think that's something that's that unusual.

Q. Okay. The story at the beach. I love this story in the book actually. The kid who's drowning and needs to be saved by the lifeguard and ... go ahead, keep telling the story because it's actually emblematic of a problem you had with the labour movement.

A. The woman's baby is washed out to sea and she goes down on her knees and prays to God and says, you know, "Please. Please, I'll do anything. Just bring my baby back," and the baby comes back on the next wave. The wave clears away and the kid's on the beach and she picks him up and she looks up to heaven and she says, "He had a hat."

Q. And, of course, the people you're talking about here are Buzz Hargrove and Bob White and the other labour leaders who, despite the fact you gave them anti-strikebreaking legislation and did lots of capital projects that hired their people, you know, he had a hat, right? They didn't seem to care about that and they seemed to care more about other things where they differed with you.

Are you still mad at them?

A. No, not mad. I'm not the least bit mad. I'm more saddened by what I learned and what we saw in office and I think it's a real issue, politically. It's not a personal issue. It's a real political question as to, can the labour movement, and a whole lot of other people, housing groups — I mean, during the election campaign we had the non-profit housing coalition putting out press releases saying, "We'll give the NDP a D+ or C-," or something, "We'll give the Liberals a D and we'll give the Tories an F."

And you sort of turn to them and you sort of say, "You realize what you're doing? I mean, you realize that the extent to which you sort of just demolished us or put us in the same package with everybody else is the extent to which we're not going to be able to win. You're going to end up electing someone else."

And I think that's a large part of the political culture of the province, with respect to interest groups generally, that if you practise pure and simple kind of, you know, pushing your interest and saying, "Well, you give me this much," and without looking at the broader political context, you pursue that at your peril because what I think has happened is that people I don't think sufficiently appreciated how high the stakes were.

Q. So they were so adamant to punish you they didn't care if the Tories won and that's what's happened.

A. Yes. And you — yes.

Q. And are they worse off now?

A. Yes. I don't think there's any question. I think there were a lot of people who wanted to get even because we didn't do absolutely everything they wanted us to do or, in the case of some parts of the labour movement, because of the Social Contract.

And getting even is never a good basis for politics. Because yes, they got even with me. Okay. I'm out of it now. I'm retired. Congratulations. And there's your successor, what I think I called in the book, the starless sky. I mean, you've won. Thank you, very much. Congratulations. And I think that's a real problem.

Q. You know, they used to say about Frank Miller that he was a nice guy but just the wrong guy for the time. Can they say that about you?

A. Oh, I think they'll probably say a lot of things. I try to describe as candidly as I can the mistakes that I've made, and I've certainly made my share. But I think, in fact, we were a good government for the times. I think history will look back and say that we were sort of at the beginning of a big change in the province, that a lot of people who start the change or are first caught up in it have a difficult time, kind of, on that wave. And I think that's certainly what happened to us.

But I think that we anticipated a lot of changes and we did things in a way that was far more progressive than our successors. And I don't happen to think that what the Tories are doing is sustainable. And I think that it's more than likely that another government will replace them.

Q. Now, why do you say that? Because, you know, former premiers Peterson and Davis don't generally, as ex-premiers, comment on issues that are sort of around today.

A. Because I think what's happening is something — no citizen can sit back and say, "I don't have an opinion on what's happening."

Q. They do.

A. Well, that's their privilege. I don't intend to do that.

Q. It's not as true for Mr. Peterson as it is for Mr. Davis, but his attitude is, you know, "If I want to go off and comment on the issues of the day like this, I should stand for office again."

A. Well, I think it's important not to interfere in the day to day. But I think that — and certainly the day-to-day management of the party or what the new leader is doing but, as far as I'm concerned, it would be irresponsible of me not to say that I think that what Mr. Harris is doing is wrong. I think what he's doing is wrong.

Q. Let me ask you another one of the real smart-ass questions to close off with here and that is, you know, I know John Donne said no man is an island but can I suggest that maybe you are? I saw you at the NDP leadership convention that chose Howard Hampton, your successor, and you seemed like an island.

You're not as comfortable with that kind of group of people as you once were because of the five years when you governed and you had those choices to make and so on. And now you're — I know you're a Yonge Street lawyer [at Goodmans] but, for all intents and purposes, you're a Bay Street lawyer nowadays and you're dealing in the world of international trade and high finance, making a good salary. But my suspicion is that those big-money Bay Street people don't see you as one of them either.

Are you kind of a stateless soul in a way?

A. Well, you're putting it a little harshly. I mean, certainly a little more lonely than I like to think. I have a lot of friends. I mean, if I listen to your program, I have no friends I used to have, I don't have any —

Q. You know what I mean.

A. — friends in the party and I don't have any friends on Bay Street. Life isn't quite so bad. I wouldn't be enjoying myself so much if I didn't have any.

But there's an element of truth in what you say, not in the sense of being personally lonely, but in the sense of feeling that, you know, being in government did change me and knowing full well that I don't want to become a pillar of Bay Street or anything of that kind and no, that's not my shtick. It's not what I want to do at all.

At the same time, within the party, I think that there are a lot of people who probably say, "Well, you know, you've done your bit. Now, you know, make space for others to do theirs," and I think that's right. I think that's the right thing to do. So it's a chance for me to play a different role in a different way.

But I certainly don't feel politically homeless. I mean, I feel quite at home saying that I'm a New Democrat. I'm a proud member of the party and proud to be associated with it, but we're in the middle of a very dramatic change across the country. I think we all recognize that, and a dramatic change in Canada. Some of the old political formulas don't work as much as they did and have to be changed and have to be looked at.

I've always been an independent spirit and I think the thing that's true about my life, the reason I wrote the book is because I always have taken my own counsel a great deal. And I think that has its minuses but it also has its pluses. It means that I can speak my mind, say what I think, say what I feel, say how I feel, and be loyal to the people and the things that I really believe in.

Q. We wish you well in your new career.

A. Thank you, sir.

Q. And with your book, *From Protest to Power: Bob Rae's Personal Reflections of a Life in Politics.* Thanks for being here.

Ironically, Bob Rae's program to fight the recession — the Social Contract, freezing teachers' positions on the grid, unpaid days off work to save jobs, and dramatically ramping up spending to keep some economic activity going — was portrayed as utterly ridiculous and controversial twenty years ago. Today, it has become standard operating procedure for governments all over the world.

Once the Great Recession of 2008 arrived, governments everywhere primed their pumps and let deficits rip rather than watch their unemployment rates triple or quadruple. Every major bank economist

I interviewed on this approach acknowledged it was the only option today's governments had. Furthermore, other jurisdictions and private sector companies have imposed their own version of "Rae Days" in order to save jobs during these tough times.

In 2009, as the Great Recession was instilling fear in citizens around the world, we invited Bob Rae to revisit those decisions of a decade and a half earlier, when his government implemented the Social Contract. He joined us on the line from Ottawa.

STEVE: Joining us now, Bob Rae, the former premier of Ontario, now the member of Parliament for Toronto Centre. How are you doing tonight, Mr. Rae?

MR. RAE: Very well, thank you.

Q. I want to take you back to a really fun time in your political career.

A. They are all fun.

Q. Mid to early 1990s. You know what the recession is doing, you know what the unemployment figures are like, you know what the deficit is like. Where did the idea of asking public servants to take some days off without pay come from?

A. Well, it was part of a big package of things that we had to think about. It wasn't just a kind of a one-off. I think the real concern was, as we were heading into the third year of our government, although the worst year of the recession was 1990/1991, the recovery in terms of revenues and employment coming back, '92 was not as good as we had hoped. So, we started to really have a hard look at public finances, at where we were going. And I think … the critical sense came when we began getting reports from the treasury in the fall and winter of 1992/1993 that we were really looking at a $17-billion deficit number rather than a $12-billion number, which had kind of been the working assumption for quite a while. And that happens in a recession, but when it does, it has a way of focusing the mind.

Q. Yes, I had a feeling you were going to use that expression. You called it the Social Contract, the idea being if a million publicly paid employees take a few days off, unpaid, that will avoid you having to fire tens of thousands of people in order to save the money. When you invited all the union leaders into your office to have a discussion about this, what was their reaction?

A. Well, it was a long discussion. First of all, we had to have an internal discussion, because there was a lot of people in the government who were very concerned about it. We had had a series of dialogues with the trade union leadership that had gone on for some time about a number of other things we were doing. I mean, we were determined to maintain our investment in housing, we were determined to keep up our investment in infrastructure. We didn't want to get into huge cuts on the poorest of the poor, in terms of people who are on welfare. And about 65 percent of the provincial budget is made up of salaries.

When you are saying, "Well, how are we going to have an effective expenditure control program over the next three years if we don't deal with the issue of the size of the public sector, its compensation, and so on?" And that started out as sort of a discussion. There was some negative reaction, a lot of people who were unhappy, some people who said they could never consider it.

But I was persuaded that it was worth trying, because I thought the alternatives were, as often are in politics, it is not like choosing between really good things and really bad things. I haven't had too many of those days. I think what you are often doing is choosing between something that is less good and something that is even worse. And that is sometimes the choices you have to make.

Q. You gave the job to Michael Decter, one of your top civil servants, to open up negotiations with all of the trade union leaders, including the Ontario Medical Association, as well. And I guess I wonder, what made you think that there was the possibility of negotiating something, rather than just unilaterally bringing down the hammer on this?

A. Well, because I felt that people would see the nature of the choice. And I think that was always the battle all the way through, was persuading people that the numbers were what they were, that it was not going to make sense for us to simply increase borrowing, in a budget of $50 billion or $55 billion to have a $17-billion deficit, or to continue with really high deficits without any prospect of them going down didn't strike me as very smart, and I thought ultimately become unsustainable.

Don't forget, we still had real interest rates; I mean, they weren't what they are now. We didn't have negative interest rates, as we do now. So, the cost of borrowing was high, and I felt that as we were coming into recovery, which we were in '93, and as things were starting to improve in the private sector economy, it was going to be important for us to be able to keep things under control in the public sector.

And I didn't want to take it out of infrastructure. I didn't want to take it out of capital, because I thought that was wrong, because we would end up slowing down other things that we needed to do.

So that was the choice, and politically it was obviously a difficult thing to do. But again, we were determined to build new subway lines, only one of which ended up being built by Mr. Harris — others were cancelled. And one of them, in fact, the one that was cancelled is now being renewed by the McGuinty government with the support of the feds. So, fifteen years later we are going to get the York University subway when we could have had it in 1996 or 1997. So, I do think that we made some choices. Our successors made other choices and we live with the consequences.

Q. And when you watched TV the night the negotiations broke down, and you saw the head of the Ontario Federation of Labour and the head of the Ontario Medical Association locked, arm in arm, singing "Solidarity Forever," what went through your mind at that moment?

A. Well, we were obviously disappointed. I mean, it was a very tense moment, because I am sure Michael Decter, if he is coming on your program, can tell you, I mean, it was quite a close-run thing. We did make a lot of progress at a lot of the tables, and we came very, very close. And you still wonder, going back in your mind, is there anything we could have done differently? You always think that: is there something we could have done that would have made that negotiation come to a better conclusion?

I don't think people were fully aware of the fact that if it didn't work that way, we would have to do it another way, which would be more complicated and less desirable. But we were determined to get to where we needed to go.

I think we were asking the unions a lot. I think it is hard for union leaders to actually ask people to take less. I think in the public sector, it was probably the first time that it had been tried to be done through a negotiation.

In the private sector, you can get into bargaining about tougher alternatives, because the alternative is very clear: the padlock is on the gate, the banker is at the door, the choices are there. We did that in Kapuskasing, we did it right through Northern Ontario, we did it at Algoma Steel. We had to make very difficult decisions, and the workers ultimately bought in because they could see the plus side. They could see the fact that the alternative was going to be much, much worse.

But to do that in the public sector is hard because it is the government, and the assumption is, well, the government is always going to have money, and the government is always going to come up with the cash. So, I think in that context, I think it is hard to get public sector workers to agree to make concessions.

Q. I don't know if you saw Michael Decter's piece in the *Toronto Star* recently; he did an op-ed offering some advice to the current premier.

A. I did.

Q. Well, you must have loved this line; I am going to quote it here: Here is some advice from Mr. Decter, which says:
"Do not, as Bob Rae did privately, refer to the key public sector labour leaders as 'The four windbags of the Apocalypse.' This will make your negotiator's task harder."
Did you really say that?

A. I don't remember saying it, but if Michael says I did, I did. But I think he says it in the article that I said it privately, but clearly that wasn't the case.

Q. Is he right when he says that in the interests of getting a settlement, that may be ill-advised, if Dalton McGuinty is watching?

A. Look, I mean, if you can't have a sense of humour in this business, then you can't survive. I think I am well-known as somebody who in both private, dare I say it, and public conversation, say what I think.

Q. Well, let's ask the bottom line question here: You brought in the Social Contract in order to save ... remember as part of that three-legged stool, of course, program cuts and tax increases and then the Social Contract, the idea being to save $6 billion at the end of the day. Did the Social Contract, in fact, save $2 billion, which was the plan?

A. Just about, yes. I think, as [finance minister] Floyd [Laughren] used to say, "Spot on." Just about spot on. We did actually effect a lot of savings in public sector compensation over that period, and we did save a lot of jobs. I mean, when Mr. Harris came in, he took a very different approach, saying there would be no Social Contract. The unions all cheered, and then, of course, we all know what happened. There were literally thousands of nurses that were fired, thousands of teachers lost their jobs.

We had basically a pitched battle in our public education system for the better part of six or seven years, and very bad relations with the municipalities, very tough sets of issues there, and ultimately I think a playing field where Mr. McGuinty was able to come in as a man of peace and reconstruction, with a relatively stronger economy, and a lot of wind in the sails of the provincial revenues. And I think that had been the situation that Mr. McGuinty took forward for the better part of six or seven years after that.

Q. Not to quibble with you, but Mike Harris won a second consecutive majority before any of that happened, and obviously you've got to ask the question whether, politically, he made the smarter decision by firing all those people. He was seen as a tough guy prepared to make tough decisions, whereas you went for what you thought was a more humane approach and didn't get rewarded for it.

A. Well, we don't always get our rewards on this earth. That happens. I am quite happy with where I am, and I am sure Mr. Harris is very happy where he is. But seriously, I think we made the right choice. I think for us it was a hard one, and particularly for a social democratic party it is very difficult in dealing with the unions in that context. And we are not the first social democratic party to experience that. The Labour Party in England went through huge changes and adjustments and difficult moments because the labour unions decided that they weren't going to support Mr. [James] Callaghan in the end of the 1970s, because he was making similar demands and requests, and they decided to go with Mrs. [Margaret] Thatcher.

Mrs. Thatcher also won successive mandates, which I suppose from the point of view of the Conservatives is great. But when I look at how long it has taken Britain to reconstruct its public services, to reconstruct the National Health Service, to do some of the difficult things which they have had to do, I still don't believe that there are any circumstances in which the neo-conservative solution is the sensible solution, and I don't take away from that. In fact, by the time I was premier, [Manitoba] Premier [Gary] Filmon had Filmon Fridays. Many other provinces had similar circumstances and similar days and similar efforts, and I think our municipalities are going to have to make some choices and offer unions choices in terms of how to proceed. And even President Obama in his inaugural speech talked about how worthy it was for some people to give up a day's pay so somebody else could keep on working.

We didn't cut welfare by 22 percent. Frankly, I am proud of that, and I don't take anything away from that. So, you know, you live with what you do. I have no regrets. I would have liked to have had another term as premier, but a lot of things have happened since then, so I think you just keep going.

Q. Mr. Rae, as always, it is good of you to join us on TVO. Thanks for this walk down memory lane.

A. Well, you know, I have been a rising star in five decades. I am sure we will be talking in the next ten years.

Q. Indeed, we shall. Thanks so much.

A. Thanks.

Bob Rae has had one of the most eclectic post-premier careers of any of the twenty-five individuals who've so far had that job. Initially, he got himself ensconced in one of Toronto's biggest law firms, Goodmans. He offered his mediating and fundraising skills to the Toronto Symphony and saved it from going under. He mediated a dispute with Native fishermen in Burnt Church, New Brunswick. He chaired an inquiry into the Air India crash, which remains the deadliest terrorist incident against Canadians in history.

And, of course, Rae astonished many when he returned to politics, this time with the federal Liberals, seeking the party's leadership in 2006. People were shocked that he left the NDP, the party of which he claimed to be a "proud member." But it's also probably accurate to say Rae didn't leave the NDP as much as it left him. The federal party's increasingly anti-Israeli tone and doctrinaire positions on too many issues were serious problems for Rae.

Rae with Liberal MPP Monte Kwinter, now the oldest member of the Ontario Legislature ever.

He came third at the Montreal leadership race behind Stephane Dion and Michael Ignatieff. Too many Liberals regarded him as "that New Democrat who's been bad-mouthing us for years." Rae might have had more success had he joined the Liberal Party earlier, or run as a candidate in the 2006 election. But he'd committed to finishing his work on a task force examining whether a full-blown public inquiry was necessary on the 1985 Air India terrorist incident. As a result, his return to partisan politics was delayed, and that delay proved an insurmountable problem for too many Liberals.

After both Dion and Ignatieff led the Liberals to successive losses in the 2008 and 2011 elections, Rae accepted the interim leadership of the party, on the condition he not seek the permanent leadership. After much soul-searching and many Liberals telling him, to hell with his pledge, change the rules and run for the permanent job (which for awhile he seemed inclined to do), Rae told the Liberal caucus in June 2012 he wouldn't.

That seemed to bring to an end the third act of Rae's political life. But you never know. Last year, after he declined to seek the permanent leadership, I saw his wife, Arlene Perly, and mentioned how odd it seemed that her husband's political career was coming to an end. After all, I said, he'd been in public life for much of the past thirty-five years.

"Don't be so sure he's leaving," she said.

"Really?" I asked. "You can see him contesting the next federal election? He'll be sixty-seven in 2015 when the next election is scheduled to take place. You think he'd run again even if he can't be the leader?"

"It's funny," she replied. "Just the other day Bob was telling me how much he liked being just an MP. So yes, I can imagine it."

I didn't have the guts to push back on that, but I wasn't buying. The notion of Bob Rae being content as a backbench MP for a third-place party headed by someone else wasn't on, as far as I was concerned. So, when Rae announced in June 2013 he was resigning from Parliament, I wasn't surprised. Having said that, I can't quite imagine him being out of politics forever either. Rae was asked at his farewell news conference, is this it, are you done with politics?

"Never say never," was his reply. Now *that's* the Bob Rae I know.

MICHAEL DEANE HARRIS
(1995–2002)

⌁

There are a lot of "moments" in politics that make it one of the most interesting things in the world to follow — an unexpected election victory; a leadership convention that takes an unanticipated turn; the unveiling of an exciting, fresh new policy idea; a great speech in the Legislature; a witty exchange during question period; a scrum with journalists that gets particularly intense; a question-and-answer exchange during a television interview that goes off script.

But some of my favourite moments are those that happen away from the cameras. They reveal a little bit of truth you hadn't counted on. I experienced one of those "moments" with Ontario's twenty-second premier not long after he got the job.

Mike Harris could hardly have been more different from the man he defeated in the 1995 election. Bob Rae's father was one of Canada's finest diplomats. Rae liked to joke that he was born in a "log embassy" in Ottawa. He did not have a normal childhood. He went to public and junior high school in Washington, D.C. He was Richard Nixon's paperboy, for heaven sakes. He went to the University of Toronto, U of T Law, and won a Rhodes Scholarship to Oxford.

Mike Harris' father, Deane, ran a fishing camp and then a ski lodge in North Bay, Ontario. Harris attended Wilfrid Laurier University (then called Waterloo Lutheran) but quit after a year. He became a ski instructor. He went back to school, this time to get his certificate at

North Bay Teachers' College. He didn't last long as a teacher, and eventually became a golf pro.

So, when Mike Harris won the leadership of the Ontario Progressive Conservative Party in 1990, just a few months before that year's provincial election, there were plenty of people in "polite society," particularly in the corridors of power among Toronto elites, who thought he was completely unsuitable for public life.

And frankly, Harris didn't do anything in that first election run to disabuse anyone of the notion that he wasn't ready for prime time. The Tories got slaughtered in the previous election in 1987. Poor Larry Grossman, after having waited years to become PC Party leader, finally got the job just in time to see Tory fortunes plummet. He led them to a third-place finish (the first time that had happened to an Ontario Conservative party since 1919), and lost his own seat in the process (which had been held by his father, Allan, before him).

But as badly as Grossman fared in 1987, in some respects Harris did even worse three years later. Harris' Conservatives remained in third place, and actually received 1 percent less of the total votes cast. However, because of the way the votes split, Harris actually won four more seats — twenty in total, up from Grossman's sixteen. It gave the illusion that this new leader had not a bad night, all things considered. But still, no one was taking seriously this leader who dubbed his bus "Taxfighter I," and was talking up deep tax cuts on the eve of what would turn out to be the worst recession since the Great Depression.

When Harris showed up to question period, his attacks reflected a conservatism that was well to the right of where most Ontario Tories traditionally felt comfortable. Harris talked of the need for a "common sense revolution." He felt consecutive Liberal and NDP governments had lost sight of the fact that it's a vibrant private sector that pays for public services. He sensed a budding mood that taxpayers were ready to revolt, that taxes had become too high, and the government was intervening in the economy far too much.

But a lot of traditional Queen's Park watchers weren't watching Harris. The Liberals were in opposition now with a reasonably talented front bench of former cabinet ministers who were licking their chops at the notion of giving the NDP its one term in power, then getting themselves back on the governing side of the house.

Furthermore, Harris would go long stretches where he was absent from question period, prompting the "he's probably off playing golf somewhere" jokes. In fact, he and his wife, Janet, were trying to adopt a child, but insisted on keeping that private. Add to that the fact that no party had gone from third place to government in a single election in seventy-two years, and you had every reason in the world to ignore the man from North Bay.

Except that in politics, timing is everything, and at this time in Ontario's history the mood was becoming increasingly harsh and bleak. By 1994 the electorate had clearly decided it wanted no more of Bob Rae's NDP. The only question was, when would the election be called, and when would the Liberals move back in? At least, that's what almost everyone *thought* the question would be.

Michael Marzolini didn't think that. One of the brightest public opinion research guys in the business, Marzolini was the Liberals' pollster, and he saw dark storm clouds on the horizon well before anyone else did. So, while Lyn McLeod's Liberals were leading the PCs and NDP by twenty-five points on the day of the 1995 election call, Marzolini had already shared with me his deep sense of foreboding that this was not going to be an ordinary election.

He was right.

A sizeable chunk of Ontarians didn't want the Liberals back in. They wanted a significant course correction from the previous ten years — the "ten lost years" as Conservatives often referred to the Peterson-Rae interregnum of 1985–95.

And so, on election night, 22 percent of the voters who were with the NDP and Liberals in 1990 abandoned those parties, and parked their votes on the right with Mike Harris' PCs. Harris captured almost 45 percent of the total votes cast, a higher number than even four-time winner William Davis ever garnered.

Yes, the public was fed up: with what they perceived as exorbitant taxes, sky-high deficits, welfare rates that continued to go up (even in good times), the sense that public sector unions were being too coddled, and photo radar, which kept the speeds down on the province's 400-series of highways, but much of the public saw it as a tax grab in disguise.

With Harris promising lower taxes, smaller government, a more than 21 percent cut in welfare rates, no more Mr. Nice Guy with the public sector unions, an end to Ontario's "no scabs" anti-strikebreaker law, and scrapping photo radar, well, it was apparently an irresistible combination for a lot of folks. To make this new omelet, the PCs knew they were going to have to break a lot of eggs. In fact, they boasted "by the time we're done, there won't be a single blade of grass on the south lawn of Queen's Park that hasn't been trod upon by some protester." More prophetic words were never spoken at the Ontario Legislature.

So what was my "moment" with Mike Harris? It actually took place on a gorgeous, clear, but frigid day at Queen's Park. Our TVO crew thought we'd do something different with the premier. Rather than do the typical sit-down interview in his office, we thought we'd do a "walk and talk" interview with him outside the Legislature — sort of a different look.

As the crew was getting its equipment set up, the premier and I made small talk in the front lobby of the provincial Parliament Buildings. And then the moment happened. I wish I could say it happened because of some brilliant question posed by me. But that wasn't the case. Mike Harris just felt like sharing something I'd never heard him say before.

"You know," he started, "there are all kinds of people in this world, the Dalton Camps and so on, who thought I could never be premier. And yet, here I am."

With that one observation, I felt I gained a whole new insight into Mike Harris' personality. Clearly the man still had a chip on his shoulder at having been treated like a second-class citizen by the Red Tories who once ruled the Ontario Progressive Conservative Party. And it was true: Harris was never considered "one of the club." He was never part of that "in crowd" consisting of Premier William Davis, his secretary to the cabinet Ed Stewart, and a small group of close advisors that would have gathered at the Park Plaza Hotel every Tuesday morning, to go over government business before it got to the whole cabinet.

No. Mike Harris spent his first four years on the government back-benches, quite a long way away from the true corridors of power. He chaired a couple of legislative sub-committees for two-and-a-half years before working his way up to a parliamentary assistant's job. But he was always seen as too conservative for the Davis crowd.

Once Davis retired and Frank Miller took over as premier, Harris finally got his chance to show his chops. But it all ended too quickly with the Liberal-NDP Accord in 1985. Harris' tenure as natural resources minister lasted less than five months (he was also energy minister for about five weeks), and then it was on to the opposition benches for ten years.

Maybe I read too much into Harris' comment to me as we were waiting to shoot our interview. But it sure felt as if he was saying "to all you Toronto big shots, to all you media elites, to all you Red Tories, to all you socialists, and, for that matter, to anyone else who thought you had to go to the right university, had to belong to the right law firm, had to be clever and be well thought of in polite society, and, above all, couldn't be too conservative — well, screw you. Here's a golf pro from North Bay with nothing but his convictions to draw upon. And I'm the premier. So take that!"

That's what I inferred from Mike Harris' comment. And nothing I've seen in the more than a decade and a half since then has persuaded me that I'm wrong in that interpretation.

Mike Harris won his first election in the summer of 1995. In the spring of 1996 he came to TVO for an interview. While the relatively new premier wasn't keen on my introduction, which included noting his historic achievement of going from "worst to first" in the Legislature, he was in fine form as he took calls from our viewers, demonstrating a knowledge and ease on a wide range of issues:

STEVE: To say Ontario has changed dramatically since the Tories won the keys to Queen's Park is the understatement of the season. Spending has been cut as never before. Taxes may soon be cut as never before. Public service workers have gone on strike and that has also never happened before, all of which means there is a lot to talk about with our guest, Michael Deane Harris, twenty-second premier of the province of Ontario, and we welcome you here tonight.

PREMIER HARRIS: Thanks very much, Steve. I'm not sure I like "worst to first"; maybe third to first.

Q. Well …

A. I never thought I was worst.

Q. If I check the standings, that was … okay, third to first.

A. I was three out of three, so I guess that's …

Q. True enough. Outhouse to penthouse; do you like that better?

A. Okay.

Q. Okay. What have you learned? You know, there are literally contracts for hundreds of thousands of government employees coming due this year. What have you learned about these negotiations that you think you can apply to those future contract negotiations when they come due?

A. Well, you know, we are personally responsible for negotiating two directly, and we have successfully negotiated the AMAPCEO (Association of Management, Administrative, and Professional Crown Employees of Ontario) union contracts. I would not call, even if we get a negotiated settlement, this hasn't been successful. When you have a strike, it is not successful. But I believe it will probably set a pattern for other public sector contracts which our transfer partners, many of them will have to deal with that will …

Q. What's the pattern, though?

A. Well, that times have changed, that we need to be fair, we need to be reasonable, we need to understand that our civil servants work very hard in their jobs, and they need to be compensated properly and treated fairly. But there is a myth that's out there in the public area, in a couple of sectors, though, some in the public, some in the private, that they've been immune to the downsizing or that there's a guaranteed job for life, or there's sort of tenure. That has never been the case, but it's been more so than in the … perhaps the private sector, and it is not the case today.

Q. I guess what people are wondering is … there are going to be teachers who are going to see their contracts expire soon. Are we going to see thirty-two-day strikes every time one of these deals comes up? Is that the climate we're in now?

A. Well, I hope not. I hope we don't see any strikes. It's certainly not our goal.

Q. Will anything be done differently next time around?

A. Well, we hope there won't be a strike. We didn't go on strike. We didn't want a strike. And at the end of the day, let me say this, and I think there has been a shift, and I believe that the unions we're dealing with and our employees and perhaps our transfer partners have come to understand that the old way of doing things, that if government said, "Well, we're going to downsize a little bit," the old way was scream and yell, hit them where it hurts, and I give you an example: We early on made a reduction of 2.5 percent to transit systems, and TTC responded, "Oh, we'll cut WheelTrans. We'll cut the handicapped. That'll bring them to their heels. They can't cut us."

Q. And it didn't work?

A. No. It used to work.

Q. Yes.

A. You see? And we said, "No, cut something else. That old style stuff does not work." And so we want our transfer partners, and those that have played by the old rules, and some of the union tactics are old, some of the management tactics are old rules; they're out.

Q. Let me ask you my first sort of touchy-feely question of the night, if you like: The polls say you're as popular today as you were on election day back in June. You must be pleased with that. On the other hand … and listen, maybe this is just my sense and I'm alone in this, but when I run into people, the sense I get is that yes, people understand you've got to do something about the deficit, yes, people understand, they hope you're going to make good on your tax-cut pledge, yes, people understand a lot of that stuff. But they're not real comfortable with the air of confrontation that has taken over. They don't like seeing their premier behind concrete bunkers when he has a convention in Hamilton. They don't like the OPP riot squad being called in for stuff. What's your gut feeling about how comfortable Ontarians are with what's in the air right now?

A. Well, I think by and large the public actually, far more so than the election, are supportive of the direction we're going in or are supportive of the agenda. We see that anecdotally, we see it in polls, that they may say that we like another party better than Harris' party, we like someone better than Harris, but by golly, we are supportive of the direction, and that actually is increasing dramatically over this last period of time.

There is an understanding that it has to be done. Do it fairly, do it, quite frankly, quickly. I hear some say you're going too fast, but most people, usually that's when they're being affected.

Q. It has to be done, but done like this?

A. Well, I mean — I mean, done like what? It has to be done, and if some people say, "You'll do it over my dead body," as [the Ontario Federation of Labour's] Gord Wilson has said, unfortunately it has to be done. And I don't like drawing lines in the sand. I think that's old-style confrontational politics, union-management relationships. We're not into that. We're into negotiating fairly and reasonably, and we would like to consult, and we'd like to work with people.

Q. But there's a change in the air, you know? I mean, three hours ago, the OPP came to this building to sort of sniff it out and make sure it was secure. You've got three OPP in here tonight? Premier Rae, when he came here, used to have one guy, and —

A. I actually have one less than Premier Rae had on full-time staff, because we're short one, so …

Q. But I mean here, tonight. You presumably think that being out in public is a security problem.

A. No, I don't. I don't have anything to do with security at the Legislature, or here. And the detail assigned to me is the same complement as was assigned to Premier Rae. We're short one, I think, at the moment, and it's probably 10 percent or 5 percent of the prime minister.

You know, I think it's sad that any politician requires security. I think it's sad that some of our leaders in industry require that. That seems to be a reality today, and it's unfortunate, but it's not my wish or my desire.

Q. Premier, what has your government, in your judgment, done really well so far, and what has it done badly so far?

A. I believe, we've stayed focused. We listened for four years, we put a plan together, we campaigned on it, and we won on it, and we have stayed very focused on that, and implemented a large number of the items on that agenda. And I feel good about that, that we're doing what we've said we would do. I feel very confident that they're the right things to do, that in the long run this will be a more prosperous province. There'll be a better future for our children, as well as ourselves.

You've touched on a couple of things. I regret that some feel so strongly against the changes, and also so strongly, I might argue, in my view, against democracy, that they think that for some reason or other we're doing something we didn't campaign on, or weren't elected, people didn't ask us to do. I feel badly about that…

Q. That doesn't speak to what you think you've done badly, though.

A. No, but I feel badly about that. What have we not done? MPP compensation, scrapping the pensions. There's some things there that I wanted done before Christmas, and we haven't got done yet.

Q. How come?

A. Well, we got off on other agenda items. I want to do those things fairly and in consultation with the other parties. They're complicated. They affect people's past and future when we scrap their pensions, and we want them to be treated fairly, you know, in that period of time. I think we have something pretty close, and I think we'll be done in the spring, but I would have preferred that be done sooner.

Q. You're still going to go from 130 seats to 103 seats before the next election?

A. Yes, we had said 130 to 99, because the principle was on the federal, the number of federal seats. We'd like to have the same boundaries, and we believe we can save a fair bit of money working with the feds, and actually we are now in some good consultations with the federal government on how we can share enumeration lists, have a permanent list, how we can share election costs. And their new number of seats for Ontario is 103, so it will be about 20 percent fewer politicians. We need to have that ready for the next election.

Q. I want to ask you one more question before we go to the phones, because they're all lit up. You have done something that I think is unique. You've had all the ministries make up business plans, write mission statements, basically try to rediscover what businesses they ought to be in and what businesses they ought not to be in. And I am wondering if I can just get some of your thoughts on this tonight to see how far this has progressed.

A. Well, I don't want to get into the details.

Q. I want you to get into the details.

A. I know you do, but the business plans are still in the development stage, and still require approval of committees of cabinet and of cabinet and to come forward. I can tell you in general terms that it is new, and it is different, and it is more how the private sector functions.

What we have found is that the senior bureaucracy that has been working their way through this have really discovered a lot of things and said, "You know, we don't know why we do that," because they had to justify —

Q. Tell me one thing that government —

A. Well, no, well, I mean I —

Q. — should or shouldn't doing.

A. Listen, the other thing that is going to be very unique, all these business plans will be published, they will be made available. They'll be up for public scrutiny, just like an annual statement of an agency. But the kinds of things where we asked every ministry, justify this program. And when we actually got into trying to give measurable and tangible results, in many cases they said, "Well, you know, we just did it because it was there last year and we carried it on this year."

Quite frankly, when we consulted client groups, they said, "We don't need the program." Well, I am not letting anything out of the bag, but the business grants, where we committed to cut out to a large extent the grants to individual businesses. And we set a target of a couple hundred million dollars, where the business plan will come out in excess of $200 million. Many businesses, and when the ministry started to consult with them, they said, "Well, as long as you don't give this grant to our competitors, we don't need it."

Q. Our first call tonight is from Orillia. Mary Beth, the premier is here for you. Go ahead.

MARY BETH: Yes, Premier, I was just wondering, and I know [you are] likely not able ... to answer for Mr. [Dave] Johnston, but on a technical point, I would like just to know why Mr. Johnston was giving info to the media during a blackout and still continue his press conferences?

A. I believe that Mr. Johnston tried to respect the blackout with respect to individual details. Information he basically gave out was, "Here's the offer we made before the blackout." I could ask you why, during the blackout,

OPSEU ran millions of dollars worth of ads talking about what we were doing or not. I don't think that's productive. We hope we have a negotiated settlement, and my own view is that Mr. Johnston has gained respect from a lot of people involved in labour negotiations for being fair and reasonable and up front.

BARBARA: I would like to know how you expect to eradicate the debt when you are planning on giving people up to 30 percent cuts in income tax.

A. Well, I'm glad you asked that. Bob Rae, when he first came into office, his first budget he hiked tax rates by a billion dollars in his first budget. And then he hiked tax rates by a billion dollars again in his second budget, and then he hiked tax rates by two billion dollars in his third budget. He hiked tax rates equivalent of four billion dollars, and he got fewer dollars. Why? Fewer people working. Fewer people paying taxes. More unemployment.

So, we don't believe that cutting rates cuts revenue to the province if, in cutting rates, you create more jobs, you put more money in the hands of consumers.

And so we are very confident that just as Bob Rae destroyed jobs and lost revenue hiking taxes, that we will create jobs and ultimately in the long run create more money for the government by cutting tax rates.

LISA: First off, I'd like to know, if successor rights don't cost the government any money, why is it they've been such a big issue for Mr. Harris during these negotiations?

A. Well, they do cost us money, and it is a big issue. Second question?

Q. How do they cost us money, successor rights?

A. Well, if the rights are that you're entitled to the job in succession, forever and a day, that costs money if you don't need that person anymore or you don't need that job anymore or you don't need that service anymore. So, I understand the union has said it doesn't cost money, but it does.

Q. There is apparently another guy named Mike in North Bay, because he's on the line right now. Mike from North Bay, go ahead.

MIKE: Yes. Mike, I just want to give a comment that, I just wanted to say that a lot of the stuff that's going on in the province right now, I think you're doing an excellent job. And I think a lot of people just have to give it a little time, and I don't think they're really looking at the big picture.

And, you know, I congratulate you for actually doing what you said you were going to do. A lot of politicians up to now have not been doing that. And it's funny, you're one of the first guys that have, and you're taking a lot of flak for it, and I just think it's going to have to take a little time, and I think people have to appreciate that, and you've got to look at the big picture, because I don't think they are.

A. Yeah, thanks, Mike. I appreciate it, and I know not everybody agrees. I believe, when they look at the big picture, and when they look at other jurisdictions, we have delayed a number of tough decisions that have already been done by Roy Romanow, NDP government in Saskatchewan, that have been done by Liberal governments in Nova Scotia where they just cut 10 percent across the board — actually, more dollars per capita than we're reducing.

So, we've been a little behind in facing up to this, and that's why Alberta now has a budgetary surplus, and they're now in a position to look at new spending. What a luxury they're in compared to our situation. But they moved sooner than we did.

On the other hand, the federal government, ourselves, the Quebec government, we've been the slowest, Mike, to respond, and the federal government's responding now and so are we. And we don't have any choice.

Q. Getting a call from North Bay has put a question in my head. I am told, and I've seen it, one of your great skills is that you relate extremely well to folks. You've got a real good common touch with people, and presumably some of it comes from the fact that you're not the Rhodes Scholar, silver-spoon-in-the-mouth type of background. You have relatively ordinary roots and upbringing.

However, Premier, you've moved your family from North Bay to Toronto; that is a new thing. You are now the premier, your day is completely planned by staffers. You are in the cocoon, you've got security people around you all the time. Do you worry about losing your common touch?

A. Yes. And we try very hard to get back to that. I'll often stop on the road into a doughnut shop and just go in and try and chat with people where there's no organized brief for me or protest. Some people who protest, blow whistles in my ear, and scream and yell and say, "Why don't you stop and chat with us?" I said, "Well, it's hard to hear you over the whistles and everything." So, I try and do that.

During the March break, I was at a hockey game with my sons. Sitting beside me was an OPSEU worker who was on strike with his son. And sitting on the other side of him was another worker who worked at the psychiatric hospital, where the one was, and he was crossing the line, see? — and had to cross the line.

So, there were three different people all from North Bay, all with their sons, all watching an oldtimers' hockey game.

Q. What happened anyway?

A. Well, we didn't agree necessarily with everything, but we agreed that we had some friendly chat about it, and it was a surprising number of things that we did agree on. So, I have learned a lot that way, and tried to stay in touch with people that way. And while my family's in school here in Toronto, we still spend a fair bit of time in North Bay.

Q. The story I've heard about you that I like so much is the one where ... I think you were still leader of the third party at the time, and you're about to go into the Legislature to give a speech on the Social Contract, which the NDP, of course, brought in, and you stop in for a haircut with Frank the barber —

A. Frank, sure.

Q. — in the basement of the Legislature. You're in conversation with Frank. He says something to you, and suddenly something registers. You decide to change your speech on the basis of what Frank the barber tells you.

A. Frank the barber's a smart man.

Q. I only raise it to say that that ain't going to happen anymore, is it?

A. Yeah, it still happens. When I was in North Bay, I stopped in to see John and Dom in the barbershop in North Bay where I used to always go. We still talk to a lot of people in there, and I said, "You know, what are they saying? What are they talking about? What are people concerned about? What advice do you have for me?" And I do that with cab drivers any time I get a chance to ride in a cab or standing around at the airport.

The Common Sense Revolution came from people — open houses, town hall forums, doughnut shops, talking to folks. And I still believe it's a very valuable way to see what people are thinking.

MARK: Actually, I was just calling to give you a bit of praise on what you've done. I think it's helping bring back foreign investment, and in dealing with unions the way they need to be dealt with, because I think, in a lot of cases in the private sector, they're holding us down.

And my question is with the economy: how do you feel it's going to move?

A. Well, one of the results of being a high-tax, high-regulatory area is those businesses that have survived have been real good. They've been able to survive in that and they're very competitive. And so, if we can reduce the regulatory burden and deal with tax issues, payroll taxes, and income taxes — and we will begin that process in this budget — I think they'll do even better. The low dollar is in our favour right now. This is a double-edged sword; providing we take advantage of that to bring about other reforms for the long term, it is an advantage for us.

I believe Ontario will do even better than the economists say. I think a lot of these decisions of investors are kind of still gut decisions. Do I think

Ontario will be a good place next year, the year after, the year after that? And the more we can develop that confidence, it'll mushroom and grow, I am confident.

CHRISTINA: Yes, I have two girls on mothers' allowance, and we are just getting by. Now, I can't understand, are you going to help the poor, or are you going to discriminate against them? It seems to me that you're not helping the poor and you're not helping the middle class, but you're helping your big shots. And I don't think you're being fair to the people that are on unemployment, that are on mothers' allowance.

STEVE: Christina, let me jump in. Who are the big shots he's helping right now?

CHRISTINA: His own caucus. Like, he is not helping the people that need it the most. I don't feel that. My daughters have to come to me and ask me for money to keep them going for the month, in order to have something to eat.

A. Yes. Well, Christina, it is a good question. Our goal is to try and target our help to those who need it the most, as opposed to universally giving everything to everybody. We made some changes to those who were on welfare. We still are paying 10 percent higher than the average of Canada, about the highest in the world, and we have allowed everybody, even at minimum wage, if they work four or five or six hours a week, to earn back the difference without penalty. We're bringing in workfare and training fare. We'd like to give people a hand up, but ...

Q. When is workfare coming in, since you mentioned it?

A. Well, I think you'll see some announcements this spring.

Q. The spring's a long time, Premier. When's workfare coming up?

A. Well, the minister is working hard to have something in place this spring.

Q. Has Cabinet approved it yet?

A. And we'll … no.

Q. Has Cabinet seen a final proposal yet?

A. No, no.

Q. No?

A. No. If Cabinet had approved it, it would have been leaked out and you'd know about it, because that seems to be the norm these days.

I guess if your question is do we plan to pay as in the past, more and more money for more and more people to stay at home and not work? No, we don't. If you ask us are we prepared to be generous and helpful in trying to help people help themselves, yes, we will. And that is a little bit of a shift from the past, and by and large we've received good plaudits from a lot of people on welfare saying, "We like the direction. Get on with it," and you know, kind of saying, as you are, Steve, "When do we see workfare? When do we get these opportunities?"

Q. Having said that, the head of the Daily Bread Food Bank, Gerard Kennedy, held a news conference in Toronto today, saying that business for him is up 50 percent since the welfare cuts, and this is not a business, obviously, that you want to see go up 50 percent.

A. No, it's not. This is the same guy that campaigned and helped destroy us bringing the Olympics to Toronto, which would have created a massive number of jobs here in Toronto.

Q. Well, okay, but speak to his point.

A. So, philosophically, you see, I think that had we done a lot of things differently in the last ten years, we wouldn't need a Gerard Kennedy or a food bank, and I regret that we do, and we do. I acknowledge and admit that.

Q. Does it speak to a failure of your welfare-cut policy?

A. No, it speaks to a failure of society over the last ten years to be able to generate the number of jobs that we need here. It is probably the last fifteen years, if you like. And to expect that in a short period of time we can pull $12 billion dollars to balance the books out of the economy without it having some effect in the short term is not realistic.

I say to Gerard Kennedy to do nothing is the cruellest thing we could possibly do to those people dependent on the food bank today.

FELICITY: Yes, good evening, Premier. Actually, my original question was what would you do, and your government, with your MPPs' fat pension? And then all of a sudden you mention that it's so complicated to deal with. But then how come that you cut and slash funding for all levels of the government in Ontario, and yet you're not moving fast enough about the MPPs' fat pension, which is the great suckers of taxpayers' money.

A. Right. We've said we will scrap it, and we'll do it retroactive back to the day we were elected. So, I believe that will be dealt with this spring. But if it takes an extra month longer it will be retroactive to the day we were elected; the pension plan will be gone.

FELICITY: Would it be really possible that the public would really know about this, that there won't be nothing to be happening behind closed doors when it comes to dealing with your fat pension?

A. I think we will probably shout this loud and clear.

Q. I was going to say, trust me, Felicity, they'll have a news conference on this one.

A. I don't think we're going to hide this.

ROB: My question to you is car-insurance rates. They just keep going up, up, up, and up. Is there anything that you can do about it?

A. We hope so. We believe there are some things we can do, and there are some things we can't do. We believe that some of the changes, legislatively, that have been made, quite frankly, have contributed to some of the rates going up. To be honest with you, we believe there is more fraud in the system than there used to be, when they went to the universal no-fault benefit; some of them are very open-ended. There's not a lot of incentive to get back off of the universal benefit. Let me give you an example: The benefit rate went to, I believe, $1,000 a week.

ROB: That's a little high, isn't it?

A. Well, it is if you're a student earning nothing, or if you were earning $500 a week. What incentive is there if you were injured in an accident, call it whiplash, which is a common one, difficult to assess, there's not great incentive to get back to work at $500 a week when you're getting a thousand.

So there were some things that were made that we think didn't make a lot of sense, and we want to make legislative changes to deal with that. I don't want to commit to you rates are going to go down. I think we can control the growth in rates through some of the legislative changes. We are prepared to make those.

The second part of it is that we need competition, and there's some areas where there's still not enough competition. I'll give you an example. I don't drive a motorcycle, but motorcycle drivers tell me that there's only one company left insuring motorcyclists, and they've got a cartel and a monopoly. So we have to try and do everything we can to get competition into the marketplace to help control some of the prices, as well. So we're doing our best.

Q. How about a private university for Ontario?

A. Well, Steve, I personally am not opposed, and I have said that.

Q. Well, something tells me if you say it's okay, it's going to happen.

A. No. We are looking at a number of reforms within the current system, but I don't see anything wrong with a private sector or a private university system. No taxpayer dollars. They'll have to meet standards and set those standards. I personally believe the competition might be good for our other institutions.

Q. So your old cabinet colleague, Bette Stephenson, who's been trying to get this private university northeast of Toronto, she's got the green light from you?

A. Well, no. I wish that I could say that. I'm not the minister of education, and there is consultation, and I don't want anybody to think, "Oh, you know, Harris is going to dictate policy." I am giving my personal view. We have other things that we are dealing with that we believe are important, but before the mandate is out or before I retire, it's something I'd like to put before the people.

BOB: Mr. Harris, my question is why would you consider privatizing Ontario Hydro if it is now turning a profit and could be used to help pay down the provincial debt?

A. Well, it's got about a $31-billion to $36-billion debt of its own to pay down, first. It's interesting, our whole philosophy on privatizing is we should look at it. If we can get a better deal in the private sector, we should consider going that way. If we can't, we won't. And there are a number who have a philosophy "never." It should always be government. It should be government ownership. Only government can sell booze. Only... let me say something here: Only government can run TVO, and I am not convinced that's so. I like TVO, but I think we should explore, is there somebody else can run it and own it and operate it?

And if they can do it more effectively, provide better service, make a better profit, run it more efficiently, surely you would want us to at least look at it.

Q. Has your thinking evolved on it at all? Because, frankly, from what I've been able to tell, what you said in the *Common Sense Revolution* during the campaign and what you said last week isn't that different. You have said all the way along, you're looking at whether or not it is feasible.

A. Yes, we come at this not with a philosophy that you must privatize, but with a philosophy that you really must look at all options and alternatives.

Q. Should the government be in the TV business?

A. Well, I'm not so sure that we should. I think we should be into a lot of things, though, that TVOntario does, in educational TV and in …

Q. Could the private sector do those things better?

A. That is what we're examining. And what role for us is there, then, within that as government? I am sure there are some things that the private sector say, "Well, you know, Polkaroo's nice, but we can't make a profit on Polkaroo." Well, if you think Polkaroo is good, educational-value programming as part of school readiness and early childhood education, then we would like to see that continue, for example. And I don't want to pick one or the other, but it is that type of analysis that we should look at.

And I like public broadcasting, and I like a lot of things that they're able to do, but the question comes down to, does the government need to be the sole shareholder and principal? And I'm not convinced that's the case.

Q. I was going to say, at the risk of sounding a little self-interested here, do you know what the answer is yet?

A. No. If I knew the answer, we'd announce it. We don't hold things back, we've had a pretty ambitious agenda, you know. We've been a pretty busy government.

And I might add, you know, that when you look at TVOntario, this isn't a make or break for the whole government. There's $50 million or $60 million a year that we spend on it, and it's something that we need to take a good hard look at, and we are. We have had other priorities that we've moved on quicker and faster and … but in the fullness of time, we will discuss —

Q. How about booze? Does the government need to be in the booze business?

A. I don't think so, but we need to regulate it. It is the Liquor *Control* Board. The public wants us to control it, and I believe that's very, very important that we do that. Do we need to own it to control it is the whole issue.

Q. What's the answer?

A. Well, I don't think we do. I've said that all along, but again … and it's not a philosophy that we have to …

Q. Sorry to push you here, but what are you waiting for? If the first minister of the province doesn't think we need to be in the booze business, how come his minister of consumer affairs, Norm Sterling, hasn't even appointed the members of a task force yet to look into selling privately?

A. Well, they've been looking at it, and the ministry have been trying to assemble information. They've been looking at other jurisdictions, and they've been studying it, and the union's been running ads against it, and the same as Hydro and …

Q. A lot of private TV stations are getting rich off union ads these days, that's true.

A. When we're confident that we have an answer that makes sense, we'll move on it.

JENNIFER: Hello, Mr. Harris. I wanted to know if you're going to do anything about kids that have to move out and their parents are alcoholics, and I couldn't go back to school. I had to have a job, and I would like to go back to school, and I'd like assistance. But I had problems getting that assistance because I'm underage, like I'm seventeen. And you have to be eighteen or something.

Q. Jennifer, can I just clarify here? You used to be able to get welfare at the age of sixteen. The Conservatives changed the policy; you now have to be eighteen. You're saying you're living in an unhappy household, I gather?

JENNIFER: Well, I moved out of my parents' household because they were alcoholics.

Q. You moved out? And you can't get social assistance anymore, and therefore...

JENNIFER: I would like to get social assistance so I can be able to live and go to school.

Q. Does this person have a case?

A. Could have. And actually, what I think you should do is you should call your MPP or call my office if you like. I mean, any individual case we would like to take a look at, and we would like to be helpful. And if the system for whatever reason or other is not responding to that right now, we'd like to look into it, and if you do that, I'd be happy to look into that for you.

Q. You said during the campaign that kids who, I guess, were freeloading would not be eligible for social assistance anymore after the age of sixteen. But this clearly appears to be somebody in an abusive situation. Would she be eligible for welfare?

A. Yes, she is. And, you know, what we did say is, I don't think it's fair that somebody says, "Hey, I don't like living at home anymore. I'm sixteen. Give me an apartment." And, in my view, what is probably required if it is legitimate abuse at home, or a situation that is intolerable, what is probably required is counselling and help and perhaps foster parents or other assistance.

I don't think a sixteen-year-old, quite frankly, is in a position to go out and live on their own under these circumstances. But I think they need help, and if we can help Jennifer, we'd like to.

Q. We are literally down to our last minute here, and I wanted to ask you one last thing. We like to think of our politicians as being somehow extraordinary. I mean, there's a reason why there are four politicians' faces on Mount Rushmore in the United States. John Robarts, "The Chairman of the Board," George Drew, "The Colonel." I mean, we like these people to be somehow larger than life. *Extraordinary*, really, is the word that comes to mind. Can you tell us how you think you are extraordinary?

A. I don't think I am. I don't think politicians are. We build them up to be. We try and make them that. When I first was elected as an MPP, it was amazing the people that came to me and asked me about problems that they might have asked their doctor or a lawyer. We're ordinary people. We're the people next door.

Most of us, regardless of party, I think, have a desire to help people and try and make Ontario a better place, but we are not extraordinary, and there are many people in everyday jobs who … some will stand out more than others as politicians, but so will a lot of teachers stand out more than others. So will a lot of civil servants. So will a lot of policemen. And so, perhaps we expect too much from our politicians. We're just ordinary folks.

The Harrisites made good on their boast. As the province approached 1999 — the year they would render their judgment on the PC government at the polls — there truly was not a single blade of grass on the south lawn at Queen's Park that hadn't been trod upon by teachers, public servants, unionized employees, or labour leaders.

It was with that in mind that Premier Harris and I did a "walk-and-talk" interview on that south lawn, which was covered in snow on a frosty winter day:

STEVE: For six straight years, since this program debuted, the premier of the day has consented to an annual conversation on the state of the province and the government. Premier Mike Harris and I had this year's chat a few days ago on the snowy south lawn of the Ontario Legislature:

Q. As we look ahead to 1999, I just want to know what is on your plate; what is your top priority before the next election?

PREMIER HARRIS: Really, what we have done is try to get Ontario back on top.

Q. Do you think it is, yet?

A. Well, it is on top in Canada. The job creation record is very, very positive, another 5,000 people are off the welfare rolls today, in December, and we are now over 360,000 people off the welfare rolls, over 460,000 new jobs in Ontario.

Q. Do you know where they have gone, though? If they are off welfare, are they definitely into jobs?

A. Well, two independent surveys that were done indicate 60 percent of them into full-time jobs, and a lot of the new jobs being created are not minimum-wage jobs. They are jobs that are good-paying jobs, so we are seeing people who were sort of caught in this cycle of dependency breaking free and getting hope again.

We see 1999, and the tax cuts, I think, I have contributed to this. I think the policies of our government have contributed, I think the federal government has helped. I think getting books balanced has restored confidence and investment confidence.

Q. Are you just the right guy in the right place at the right time, though? Or would this not have happened had you not been in the chair?

A. Well, I will allow others to pass judgment. But certainly I think the record is clear that our policies of reducing taxes, not increasing them, or reducing red tape, of encouraging investment, has produced a dramatic, different result than, say, British Columbia, which went in a different direction, or even some of the states that we have competed with. We think we have contributed positively, but so has the private sector, so have Ontarians rallying together, so has the federal government.

Ninety-nine we see as the year ... we have called it the year of the middle class, and the working class ...

Q. It sounds like a good election slogan.

A. Well, we want to see more people come into middle class. Those that are not working we want to see working, those who we classify as working poor, who don't have incomes that we believe are strong enough to be able to meet their objectives and their goals. We would like to see them move into the middle class, we would like to see the middle class keep more of their own money. So those will be our policies.

Q. So which taxes are you going to cut in the next budget? Can you tell us?

A. Well, no, I can't tell you that; you have to wait for the budget for that. We are watching the federal budget right now. Our goal is to make sure that the federal government doesn't undo some of the good we have done. If they will cut some taxes, and they are in a $10-billion to $14-billion, $15-billion surplus next year, this will benefit Ontarians as well. And we will take a look at our fiscal situation. We are still a couple of years away from balancing our books; we still have substantial investments to make in health care, as you know.

If the federal government comes through with what it should do, give us our health care money back, reduce taxation in some areas, then we will take a look at how we can complement that, and it will be a double bang for the buck, and I think Ontario will do even better.

Q. I think I, like you, take a lot of my cues about politics from my hockey buddies. You are sitting around the dressing room after the game and you want to know what people talk about. I have got to tell you, a lot of them are complimentary. They like the fact that you came through on the tax cuts and that you got rid of photo radar and you did what you said you were going to do on welfare.

The other side of this, though, is that they are concerned that stuff that wasn't in the *Common Sense Revolution*, the stuff you didn't campaign on, like, for example the creation of the Megacity or Bill 160, or maybe the way you handled the Dionne Quints' situation, that has been subpar.

Do you acknowledge that as many areas as you like to think you have done well in, you have blown a few, too?

A. Well, I think in a lot of the big areas we have done well, and I think, when you talk about one city, we talked about fewer politicians. We talked about restructuring in municipalities so that we could get more for less. We talked about those areas, so —

Q. But I am looking at the general principle here, not the specific, the general principle of what you campaigned on, what you knew about for the past three years, you were good at.

A. Yes.

Q. Stuff that came along later, you weren't so good at it. Is that a fair criticism?

A. I think some of the things we didn't handle nearly as well as we wanted. Listen, we will make mistakes every day, when you look at the myriad of issues that we have to handle. But they are well-intentioned mistakes. We haven't had a lot of cooperation from some unions in some of the reforms that are better for their union members, bringing them more jobs, bringing their companies more money so they can get more money. The same in the public sector. So we have had a lot of misinformation out there and campaigns trying to fight us along the way, and perhaps we didn't spend as much time communicating what we were doing and why we were doing it and how this would lead to a more modern, better health care system or education system at the end of the day.

Q. My suspicion is most new governments when they come into office they hope they have unifying rather than a divisive effect on the public that they serve. And I guess the knock I hear about you guys all the time is that hasn't been the case for you, that your government, because it came to power with such an agenda, has polarized this province more than it has helped unify it. Don't you think that's the case?

A. Well, I think there are some who feel that they have been polarized but, really and truly, I think there are some, the vested interests I would call them, the special interests, who kind of had their way. As soon as they raised a voice and they knew how to access government, they knew how to get to media, government always backed down and gave them whatever they wanted.

And we resisted that. We resisted the temptation to play into that. And certainly it has not been our goal, you are quite right; every government, including Mike Harris' government, including me personally, wants to represent all the people, it wants to be a unifying force.

Q. I guess one of the last things I want to find out from you is whether or not you think the main thing you came into government to do, which was basically get it a little bit less into people's lives — shrink it, whether you have in fact achieved that? — because the Ontario government is still spending more than $50 billion a year. You haven't cut spending all that much. Have you failed to do the chief thing you came into office to do?

A. Well, we have tried to cut out waste. We have certainly controlled spending better than it was. It is not accelerated, and we have tried to in a number of areas cut out waste and then redirect it into more programs or better programs or areas that we believe are important.

Colleges and universities, we reduced some money initially, in the first year, and said, you know, "We want you to take this out of administration. We want you to look at how you cut the fat, not the programs." And then we have substantially reinvested back into colleges and universities, in research and development, and science and technology, and a whole host of areas, that —

Q. Is government too unwieldy?

A. It is still … listen, I think we have had some success. We have cut a lot of red tape. Have we done enough yet? Is there more that can be done? I think it is a constant exercise. There is a lot more to be done. I believe this province, we have gone, actually from the last in Canada in a number of categories important — the most people dependent upon welfare in the country, per capita. We were the worst; we are now moving toward the best. The job numbers down now, below 7 percent unemployment rates; we were up over 8, pushing 9 percent.

We have done better in a whole host of areas, but there is still a lot to be done.

Q. I know all this because "the tax fighter's" on TV with commercials telling me this all the time. I can't turn on the radio or TV without seeing you these days.

A. Well, people have said we want to hear from you more, we want you to communicate more, and the opposition and the unions have done a better job of communicating some of these things, and oftentimes their information is —

Q. You are not worried this is backfiring? Spending public money to make these ads?

A. Well, we spend some public money. We are probably back to the level that the Liberals and the NDP spent — not even counting indexing for inflation. We didn't communicate a lot in the first year or two and perhaps we paid a price for that. We are certainly not communicating, if you like, or spending more than previous governments did. But we are doing a little more than we did in the first two years. We were so busy getting things done that perhaps we didn't do enough in those areas.

Q. Okay, I apologize; I took you off course there for a second. But tell me again, why does government need to be smaller? Why, philosophically, is that important?

A. Well, it is not just philosophically. I think you want government to be as efficient as it can possibly be, and when you do that then you leave more dollars and more opportunities in the hands of the hard-working middle-class, working-class, working Ontarians. And the more they have, the more they spend, the more jobs they create, and the more secure they are and the more prosperous the whole country is.

Q. You really think it turns out that way? I know you have been going around the province with your jar of loonies, showing people how much they have saved under your tax cuts. However, there are more co-payments, there are more user fees, the federal government has moved into areas where you have reduced taxes. So we are no further ahead then, maybe?

A. We are a lot further ahead than if we had not, and we are further ahead in so many areas. I mean, listen, if some people have said, well, property taxes have gone up. Property taxes have gone up the least under our administration than they have in the last twenty years, in many cases, they haven't even gone up the rate of inflation. So, certainly collectively, we are better off, and we are so much better off than we would have been had we had another ten years of the spending we had in the ten years previous.

Mike Harris called an election for almost four years to the day he won his first mandate. Unlike in 1995, when he came out of nowhere to win, his opponents were ready for him this time. They knew Harris' agenda and they feared he would win a renewed mandate. So, when the premier and I met up for an interview in Whitby during the campaign, that was the focus of our conversation.

Q. I don't know if you got a chance to see the newscasts because you are obviously on the hustings all the time, but if you watch the local newscasts, it is very little about Mike Harris getting the message out about tax cuts and a great deal about all these protesters that you have to run through in order to get to where you are going. Have you had trouble getting the message out because of that?

A. Well, no, I don't think so, Steve. I think people know I am the tax-cut guy, even Dalton McGuinty says, "Harris is the tax-cut guy, not me. I don't cut taxes. I am against tax cuts." He says that, so that helps.

Q. Well, he says he is against tax cuts until the budget is balanced, in fairness to him.

A. Well, okay, but he opposed sixty-nine tax cuts that we brought in, voted against them, said they were terrible, we shouldn't have done it. And that is, as we saw today, you know, when we visited three plants, that is one of the reasons those three plants are going and these people have these jobs. So, really and truly, we believe we are getting our message out. I think they know who Mike Harris is. I think they know they can trust me. If I say I am going to cut taxes, I cut taxes. And I said the same thing eight years ago, and I said the same thing in the '95 campaign, and I did cut the taxes as I said I would, and I will in the future. And I think people know that.

To be truthful, the protesters probably help us. They probably do point out to voters there are some people there, there are some union leaders, there are some vested interests who used to get their own way when we had weak leadership in this province, and they are not getting their own way now. In fact, this premier is listening to all the people of Ontario. And I think it does, in a strange kind of way, actually help point out, yes, Mike Harris is a strong leader.

Q. Okay, but the flip side of that is I remember you in 1995; you could main-street, you could go out in public without a whole horde of OPP surrounding you, worried about your security. You can't do that anymore. You don't meet any normal people anymore.

A. Well, strong leaders can't do that in campaigns, when cameras are around. I was out shopping today; I bought a couple of Maple Leaf jerseys for the game tomorrow. I mixed with people. I am going to the game; I am going to take [my son] Michael. But when all the cameras come and the protesters come, they see it as a good photo op, and I understand that. But my advice to them is get your own photo op. If you've got something positive to say the media will cover it. I have found the media in Ontario very fair. If anybody has a new, original, good idea, they cover it. And they will also cover people who disagree with me. Either way, I believe I am getting my message out.

Q. I don't know if your staff has told you this, but you have got to know that the big concern before this campaign started was that Mike Harris' legendary temper was going to show itself on the hustings and, when you walk through some gauntlet of protesters, someone was going to take a whack at you and you were going to blow your stack and lose it. How much do you worry on a daily basis about doing that?

A. I rarely would lose my temper in public. I don't suffer mistakes, if they are caused by a lack of preparation or if somebody slept in; that concerns me, and I let people know that. On the other hand, if people make honest mistakes, then they make them. And do they learn from them and do they go on from there? I mean, nobody has made more mistakes in life probably than I have. I am a human being, and I have tried to learn from them.

Q. Are you confident you are back with a majority?

A. I am confident that if we can get our message out, it will be good for Ontario, and I think if it is good for Ontario, Ontarians will want to vote for it. So we will work hard to get our message out, we will work hard to deserve to be re-elected, and we will accept the decision of the electors as we always do.

The 1999 election campaign was another good one for the Conservatives. Harris kept his coalition together and garnered exactly the same 45 per-cent of the total votes cast as he did in 1995 (actually, a touch more). Brian Mulroney used to say "ya gotta dance with the one that brung ya." Harris did, keeping faith with his supporters and, critics would argue, saying tough luck to the majority that voted against him.

But there were two stories related to the outcome of this campaign. Yes, the top story was that Mike Harris was back. But the other story started developing with just a few days left in the '99 campaign. Harris looked as if he would romp back into power, given how unimpressively the rookie Liberal leader, Dalton McGuinty, was performing in his campaign. And the electorate was certainly not ready to return the NDP to power under Howard Hampton, just four years after getting rid of them.

But McGuinty caught a break in the dying days of the campaign. Many of those who wanted Harris out abandoned the NDP and fled to the Liberals, not out of any love for McGuinty, but rather because the numbers screamed the obvious — only the Liberals could threaten the Tories' hopes for a second consecutive majority government. And so, on election day, the NDP found itself with an unusually low 12.6 percent of the total vote, while the Liberals, despite a lacklustre campaign, captured almost 40 percent of the vote. The Tories lost twenty-three seats while the Liberals gained five. It wasn't enough to deny Harris his majority. But that strong Liberal showing beat back the "Dump Dalton" forces that were gathering in his party and saved McGuinty's job. It also gave McGuinty four more years to learn how to be a successful politician, and learn he would. But that's another story for another chapter.

Harris' second term was a lot different from his first. His PCs were no longer the folks who came to fix the government. They really *were* the government. It also soon became apparent that the revolutionary zeal with which the party came to power was giving way to a more mundane managerial approach to issues.

In addition, less than a year into their second term, the Conservatives became mired in one of the worst crises in Ontario history. In May 2000 the water supply in Walkerton became contaminated thanks to a series of appalling screw-ups, some but not all of which could be laid at the feet of the cost-cutting Conservative government. At least seven people in a town of just 5,000 died. Harris became the first premier since George Drew in the 1940s to have to testify at a public inquiry.

It soon became clear that the premier was simply running out of gas. He looked as if he was enjoying the job less. The endless protests, media criticism, and sniping from the opposition side seemed to be taking its toll. In fact, one day during question period, Dalton McGuinty went after the premier so hard, Harris responded by violating Rule Number One: he went after McGuinty's family, essentially saying it was a good thing McGuinty's father, Dalton Sr., was dead, so he wouldn't have to see what a disgraceful performance his son was putting on during this interrogation.

It was an extraordinary violation of the Marquis of Queensbury rules, particularly since Harris' own father, Deane, had only recently died. Going after someone's dead father crossed the line. A skillful politician would have crucified Harris for his misstep. McGuinty could have expressed how shocked and appalled he was that the premier would make such an attack. He could have threatened to cross the floor of the Legislature and bash the premier's face in.

Instead, he froze and said nothing. Dalton McGuinty still had a ways to go before becoming the leader who would win three consecutive elections.

And yet, when Harris announced his intention to resign from politics, effective the spring of 2002, it was McGuinty who surprised observers by giving a generous speech about Harris during the MPPs' tributes in the Legislature. When it was his turn to respond, Harris had a written text to read from, but his staff purposely left blank the part of his response dealing with the Liberal leader, because they were so unsure of whether McGuinty would praise the outgoing premier or take one last chance to castigate him.

Harris' departure from the scene also meant one more interview for us at TVO, in April 2002, on the eve of the convention to find a new PC Party leader:

STEVE: Thousands of Tories are gathered tonight at the Metro Toronto Convention Centre to say thank you to Mike Harris. It will be the last time the premier will have the spotlight as, tomorrow night, the process begins in earnest to find his replacement.

Mike Harris' story is by now well-known: From worst to first in 1995, two majority governments, tax cuts, balanced budgets, Walkerton, Ipperwash, wars with the feds, wars with teachers and other public servants. One of the most successful and divisive premiers in this province's history.

I sat down with Ontario's twenty-second premier to find out what he might have done differently, and what he might do next.

Q. Frank McKenna once told me that as he got closer to the end he started to have second thoughts. How about you?

PREMIER HARRIS: No, no second thoughts. I will miss the job, I will miss the excitement, I will miss the people. I know that, I know I am going to do that. I have also met with a number of former premiers and discussed how they felt, and the life of transition out of politics and into the private sector. So I have some idea. But they tell me, "No, it will hit you and it will be different."

But I don't have second thoughts, I don't have regrets. This has been a fabulous opportunity for me. I will forever be grateful to my party and the people of Ontario for giving me the chance as leader and giving me the opportunity to be premier for the past just about seven years.

Q. I understand that, given the information you had and the circumstances you were in, you made what you thought were the best decisions at the time. But now, with the advantage of hindsight and with more information and the passage of time, is there anything you would have done differently?

A. No. I don't dwell on that. I might have done lots of things differently. I mean, I … I …

Q. Name one.

A. Well, you know, I … I … I … I don't have one coming to mind. I would have certainly wished that classroom teachers understood, I am on their side. I am not on the unions' side, I am not on the boards' side, I am not on the administration side; I am on your side, to help the kids. I never seemed to be able to get that message through, and others were able to confuse the message.

I am sure some would say that I wish I was running the water system in Walkerton and could have fired people before a disaster struck. But, you know, $600 million worth of budget and all those people weren't able to determine that, and so some have said going to $350-million budget should have accomplished that. I think that is nonsense, quite frankly. You learn from experiences, and the people of Walkerton, you know, I feel for them, but they should feel and I hope that there is some good came out of what was a disaster that took place there. But, you know, hindsight is great.

Q. I don't know how much premiers care about what's written in the history books about them; but I think most people have a general understanding about what's going to be in that first paragraph of you in the encyclopedia: the guy who came in, horrible fiscal situation, cut your taxes, balanced the budget, a lot of that stuff.

If Mike Harris is writing that first paragraph, and since you have raised it, is Walkerton in that first paragraph?

A. No, it is not in the first paragraph. What I will talk about and would hope is written is the motive. Why did Mike Harris seek the leadership of the party, why did he come out with a common sense revolution? Why did he make the changes that he made to the province of Ontario? And I think one of the things that I think is very unfortunate in politics is those who will impugn a motive that actually is quite silly, and very disrespectful of people. I disagreed with Bob Rae, I disagreed with David Peterson, I disagreed with Jean Chrétien on many issues. But never for a second do I doubt that they are doing what they think is in the best interests of the province or of the country.

And I am the same. And so I hope the history books and those writers will understand that — that I came to try to make this a better place for my children, for their children, for the next generation, and I believe I have accomplished that in a very significant way.

Q. I want to talk a bit about the race to succeed you, but I am not going to ask you who you are going to vote for because you are not going to tell me that anyway, are you?

A. You haven't asked me.

Q. Who are you going to vote for in the first ballot, Premier?

A. I am not going to tell you.

Q. I thought so, yes. You did say at the outset of the campaign, you wanted a healthy debate about ideas and about where the future of the party should go and, to be sure, that has happened. It has also gotten very personal. Do you think it has gotten too personal?

A. I don't think you should make that assessment today, right in the heat, in the middle of a campaign. You will find out afterward, are the parties able to come together?

I mean, I can remember in my leadership in 1989 and '90, I felt at the time that Dianne Cunningham said some spurious things about me. I can recall a couple of speeches, and I thought, well this is horrendous, this is terrible. You know, we've all got to come together afterward. Why would her campaign allow her to say a thing a like that? Or who wrote that for her? I can remember feeling that at the time.

Afterward, we were very good friends. And we worked very, very well together, and we did a lot of good things together. So, ask me that question in three, six, twelve months, and I will give you an answer.

Q. I take you at your word when you say you have not obviously made any decisions about federal politics at this stage of your life, and why would you? You are just about to get out of provincial politics and it is quite a mess at the federal scene. In case you weren't aware of that, I just thought I would let you know.

But what are your thoughts on that? Federal politics someday, once they get their act together, the conservative movement in Ottawa, is it a possibility?

A. Well, lookit, the rate they are going, I don't know whether I want to run when I am ninety. So that is perhaps a telling comment. I don't see any sign, yet, that the right conditions exist for the centre, centre-right, Progressive Conservative/Alliance/Reform Party to put whatever differences they have aside and come together, as you have to do under our rules.

My message to them is get your act together and figure it out, put some of your differences aside because you've got a lot of things in common. And I tell you, many, many, many Liberals who still plan to vote Liberal are not happy that there is a virtual monopoly out there that allows a party to run and to act and to govern virtually unchecked.

Q. Is there anything that you have done as premier over the last seven years that you think will outlast you? In other words, "these changes I have brought in are permanent, we can't go back."

A. I think it will be very difficult to raise taxes in the province of Ontario. I think it would be very difficult to change the workfare programs, restoring the work ethic, those things that brought a little different philosophy to government. I think it will be difficult to go back to the days when government was supposed to see how many people it could hire and keep employed, as opposed to government is supposed to, as efficiently and effectively as possible, provide excellent services to the people of Ontario and seek solutions for that.

I think it will be very difficult to go back to the days when you no longer test to find out if your kids are actually learning anything. I think it will be very difficult to run deficits, certainly for any sustained period of time, so I think there are lots of those things.

Labour legislation was terribly skewed, I believe, in this province, before we scrapped Bill 40.

Q. It was the anti-strikebreaker law.

A. Yes, yes. And against business. And I think we restored balance. I think it would be difficult to go back to those days. So I think there is a sea change. You know, the taxes, Liberals and many Conservatives said, don't cut taxes, balance the books. Many economists said that. And I said, you will never balance the books till you cut taxes and get more jobs and growth in the province. That, I believe, is a prevailing philosophy across Canada today regardless of which party you run for.

Mike Harris was one of the most consequential premiers in Ontario history. Those who approved of his *Common Sense Revolution* really loved and admired him. Those who didn't, really despised him. Not just disagreed with him. Despised him. I saw a good example of that fully *ten years* after Harris left the premier's office. His friend Ralph Lean, who teaches a business course at Ryerson University, invited Harris along with another former premier, David Peterson, to come to his class and guest lecture. As soon as Harris began his remarks, "students" began heckling him. It became clear they weren't really students, but rather protesters who'd infiltrated the classroom. Harris stood silently at the front and waited what felt like an eternity for security to show up and escort the protesters out. (Ironically, it was a former Liberal cabinet minister, Marie Bountrogianni, who came to Harris' defence and urged the protesters to shut up so everyone could hear, then question Harris.) How many politicians, a full decade after leaving office, still inspire such anger? Mike Harris did and does.

For a guy who at one time seemed adamant about selling TVO to the private sector (he studied it but ultimately decided not to), Harris never seemed to mind making himself available to the public broadcaster. In the summer of 2010 we asked Harris if he would consent to five consecutive fifteen-minute interviews on the subject of leadership. Even though he wasn't a lawyer, he was ensconced in one of the biggest Bay Street law firms as a rainmaker, and sat on a number of boards of directors as well. And yet, he cleared his schedule to talk to us, knowing full well most of our viewers and close to 100 percent of our employees would have opposed everything he stood for in public life.

And yet, he did it. And we got some fascinating new insights into one of Ontario's toughest leaders. Here are excerpts from our five-part series.

Mike Harris in the studio.

* * *

Q. We are going to be exploring different aspects of leadership all week long, and you, as a guy who won back-to-back majority governments, would know something of what it takes to be a leader in politics.

And I want to start with life before politics because, obviously, a lot of our audience is new. They won't remember that you didn't just show up and become premier; you actually got elected in 1981. So before that, there was a lot.

And I want to know, going back to your teenage or early years, whether there was anything in your background that suggested to you, "I am destined to be a leader"?

A. I don't think so, but as you reflect on it I suppose, there were a few moments. I mean, in the beginning, I had a very strong-willed father who clearly led; he was a small businessman, he led in everything that he did, in the tourist business, he became president of the association. You know, he was a doer and people followed him. And, by the way, we kids followed him too.

Q. Because he was tough.

A. He was tough.

Q. Deane.

A. That was Deane.

Q. Deane Harris.

A. And he instilled a lot of things in me, between he and my mother. Now I would say part of his leadership was fear, which I don't think is the right kind of leadership. But it worked for me.

Q. So you feared him?

A. Yes, I did. And when you get into different leadership styles, fear is one of them, bullying is another. And yet I think my mother was never that way, and yet my mother really led without my father knowing it.

Q. I want to follow up on the fear angle, because that is very interesting to me. Was it a fear of disappointing your father? Or was it a fear of the belt?

A. Yes, it was both. But ultimately, I guess, it was the fear of the belt, I suppose, but later on, it was a fear of disappointing; there is no question about that.

Q. Did you get the belt from him?

A. I did, and from my mother. Although my mother hated it, and of course she would say, "You wait till your father comes home." A lot of my generation went through that.

But the stronger motivator, on the negative side, was the fear of disappointment. And I think what you learn in life and in leadership roles is that, as part of team-building, it is the positive aspects of leadership that truly motivate people to follow and accomplish great things.

[Eventually, after several years of working in the family business, and as a teacher, Harris, at age thirty-six, runs for a seat at Queen's Park.]

Q. Eventually your private sector experience leads you to running as an MPP. You win in 1981 and become the MPP for Nipissing. I guess four years later you were in the cabinet for a little while, weren't you, for Frank Miller?

A. Yes, I was. I was a committee chair, and then a parliamentary assistant, and worked my way up through that progression, if you like. I was natural resources and energy, briefly, under the Frank Miller administration.

Q. This was right at the end of the Tory dynasty. So you finally made it to cabinet, and then the dynasty ended.

A. And there it ended. That's right.

Q. Not great timing. What do you learn as a cabinet minister in terms of leadership? The reason I ask is you are in an odd place. On the one hand you are not the premier, so you have to take direction from somebody else, but, on the other hand, you are running a big department. How does that work in terms of being a leader?

A. Well, I can tell you how it works. I mean, to be honest, I wasn't there that long. I often joke that I spent a third of the time learning what went on in the ministry, so it was all intake — them educating me. And then about a third of the time we had an election, campaigning, and then I joke, the rest of the time shredding, because we were getting ready, after forty-two years, to turn the government over.

But you clearly are part of a team, and while you will have files and areas that are your own, as you get more credibility around the cabinet table, the better job you can do in leading the ministry in the direction that you wish to lead it.

It was about a five-month sojourn with an election in the middle and all the shenanigans that were going on about the coalition that formed. So those experiences didn't teach me as much. I was parliamentary assistant to [Sarnia MPP] Andy Brandt, and he gave me a lot of responsibility. So working there, I perhaps learned more about what you can do, and sometimes the premier's office sets a little different tone than you might have wanted taken, so you bide your time.

Q. Now what does that mean?

A. Well, that means there are some things you want to do that cabinet collectively, or the premier's office, says no, that's not our priority at this time and we have other priorities we are going to use political capital on or dollars on. And that's fair. And you know what you learn from that, if you really think it's important? You go back, and some lick their wounds and get upset. What I would do and encourage people to do, you go back and say, "Okay, how can I make a better presentation next time?" And there will be other opportunities. There always are.

Q. In terms of your development though, as a potential leader of the party, you are in government for four years; you are a minister for about five months of that. How much of any of that helped you become the eventual leader of the PC Party in 1990?

A. Well, immensely, because I learned what it was like to be a soldier. I learned what it was like just as an MPP. And I learned those ministers that I thought treated me fairly and those that didn't. So I think it is an important part of the process.

And, you know, when Bob Rae took over, unexpectedly, I think that he and his team, he had a lot of rookies, who didn't have that government experience; they had opposition experience. And I think it showed in many areas. I don't want to get into the issues of the day.

Q. He wouldn't disagree with you.

A. But he wouldn't disagree with me. And David Peterson to a certain extent faced the same thing. I think he expected to win, and he did, but still, they hadn't had that kind of government experience.

So it was very beneficial to me ten years later, and maybe as leader of the party, it wasn't quite ten years before I became leader, but it was ten years before we won the government back. So in that period, it helped me immensely in getting a caucus and candidates and a team ready and getting them all on the same wavelength and ready to follow. And so it was of great benefit to me.

Q. We are going to drill deeper in the days ahead on how you became leader and what you did as premier. But just give us a sense of when you got the job as premier of Ontario, in 1995, what did you see as the essential part of the job that you and only you could do?

A. Well, leaders have to make decisions. I mean, at the end of the day I made them. And I think good leaders make decisions and dithering leaders are not successful. And you see that in business and you see it in politics.

I had the benefit of a lot of research, if you like, a lot of time thinking about what it is we were going to do, but at the end of the day it is still timing, what comes first, what gets priorities. And you know all the leadership qualities you have to have. I mean, integrity is number one, and you have to know where you are going and the team has to know where you are going and they have to be ready to follow, and they have to trust your judgment.

I was fortunate enough because of the preparation that we had done in that four-year period leading up to the election ...

Q. I think you might be referring to this thing [*holding up the* Common Sense Revolution].

A. ... and the *Common Sense Revolution*, which went out a year before. By the way, we thought it was going to be six months before. Bob Rae hung on, as you know, by his fingernails, as long as he could.

Q. So it turned into a year?

A. So it turned into a year. But our plan was, let's get it out there six months before, we will defend it, we will get it known. And so I had the advantage of that. So I was able to take that document the day I became premier, in to my staff and in to the deputy secretary of cabinet, and say, "Here's the agenda. Now, how are we going to implement it?"

And I've got to say this: You know, Rita Burak, when we interviewed —

Q. Head of the civil service.

A. — head of the civil service. When we interviewed her for this top job, Rita Burak brought a copy of the *Common Sense Revolution* to the interview — this is before we were even sworn in as government — and she said, "We can do this. And I could lead the civil service to help you implement the *Common Sense Revolution*."

Q. And that is how she got the job?

A. And that is how she got the job.

Q. I never knew that story. Well, people may remember you as premier. But what they may not remember is that you didn't just sort of show up and get that job. You were the leader of the third-place party going into two elections, 1990 and 1995, when you only had a small, hardy band of about twenty, when you first got in. So let's start there: What are the keys to leading a party when there are only twenty of you and you know that probably half of them think that they can do a better job at leading than you can?

A. Yes, it was an interesting challenge. We had been decimated as a party back in the '87 election. And that's when we really did a lot of introspection. We had time, because we had this huge majority government led by David Peterson. We thought we knew we had four or five years. Andy Brandt was the interim leader. And there was a team of us: Tony Clement and a number of party people that believed the old power politics of the past, it was time to revamp it. We had some examples with the Reform Party. I think it might have been the PQ in Quebec that went one member, one vote.

Q. For picking a leader.

A. For picking a leader. We were kind of the first mainstream party, at least in the east, and we went to one member, one vote. We got rid of that backroom politics. Senator Norm Atkins' vote was the same as the guy that just signed up two weeks ago. I always used to express it that way, and I think that was an important part of what gave us the opportunity.

So then, when we did have the leadership, it was under this process. And at the end of the day, it was just Dianne Cunningham and I; we were both new. All the old loyalties disappeared. There is a great lesson in this, by the way, for the Chrétien and Martinites, because they are still there; you know, the old Chrétien people, the Martin people, they didn't like one another, they fought. Then one became Rae supporters, one Ignatieff, and they are still fighting. They will never be in government, by the way, until they get rid of all that and they go to the next generation, and everybody has to pick somebody new. That's my prediction.

Q. And it was your experience. Because you had two new leaders.

A. We had two new leaders; we were the next generation of leader, if you like. And so the old [Roy] McMurtry people or the old [Dennis] Timbrell people, they all came together under this leadership.

Then David Peterson called a snap election, right after my leadership. We had no money, but we set the agenda in that campaign. We knew we couldn't win the campaign; they didn't know who Mike Harris was.

Q. This was the spring of 1990.

A. This is the spring of 1990. And so this is my early leadership days. So we set the agenda. We became the tax-fighting team. We had the tax-fighting buses. And it was taxes, and tax increases, that really did in David Peterson. And I don't know if you recall, on the back of the bus, about ten days before the vote, they could see what was happening, and they offered to reduce the sales tax that they had just increased, when they lost all credibility at that moment in time. I was not ready to be leader, the public didn't know who I was, and Bob Rae came up the middle and became premier with, you know, 37 percent of the popular vote, majority government. But we set the agenda. And I think the small band of caucus, if you like, said, "You know what? We didn't win, Harris wasn't ready. But he deserves another shot. He set the agenda in this campaign." And we got four more seats or something, at the time. They saw enough in me that they entrusted me with what we did over the next four years.

Q. Let me follow up on something you just said, because I think it is a real insight into where you were at the time. You said Senator Norman Atkins' vote — Senator Atkins, a member of the Big Blue Machine, had been in the party for decades and decades — is worth as much at that convention as the person who joined two weeks ago. You're not saying it, but it's true: you were not part of the PC Party establishment ...

A. No.

Q. You weren't part of the Big Blue Machine.

A. No, I wasn't.

Q. You weren't part of that long forty-two-year history.

A. No.

Q. You were on the outside, looking in.

A. I was.

Q. So what leadership qualities did you have to bring to bear to not only take over a party that had, let's face it, marginalized you in the past, and get to a point where they are now prepared to say, "Okay, yes, you're the leader and we accept that." How do you do that?

A. Well, it evolves. I was still not particularly well-accepted in Toronto, if you like, or amongst the establishment. So you go to where you can, and you start building the base all across the province. Brian Mulroney did the same thing, by the way — not particularly well-accepted by the establishment when he took over. He didn't come from the establishment. In fact, he overthrew the establishment to become leader. He started travelling the country, into all the small legion halls, all the small towns.

And then the stories would start to build, and you start to build credibility. And out of that, all of the sudden it is kind of like a shock to the establishment when they see the amount of support that's there. It's sort of like Rob Ford, by the way, if you want a current example.

Q. The Toronto mayor's race.

A. I am sure it was absolutely shocking to the *Toronto Star* and the CBC and all the elites here in Toronto that figured they understood Toronto politics; Rob Ford, now, amongst the leaders, perhaps going to be the next mayor of Toronto, he came out of, they thought, nowhere. But Rob Ford knew his constituency, knew who he was speaking for, and slowly built that credibility.

By the way, Norm Atkins and Hugh Segal and folks that didn't support me in the leadership were very supportive afterward. You know, the big tent came.

The other interesting thing is, it wasn't that I didn't know I had to win over Toronto, and I had to win these people over and it had to be a very broad coalition. It is just that you start where you can, and you start building where you can, and you start building credibility where you can.

And the other fact that very few people understand is that in 1995, when we built that coalition, I won more seats in the 416, a higher percentage than I did outside of the 416. People today are shocked when I tell them that.

Q. You won seats in the 416; I remember it well. Well, here was the biggest transition: When you eventually win that election in 1995, you are not the head of a caucus of twenty anymore; it is now eighty-two. How does one wield leadership prowess when it's not just a hardy band of men and women, all of whom you know reasonably well? My bet is, on election night, there were some of those eighty-two who you probably didn't even know.

A. No, it's true, I didn't. I had read their names, or heard of them, or campaigned with them, but I certainly didn't know a lot about them. And that two-week transition when you've got to pick your cabinet, who is going to lead the civil service; those are all the things we had to do. Those were twenty-four-hour days. They were in many ways much scarier than being in opposition, scarier in the sense that you've got to assemble as much information as you can as quickly as you can, and you ultimately have to make those decisions. And there are eighty-two people who probably all thought they should be in cabinet, or deputy premier, minister of finance, whatever it is.

It's a great credit, though, to that caucus, that when I did make the decisions, they all accepted them. And it is not always the case. But they all accepted them.

Q. Why do you think?

A. I think because of the campaign. We had built a great deal of credibility in the year leading up to the campaign and in the campaign, and they had a great deal of confidence in the whole team. The Tom Longs and the Leslie Nobles told all the candidates, "This is what is going to happen, this will be the first week." We did unusual things in the campaign. We shared the whole thing with all the candidates, all the campaign managers.

Q. You were twenty-five points behind when that campaign started.

A. Yes, yes.

Q. And were halfway through.

A. And we were. And we told the candidates, (a) we are going to win, here is how we are going to win, here's when the polls will move, and all that unfolded within a day or so of what we predicted. So there was a bit of magic, I think, there, that a lot of people said, "Well, you know what? If Harris doesn't know what he's doing, this team knows what they are doing." But it was a collective thing, and so I was given a period of grace.

Those that didn't get in cabinet, right away, you know, I think took the attitude, "Well, by golly, I trust his leadership and I am going to earn it and deserve it and get in there later."

Q. Chris Stockwell didn't. Chris Stockwell went to your office and swore a blue streak in your face.

A. Well, eighty-one out of eighty-two is not bad.

Q. Eighty-one out of eighty-two, okay. When John A. Macdonald signed in to a hotel once, they asked him his occupation and he said "cabinet-maker," which is pretty clever. Here's what Teddy Roosevelt said about it. He said:

"The best executive is the one who has sense enough to pick good men ..."

Today, we would say "good men and women ..."

"… to do what he wants done and self-restraint enough to keep from meddling with them while they do it."

Did you sign on to that?

A. Yes, I think so, pretty much. Yes, I would agree with those sentiments. Let them do their jobs. In the early days, I suppose it was a little easier for me than my predecessors, again, because of the *Common Sense Revolution*.

Q. You had the road map?

A. We had the road map. So the bureaucracy had the road map, the ministers had the road map, Guy Giorno was part of the team that prepared the briefing books for all the ministers. He did become my chief of staff, but he was key, you know, one of the key parts of the campaign team and David Lindsay was the chief of staff. And every minister had binders that said, "Here's how the *Common Sense Revolution* pertains to social services, to education, to finance."

Q. What happened in cabinet, though, when a minister would say, "This wasn't covered in the *Common Sense Revolution*. It has just come up and I don't agree with the way you want to handle it."

A. That's where we had great discussions and great debates. The amalgamation stuff, of municipalities. That wasn't in the *Common Sense Revolution*. We said you've got to figure out how to do more for less, right? We can't keep spending this amount of money and we want quality services. So how are we going to do that?

And one of the ways we looked at was municipalities. We also asked municipalities to take an across-the-board, 3 percent cut in our transfer payments to the municipalities. You know, a little less had been downloaded on us by the feds, but we said, "You know, everybody's got to be part of this." And I will say this: For the most part, municipalities said, "We get it. No point having a booming Toronto and a bankrupt province."

And it's just like I said to Paul Martin: "We support the cuts. No point in having a booming province and a bankrupt Canada."

Q. Well, Toronto was opposed. Hamilton was opposed.

A. Well, there would be no city of Toronto if I had not forced it. There would be no city of Toronto today. It would be a collection of these odd-ball municipalities. Hazel McCallion never wanted a city of Toronto. She thought maybe Mississauga could take over and she might have been right, you know.

But I think it was the right thing to do. We needed a strong Toronto. If you want to be a world-class city, you had to be that size. Now, I don't agree with all the policies that followed; the council is probably too large, but that principle is there.

Q. And when the Toronto members came to you and said, "This is not how we do things in Toronto," which they did say, you then have to show leadership. And what do you do?

A. You have to find a consensus. And once you make the decision, you have got to go with it. I mean, we came up with these — which would have come from some of the Toronto members — we came up with these local councils, who could have some of the decision making on stop signs, on little street lights, speed bumps, all these little things. So we set those up. So we ended up instead of a council of twenty-six, we ended up with a council of fifty-two, which I think was a huge mistake but, you know, that was all part of the consensus to get the team onside.

Q. By 1995, my recollection is that there was a significant chunk of the press gallery at Queen's Park, probably the elites of this city, and others in the province, who not only criticized you but vilified and ridiculed you. You were dismissed as a dumb golf pro, which most politicians don't have to deal with.

How do you demonstrate leadership when you are picking up the paper every day, and it is not just criticism, it is personal. How do you do that?

A. Yes, I think they tried to marginalize me and, of course, the Liberals and the NDP, I mean, it's an old strategy, always try and marginalize your opponent. So they played into that as well.

But the advantage of that is you get underestimated. Jean Chrétien proved that — "The little guy from Shawinigan." They always underestimated him. He turned out to be a very decisive and smart leader, whether you agree with him or not. So you put your head down. I got a lot of golf pro votes and a lot of golfers' votes, by the way, at the same time.

But the truth of the matter is it was not only that; it was sort of Northern Ontario, how could a kid from North Bay possibly understand Toronto? I was never part of the academic establishment, so how could somebody that doesn't have a master's degree or a Ph.D. possibly understand people?

Q. Or a lawyer. Most premiers are lawyers.

A. Yes. But I understood people, and I understood and felt very comfortable that what we were promoting was the right thing. I don't want to be accused of, particularly on your show, of clichés or anything, but it really comes down to I had a compass, and the team around me had a compass, and it was kind of dependency versus independence. It was freedom versus this dependency. And that transcended all the policies. And what we discovered was most Ontarians shared that view and that belief.

Q. But there was a moment, I seem to recall this, where you were away from the Legislature during that period between '90 and '95; you were away for a good chunk. And everybody was joking, "Oh, he's probably up north working on his handicap." And in fact I think you were off adopting a child.

A. Yes.

Q. And you didn't want that record corrected. That's an interesting decision, you know? I mean, you would think that you would want people not to joke, "Here's why I'm away, here's what I'm doing." But you didn't — why not?

A. No. And because that was private time, and because to use that as a defence, then you bring your child and your family into it. But let me say that when they said you are off working on your handicap, it wasn't just at that time. I did have a conscious strategy not to be into the Legislature, where the Queen's Park Gallery, let's face it and I don't mind saying it — I have said that they are a lazy lot, right?

Question period is where they can get their story. They can go there, watch it for an hour, do a scrum, and it's all done. They don't have to go find the leader, they don't have to go to North Bay, they don't have to go out and see what is happening. So question period is a convenient way, and it became that.

And what I felt through a large part of this time was that there was no mileage for me at question period. We had many good critics. There was mileage for me being in Beamsville, there was mileage for me being in Fort Erie and particularly early on. So we had a strategy that said, "Now, we will go to where we have a receptive media, we have a receptive audience. We start building." You know, some would say you throw a little pebble into a pond and it ripples out. That is coming from the centre out. We came from the outside, into the centre, if the centre is indeed Toronto and Queen's Park and the Gallery. And that's how we did it.

Q. When you are no longer an opposition politician, you are now the premier of the province, it is all on your shoulders. Do you have to consciously change the style by which you lead, now that you have "the job."

A. I don't think so. But perhaps I did. Everybody evolves, and perhaps I did. But if I did, I didn't do it consciously. The job is different. You are a premier of all the people. You are not just developing strategies for attacking the government, or not just in a campaign, selling your policies. Now you are governing for all the people.

And we took on lots of things that were not in the *Common Sense Revolution*. Problems would come along that you had to deal with. I always said, once the election was over, once we are going forward, we are going to try and win every vote. Everybody is a potential PC voter, everybody is a potential Harris voter, if you like. Never successful in that, but I think if you have that, top of the mind, that's a better way to govern than not.

And yet, you know, I have been accused by some of being divisive. I don't see it that way. What I do so see is I wouldn't back down. When I was challenged by the unions, I didn't give in. And that maybe created some divisiveness. But I make no apology for that.

Q. I wouldn't have put it that way. The way I saw it was this way: You danced with the ones that put you there, which meant that the 45 percent of the people who elected you in '95 as premier, and then re-elected you by the same total vote —

A. A little higher …

Q. — in '99 —

A. A little higher.

Q. A little higher? Maybe a fraction higher … you cared about them the most. And if the other 55 [percent] weren't onside, tough luck for them. Now that was how it looked to a lot of us at the time. You don't think that's accurate?

A. No. I governed with a philosophy, and it really does go back to this philosophy of entitlement, of status quo, of dependence, really. So whether it was welfare … I mean, I never gave up on anybody on welfare. So the pessimist would look at it and say, "Well, you've got to give them more money," right? And I looked at them and said, "No, we've got to teach them how they are going to get a job, and not need welfare." And so a lot of the policies were that way.

And let's face it, if you believe in freedom and if you believe in competition, you believe in getting the best bang for the buck, you are going to come into conflict with the public sector unions; that was my main fight. It was not the private sector unions, even though they spent some money against me. It was the public sector unions. They like the monopoly, they wanted to keep it. I understood that; that was their job.

Q. We have talked about how you run a caucus, how you run a cabinet, how you run a premier's office. What about how you run a civil service, because you are the guy who basically appoints all the deputy ministers. You are the guy who is sending out the signal that, "Here is how we are going to run the government and I need your help to implement." How do you get them to follow?

A. Well, by and large, I've got to say this: I think Ontario … particularly at the senior levels, I think they are very professional, I think they are very good, I think they are non-partisan, and there will be the odd exception, of course. And there were some who had difficulty with the *Common Sense Revolution* agenda. And they either moved on voluntarily or eventually, you know, didn't end up being part of the team, which is fair, both leaving, and fair, maybe, me asking some to leave, and why would you want to work if you fundamentally disagreed with the direction we were going in. But I thought for the most part certainly they were very professional.

So the *Common Sense Revolution*, when we interviewed for the top job, one of the first questions I asked was, you know, "Have you read the *Common Sense Revolution*?" And they would all say yes. Then I said, "Did you read it six months ago, or did you read it about ten days out when the polls said I might win it?" We would have a little laugh over that, and some said, "Yes, it was kind of in the last week. I have really been boning up, you know, Mr. Harris."

Rita Burak was a wonderful secretary of cabinet. We worked closely together, we met every morning on the agenda, and I am going to tell you this: There were times when I would say to her in a morning meeting, "Rita, this isn't happening over in such and such a ministry. And we all agreed we are going to do it."

And she would come back to me the next morning and she says, "I have checked into this, Mr. Premier, and your minister is holding this up. It is not the bureaucracy."

So we worked as a team. We worked very well together. We incented, by the way, all the top levels of management. We offered all the unions' incentive pay and everything; they turned it down because it was against their principle, but we incented senior management. We respected them, with the Trillium Awards and whatnot. And I had great, great cooperation.

Q. Just finish that story. What happened to the minister who wasn't playing ball, even though the civil service was prepared to?

A. Well, there was a phone call. And the next day, he played ball.

Q. Do you want to say who it was and what the situation was?

A. No, I don't want to get into individuals, but it happened more than once.

Q. We did a program last month on the fifteenth anniversary of your election win, which was June 8, '95. And Leslie Noble, who ran your two successful campaigns, pointed this out and I thought it was fascinating because I didn't pick up on it at the time.

The first four years you were premier were pretty bloody eventful. And there were a few demonstrations, you may remember. And you got re-elected in 1999, and Leslie Noble said, "The Mike Harris who won that re-election was not the same guy who won in '95 because he was tired. He had been through the wars, and he just didn't have as much wind in his sails for his second term as he did in his first." Is she right?

A. I think she is partially right. By the way, somebody had dredged out an old quote from about six years before, that said, "Mike Harris' goal was to get elected, implement an agenda, get re-elected, and then leave."

It was the overall game plan, by the way; it was never to be a career politician, or stay there forever. So that is partially it.

Secondly, I would say she is wrong in the first year. The goal was to implement the *Common Sense Revolution*; that was the one that we had really worked on. The second agenda, "Blueprint for Ontario" we called it, was not as clearly defined, I don't believe. I think the caucus had been worn down, too. I think Leslie is right in that; it does wear on you, day after day after day. And the personal attacks and, David Tsubouchi's wife had eggs pelted at her, and there was a certain sense that, "Okay, we are re-elected. When do we get to enjoy this?" because there was a tension in a lot of the changes that we made.

And I also went through changes in my personal life. I was separated [from his wife, Janet]. With my marriage, I had things to work on there, both with my ex-spouse, who we are very good friends today, and my children and whatnot. So I think it was a combination of all of those things, and it was time for new leadership.

Q. Let's talk about trying to lead in a diverse place. This province, I think actually during your years as premier, '95 to 2002, became exponentially more diverse than it was before that, in ways that a kid who grew up in

North Bay, Ontario, could not have imagined. StatsCan says 223 different ethnic origins live in this province. And my hunch is when you grew up in North Bay, you didn't have contact with 221 of those 223?

A. I did not. You are quite right.

Q. So how do you lead people with whom you have essentially no common background?

A. Well, you try and find commonality. Again, one of the great things I think about leadership is that you know where you want to go. And then you motivate others to go there with you. And so I tried very hard to stick to the knitting, if you like. "Here is what we believe in; they are the principles of the *Common Sense Revolution*." Even after the revolution was over, they are the same principles.

I would argue most of those immigrants that have come to Canada in the early years, and then later, came here for opportunities that were not available to them where they came from. So it may have been the potato famine in Ireland or they came because of oppression. Or they came from poverty and no opportunities.

So what did they have in common with me? What did I have in common with them? Well, the principles of freedom, and opportunity to get ahead, regardless of race, creed, religion, colour. Education is a key component, one of the great levellers. I was very strong on quality, accessible education, at all levels, even though I had some fights with some of those involved. And we had some common bonds.

And traditionally, I think people had thought, well a lot of the immigrants that have come to there, and particularly first generation, were Liberal because we had a Liberal government; you used to hear this all the time.

But, quite frankly, they were looking for small-c conservative values and opportunities and those kinds of freedoms. So I would emphasize what we stood for. We reached out to the recent immigrants and second-generation immigrants, the visible minorities. I appointed Keith Norton, who had been the federal human rights commissioner, I appointed him to the [Ontario] human rights commission. We were very strong on strengthening those rights amongst visible minorities and those of a different religion. I mean, after Peterson tried and Rae tried, it was finally the Harris government, by the way, that brought in long-awaited changes for gays and lesbians in Ontario.

Q. Let me follow up there, because that is fascinating. The fact is that you ran a conservative government, but you did not run a socially conservative government.

A. Not in the least.

Q. Now why not? Because that was certainly a part of your power base, the social conservatives of this province.

A. It was, but it wasn't for the social conservative side of them, it was on the freedom side. It was on the tax side, it was on the freedom of opportunity, the competition, the reducing the barriers to entry to get in there and compete.

Q. But I think the Supreme Court made some kind of decision which required you to bring, I think, about sixty-seven laws in the province into accord with their decision, allowing rights for gays and lesbians. And you did it.

A. Of course.

Q. You say of course, but the social conservatives would have not appreciated that.

A. Well, some of the social conservatives didn't. And some would bring religion into it. And there is still to this day some discussion over abortion. And I said, look, here are the things that unite us, here are the things that we believe in. I am Anglican, my religion is different from a lot of others, and we believe in freedom of religion and go practise your religion and teach whatever you want in your religion. But here are the common things, and here is what we ask our governments to do, and here are things the government can do, and here are the things that the government are rightly involved in. And so protection of freedoms and of rights, I think that is fair. And we moved to strengthen those.

And I understand there were some social conservatives who were also part of our power base who supported us. But they quickly learned that here is the way we govern, support us for these reasons. Don't support us because you think we are going to allow discrimination or we are going to take a position on abortion or we are going to take religious positions or any of these areas, because that is not us, that is not who we are.

Q. That is interesting because, again, would you have known one homosexual man or woman growing up in North Bay?

A. It turns out I did, but I probably didn't know at the time. I mean, most weren't out of the closet at the time. I have had great discussions with my mother on a late uncle of mine who clearly was homosexual, but, "I didn't know at the time." He just preferred men, and they lived together, and not women. And we had some visible minorities. We had a fairly large Native population. We had an air base there, and as the university grew it was the first that we saw visible minorities, because they had the expertise and the excellence over part of it.

We had a very small Jewish community. The truth of the matter is, I never knew whether they were Jewish or not. I didn't understand the difference in all these things, until I came to Toronto, and there were more prejudices down here, as I discovered, against some who were different or different ethnic backgrounds.

Q. But it is probably worth remembering that I think in both of your elections that you won, '95 and '99, you swept the 905. That ring of ridings around Toronto, you won every single seat in the 905, which is where the burgeoning visible-minority population was living.

A. Yes. Particularly the recent immigrants. Those values, I mean, workfare, it was: don't pay people to sit home and do nothing. By the way, that was a Bob Rae quote; I loved using that one. He said it makes no sense to pay people to sit home and do nothing. I said, it sure doesn't; so why do we do it?

Q. But when you met them, how would they see this WASPy guy from North Bay and think, "Yes, I've got something in common with him."

A. You know, I was always able to go into Tim Hortons, have a coffee with them. I think, if you polled cab drivers in Toronto, I see them still today; they wave, they honk. "Hi, Mike." I think most of them are Asian, of ethnic background, and relatively recent immigrants. They supported the values that I stood for.

Q. Let's talk about women, because women are dramatically underrepresented in every cabinet that has ever existed, in every caucus that has ever existed, in the Legislature in general. Obviously, [women are] more than half the population, and certainly not more than half the seats in any Legislature anywhere in this country. And I think it is fair to say you ran a particularly macho government, if I can put it that way.

In which case, how comfortable, or not, did you find when trying to lead women in your caucus with such a macho agenda, when not every woman who has been elected necessarily brings that same kind of macho to the office.

A. Listen, not every guy is macho, either. And we had very talented women, not enough to be representative; it is a fair comment. By the way, where I could pick and choose, I had more women deputy ministers than any previous premier of the day. I don't know what's happened since, but we picked the talent where we could get it, really without regard to gender. And, of course, I had two deputy secretaries of cabinet, the head of the civil service, they were both women.

Q. And they never came to you and said, "Geez, Mike, do you have to be such a bully on this?" You never saw that?

A. Yes, lots of people would say, because if ten people would call me about it, they were all ten different union leaders, then we would say, "Well, are you a bully?" I mean, that was the goal; throw enough mud and some of it will stick.

And I can honestly tell you that, I never felt that way. I was as inclusive as I could be. I said to every union leader, "You want to have a meeting with me? I am happy to meet with you." Abuse the meeting, I won't meet with you again. And I followed that principle.

So if you tell me you want to come and meet with me and you want to discuss this, there will be no media, and here is the agenda, and then you come with five other people and cameras coming and everything else, that was your last meeting. The unions told us: "We are in charge, we are running this, we don't want accountability, we don't want testing. That's it." It was two years of attempting consultations before we finally said, "We can't wait any longer. Our province is falling behind." So is that being a bully?

Q. I think the toughest union leader on you actually was a woman; I think it was Leah Casselman, from OPSEU, wasn't it?

A. Yes, and by the way we had a big strike, the first strike in history. Well, that's because it was illegal to strike, when you were OPSEU, until Bob Rae gave them the right to strike. And then he took it away. He came in with a three-year Social Contract and said, "Even though I have given you the right to strike, nobody can strike for three years," right? Which a lot of them weren't happy with.

During my term, after about one year, I guess, all these contracts came up. And we had campaigned that, if we could find a better, more efficient, smarter way to provide a service, i.e., outsource, if somebody else could pick up garbage better than this contract, would it be a cheaper price, better quality, whatever, those things, and Leah Casselman's position was, "You will not outsource." And the strike went on for forty-two days, was it? "You will not outsource."

After forty-two days, she said, "I guess you can ... there will be outsourcing." And in three days, we settled, I think, a very generous contract.

Q. Let me pull you back, now, to multiculturalism: You did attract a lot of votes in multicultural communities in the two elections that you won. But if you look at the Ontario Progressive Conservative Party today, it has kind of gone back in time in some respects. It is a caucus that is on the whiter, older, more rural side, and a lot of those links that apparently you had into those communities have dissolved. What does a leader have to do to re-establish that when it appears as if the Liberals, now, can count on that vote, at least so far?

A. Well, I hope they smugly think they can count on it next election, because I don't think they can. You have to re-establish what you have in common, and I believe that Tim Hudak can do that. I think that you have to go and say, "Here is what we stand for, here is what we believe in, here is the compass, here is the direction I want to lead the province in." And I believe, very strongly, they will follow.

I mean, the media pilloried Stephen Harper as being right wing, Western based, da-da-da-da, social conservative ...

Q. Hidden agenda ...

A. ... hidden agenda, and yet he did quite well. He didn't make the big breakthrough [in 2006] but, if you look at the increase in votes in a lot of those multicultural communities, I mean, he almost won in Brampton. So it takes some time. You've got to build credibility, and I believe they believe in small-c conservative principles, of the work ethic; work hard and you get ahead. It is not fair that somebody that does nothing is better off than me who is working really hard. And, you know, immigrants to this country, they understand that and they want a fair opportunity, they want a fair break, and they want to be treated fairly. And a small-c conservative who sticks to those principles, I think, will reach out and win in those communities.

Q. I want to talk today about your legacy, essentially, the legacy of leadership that you left behind. You mentioned that one of the ways your father led was to instill in you a sense of fear, a sense of, "I didn't want to disappoint my dad and a sense of woe betide you if you do."

And I wonder how much of that was in you when you tried to lead this province for the seven years that you did?

MR. HARRIS: I think very little. I mean, one of the things I learned in the early years with my father, who was a wonderful man, that side of him was to me not the best side. And you learned that, growing up, and you tried to be a different kind of father. And you learn that with leaders.

But, to me, truly great leaders lead by example, [Brian] Tracy, who is a motivational speaker, I think he said that a great leader motivates ordinary people to do extraordinary things. I have to tell you that the caucus was united by and large throughout. Even [maverick Bruce-Grey-Owen Sound MPP] Billy Murdoch, I used to have to call from time to time. They understood the agenda, they understood what we were doing. We were a team, we evolved goals together, and we set them.

The difference was this: I didn't back down. I was not going to be bullied. And many have tried to bully me into doing things. They say, "We'll shame you, we'll do this, we'll do that. We'll call you names, we'll picket, we'll throw things at you, we'll do all those things." And I was not going to be bullied.

Q. Why not? Because most premiers will want to put some water in their wine to make the demonstrators go away. Why didn't you?

A. Because I think the duly elected representatives of the province are supposed to make the decisions, are supposed to run the province, not the unions. They were basically the ones that were picketing and demonstrating. And in the case of the teachers' unions, they wanted a hundred percent control of education. They didn't pay for it; the taxpayers were paying for it. And the taxpayers are electing people to help pay for it. And I can tell you this: that if you look back, I, in everything that I did as a teacher, as a trustee, as an MPP, as a premier, I put students first. I put quality education of students first.

The teachers' union's job is to represent the teacher. Sometimes they will put students first but, if there is a conflict there, their job is to represent the teacher. That bullying attempt on their part, and it was demonstrated again just recently with Nipissing University [*a union opposed an attempt to name the campus library after Harris*], you can't accept that. And you can't accept it in my view and sleep at night and say, "I'm a leader and I am doing my job."

Q. But some people thought that you were a successful premier insofar as you won back-to-back majorities, because not only did you know what you wanted to do, but because you knew who your enemy was and you vilified your enemies. And it made it easier for you and it frankly galvanized your caucus more, to identify an enemy and then go take him on. And that is what happened with public servants and with teachers and maybe some nurses and the list may go on.

A. Well I did take them on. If I thought they were unfairly trying to bully me, I did take them on. And I guess maybe other leaders in the past didn't, and maybe they just compromised, and maybe it was a wishy-washy middle and maybe that works for some time. In my view, it is not the sign of leadership.

I'll tell you that one thing I did do: And I think Tom Peters says that excellence is setting the agenda. I always remember this, excellence is setting the agenda.

Q. They guy who wrote the book *In Search of Excellence.*

A. That's right. And I think being a leader, and a good leader, is setting the agenda. We set the agenda. We set the agenda with the *Common Sense Revolution*, and once the agenda is set, once it's agreed on, once it's voted on, once you're elected, you've got to implement the agenda.

Q. But I think it is fair to say, most premiers in Ontario history, and there have been others who have won elections as well obviously, saw their role as not necessarily coming to office with an agenda that, "We are going to get through, come hell or high water," but they saw competing interests in society and they felt it was their job to broker, to find the compromise, to find the solution among those competing interests. I don't think you saw your job that way.

A. Well, no, I think for many times it is, but there are certain principles that you have to stick to, and yes, we made lots of compromises. We worked with lots of groups. I mean, it will shock people to know that we settled more Native land claims during my term in that office than any other premier before me.

Q. And no one will remember that. They'll remember the one dead Indian.

A. Yes, right, that's right.

Q. Ipperwash.

A. Right. And for some strange reason, because people have said it a million times, they think I actually had something to do with it, which is totally false. Secondly, Monte Hummel, who is head of the World Wildlife Fund…

Q. Lands for Life.

A. Yes, Lands for Life. We set aside more parks, more protected areas, than any other premier in history and since. And the World Wildlife Fund? Monte Hummel still gives me credit for that. But that is counterintuitive to those that want to vilify me.

Q. It doesn't fit the story.

A. Right. It doesn't fit the story or the image they want to have of that.

Q. But you earned the story; you did earn the brand, right? You did earn the brand by getting into some very high-profile, knock-down, drag-'em-outs with some people in the past who had been fairly powerful.

A. I have earned lots of brands, as the guy who did what he said he would do. I thought that's what we were supposed to do. But was I tough? I suppose I was. If it came to be bullying around, and doing what we said that we would do, and first choice is always do it cooperatively and do it with people and do it with various groups. And I would say 99 percent of the time we were able to do that. Occasionally, we weren't.

Q. This quote has been attributed to you; I don't know if you actually said it, so let me find out: "By the time we're done, there won't be one blade of grass on the south lawn at Queen's Park that hasn't been trampled on by some demonstrator." Did you say that?

A. I did. And it was probably written for me, but I think we had a sense that some of the changes we were going to make would challenge the status quo in some areas.

Q. Did you see it as a badge of honour?

A. Not necessarily. But what was important was we said this has to be done, the public agreed and we said, "No matter how hard they protest, we promised you we would do this, and we are going to do it."

Q. I remember Sid Ryan saying, "I don't believe it. We had 150,000 people out in the streets for Days of Action, and this guy's not backing down." Why didn't you want to put just a little bit of water in the wine, just to make things a little more peaceful and a little less divisive?

A. Well, I could argue that we probably did put a little water in the wine, but it wasn't enough for them. And it really came down to, who is going to run the hospitals, Sid Ryan and his union? Or are we going to put patients first and, if we can find a way to save a few bucks, to have a contractor come and sweep the halls and we can hire one more nurse or we can get one more piece of equipment in there, what's in the best interests of patients and whatnot?

I understand what's in the best interests of CUPE and Sid Ryan's union and that local; it is keeping everybody employed at the highest possible salary. I get that. But that wasn't my job.

Q. Okay. But does your style of leadership burn out too fast? We talked about the fact that, a year into your second term, a lot of the wind was out of your sails. You were out of gas. It's one thing to be a revolutionary; it is another thing to actually have to keep the revolution going forever, right? Is it hard to keep the revolution going forever?

A. Well, I don't think you need a revolution all the time. I think you have to make a transition then, into what's next? What do you have to do? And without being critical, I think I had successors who wanted to be loved by everybody, so I am going to make peace with the teachers. I am not Mike Harris, I heard them say, I am not that, I am not … no, no, come on.

I think small-c conservative principles, stick to them; I think it will win the day in every part of this country and in every part of Ontario.

Q. In my experience, it seems there have been two kinds of leaders who became prime minister or premier: There are the transactional ones and the transformational ones. I don't think there is much doubt about the fact that you were a transformational one, for good or ill. People will have their different opinions on it. When you got the job, did you know that's what you wanted to be?

A. Well, I didn't phrase it in my mind that way, but clearly, yes. Clearly I felt there were transformational things that had to be done. And I was not a transactional premier. I didn't enjoy managing as much as making change, if you like, and was change oriented. So if you wanted a premier who was just going to manage things as they came along, keep everybody happy, and here's this. Well, let's have a team of people come to a consensus on it, and isn't that nice, that is a different leader. I want to move on and do something else that is more interesting to me, more challenging to me, where I can use my skill set, if you like. And the trappings of office didn't appeal to me. And I was always astounded. I would go on these Team Canada trips with Jean Chrétien and, to his credit, he loved it. He loved meeting with queens and kings and state leaders and the state dinners and everything else. I hated them; I thought they were boring. And so that side of being premier was not for me. Rolling up our sleeves, building this hospital, you know, making this decision, getting this problem fixed, that was for me.

Q. Pierre Trudeau was a transformational rather than transactional leader.

A. Sure.

Q. Did you feel you had something in common with him?

A. Well, in this sense. I mean, Trudeau is the reason I joined the ... I voted for him, first time, by the way.

Q. In '68?

A. In '68. And then I joined the Conservative Party because of him, because I didn't think his vision of a Just Society fit my vision of a just society, and I felt he was abandoning those principles I had learned from my dad, his small-c conservative initiative, work ethic, all of these things.

But he was a leader, and he had a vision. And his Just Society, we could understand it. Fifty years from now we would all be bilingual and peaceful all across the country. There would be French spoken in Edmonton, it would be just as acceptable as English in Chicoutimi. Neither one of those were true, by the way, in either jurisdiction, but he had a vision, and he led that way, and he was not swayed from it. And, in that, he was a leader. And I admired him for that.

Q. What other Canadian leader do you see parallels with, in terms of your own leadership style?

A. Well, in a way, I don't think Chrétien had the same vision that Trudeau had, but Chrétien was a leader too, in this: leaders have to make decisions and be decisive. You consult as widely as you can, but you can't keep putting off decisions, in my view. I mean, you might get away with a period of time. I know many accused Bill Davis; he used to take pride, you know, "If I wait long enough, the problem will go away," he talks about that.

Q. "Never put off till tomorrow what you can avoid doing altogether."

A. He used to laugh at that, but Davis did make some pretty decisive decisions.

Q. He did.

A. And so did Chrétien. I mean, if you look at the Liberal Party, and I know Paul Martin's got a lot of credit, and I like Paul Martin for balancing the books. Hindsight tells me Chrétien made the tough decisions and Martin carried them out, because when Martin had the opportunity as leader, I didn't see that same decisiveness. I saw … Newfoundland wants this? You can have it. You want this? You can have it. I saw a big-spending, say yes to everybody. But Chrétien was tough. I had to deal with him. He said, "That's it," you know?

So that side of me, I think, once a decision is made, you are a leader and that's it. Perhaps Chrétien and I were very similar. We also came from nowhere. We came from little towns, and we were not part of the establishment.

Q. How about the one decision today you wish you could take back?

A. No. You know, I never go there.

Q. You're not going to play with me on this, are you?

A. I don't go there. There are many decisions that in hindsight, if I'd have had more time, all that. I mean, I used to be criticized; we'd bring in a bill and then a month later they'd say, "He's amending it already." Yes, but if I had have waited till it was perfect, I would have never got the bill introduced, you know. I was flexible.

You know, one of the key lines in the *Common Sense Revolution* is, here is what we believe in, here is where we want to go, and here is where we want to be. Have you got a better way to get there, have you got a better idea? We'll adopt it. I still believe that. There were probably lots of easier ways we could have done things, in hindsight. But I am pretty proud of the record and the transformation that we made in Ontario. I think it's a much better province because of it.

The day before Ontario Conservatives voted to replace Mike Harris with Ernie Eves, in March 2002, I sat down with Harris for his final interview as premier. Much of that conversation has already been covered, but one thing he said stuck with me: the notion that raising taxes would be very difficult for any future premier, given how Harris had so dramatically changed the political culture. As seminal a change agent as Mike Harris was, he apparently did not see a new premier entering the political scene shortly after his departure who would, in fact, raise taxes significantly *twice*, have deficits reach the stratosphere, and yet live to tell the tale. But I'm getting ahead of myself. That premier was still a year and a half down the road. Harris' successor would come first.

ERNEST LARRY EVES
(2002–2003)

∽

What would you call a guy who won his first election by just six votes out of almost 20,000 cast? Well, of course, you'd tease him about his massive, huge victory, suggesting he'd won by a "landslide." And so, Ernest Larry Eves became "Landslide" Ernie on March 19, 1981.

Given the narrowness of Eves' victory, Premier William Davis wasn't taking any chances. He immediately gave Eves the chairmanship of a legislative subcommittee and put him on two others. Two years later, Davis promoted Eves to parliamentary assistant. But it wasn't until Frank Miller took over as premier in early 1985 that Eves was promoted to cabinet. Those promotions worked locally for Landslide Ernie. When he sought re-election on May 2, 1985, he won his seat by almost 1,400 — rather than six votes — against the same opponent.

But elsewhere in the province, things were falling apart for the Ontario PC Party. Frank Miller only managed to best the second-place Liberals by four seats. And so, six weeks after that election the Tories lost a vote of confidence on the floor of the Legislature, and thus Ernie Eves' time in cabinet was rather short-lived: just fifty-six days as minister of skills development and forty days as minister of community and social services. Over to the opposition side of the floor he went.

Eves developed a reputation as a snappy-dressing Red Tory, a moderate centrist in the mould of his hero, Bill Davis. Eves loved to regale people with stories of how he'd show off Davis around his riding, then watch as Davis effortlessly mingled with Eves' constituents, remembering their names, matching their stories about rural Ontario with ones of his own. Eves could only marvel at that kind of retail politicking because, frankly, he wasn't nearly as good at it as Davis was. Then again, few were.

Like his good friend Mike Harris, whose Nipissing riding was 150 kilometres away, Eves cooled his heels in opposition for ten years. But when much of Ontario swung hard to the right in 1995 and elected a Conservative majority government led by Harris, Eves was the government's chief beneficiary. Harris rewarded him with the deputy premiership and the most important job in cabinet, minister of finance.

Harris and Eves were a perfect fit for each other. Their skills were complementary. The late Saskatchewan premier Allan Blakeney once told me that successful governments need "a mouthpiece and a bean counter." It was his colloquial prairie way of saying the premier needed to articulate a compelling vision, while the finance minister kept an eye on the nickels and dimes. That was Harris and Eves. The premier hammered home the message that Ontario would now become a place where taxes and spending were going to go down, and the days of governments yielding to whatever public sector union made the most noise were over. The Conservatives had their eyes firmly on the coalition of voters that elected them (middle-class suburban, exurban, and rural Ontarians), and the Harris-Eves combo intended to take an axe to government programs that they felt kept the province's deficit in the stratosphere (exhibit one: cutting welfare rates by more than 21 percent).

In fact, within the first several weeks of taking office in 1995, Eves and his team at the ministry of finance had given the once-over to Ontario's books with such a fine-tooth comb, he felt comfortable slashing spending by more than $2 billion in one fell swoop. Just like that. It was unprecedented. Eves was determined to count the beans more aggressively than any of his predecessors.

Around this time, I can recall bumping into the then-Oakwood MPP Mike Colle, who had just left municipal politics for a provincial seat on the Liberal opposition benches. "Back at Toronto City Hall, you couldn't remove a stop sign from my ward without my say-so," he said. "This guy just cut spending by $2 billion and I didn't hear a thing about it until I read it in the papers."

Eves' tenure as finance minister featured three things: plenty of controversy, plenty of good news, and the worst possible news any parent can get. Let's go through it.

For a finance minister who targeted so many different interest groups in society for spending cuts, Eves somehow managed not to be the target of the government's enemies. Premier Harris was such a lightning rod, and seemed to enjoy incurring the wrath of his opponents so much, that he absorbed the vast majority of the blows inflicted on the government. As a result it was Harris against the teachers, Harris against welfare recipients, Harris against the unions, Harris against the environmentalists. Meantime, it was finance minister Ernie Eves who got to revel in the good news. He cut the provincial portion of your income taxes by 30 percent and became the first treasurer since Robert Nixon a decade earlier to balance the budget.

But there was also tragedy, just horrible tragedy. One night, Eves got the phone call every parent dreads: just a few months into his job as finance minister, on Thanksgiving weekend in 1995, Eves' son Justin was in an automobile accident and killed. He was twenty-two years old.

Who knows how people summon the strength to go on after sustaining such a devastating blow, particularly if they're living their lives in the fishbowl that is politics. But somehow, Ernie Eves did. He stayed on the job and created in Justin's name a foundation that tries to help learning-disabled kids. Justin had dyslexia, so it seemed a good fit. And to this day, Ernie Eves wears his son's ring from Curry College.

Finally, after lowering taxes, balancing the budget, getting the province's finances back on track, and after two decades in public life, Landslide Ernie decided to pack it in. He would leave politics February 8, 2001, on a high note, and move into a great job on Bay Street — vice-chairman of the investment bank Credit Suisse First Boston. He was secure in the knowledge that his friend Mike Harris was sticking around to continue the Common Sense Revolution. And this was no John Turner–Jean Chrétien–Sandra Pupatello resignation from public life (in other words, a strategic withdrawal with every intention of returning). Eves was done. It was time to do something else.

There was only one problem with that plan — Mike Harris himself wasn't intending to stick around for very much longer. And so, when

Harris announced his own surprise retirement in October 2001, many Conservatives looked at the cast of characters in cabinet seeking the leadership — Jim Flaherty, Tony Clement, Elizabeth Witmer, and Chris Stockwell — and found them wanting.

Flaherty was too pugnacious, Clement too young, Witmer too dull (probably too pink as well), and Stockwell without adequate gravitas. But there was another Conservative who had a successful record in government, a solid, serious public image, wasn't too young or too old, and, with the revolution over, embodied a more moderate conservatism most party members seemed to want.

The only problem was, Ernie Eves didn't want to come back to politics. He'd only been out for less than a year when people started bugging him to return. They told him, "Ernie, you're the only guy that can keep us in power." Despite the entreaties, his initial inclination was to stay in the private sector.

And then Leeds-Grenville MPP (now a senator) Robert Runciman did a scrum with reporters at Queen's Park. He told them that in his opinion Ernie Eves was the best option to replace Mike Harris. Had Runciman told Eves that? Yes, indeed. And what was Eves' reaction? "I think he's getting in," said Runciman, who while close to the still non-candidate had no authority to say what he said. Still, if Runciman's plan was to force a quicker, positive decision out of Eves, it worked. Even though the man from Parry Sound actually *hadn't* made a decision to enter the race, Runciman's comments created such momentum behind Eves' candidacy, he couldn't say no.

And so, back into public life he came. I interviewed Ernie Eves about his change of heart shortly after his leadership campaign kickoff announcement:

STEVE: Mr. Eves, the first question is obvious: What changed?

MR. EVES: Lots of things changed. The last three weeks have really been a time of soul-searching for me. I had no intention of getting involved back in the public sector again. I have been there, done that. I was quite comfortable with what I had done in twenty years of public life.

However, a lot of my colleagues and former colleagues, and not just them, though, I think what really impressed me the most were people from all different walks of life, people I just bumped into on the street.

As I said, today, people that work at my drycleaners, a bicycle courier that dropped off a package to my house about a week ago. All kinds of people said, "Like, you really have to think about doing this."

Q. Yes, but usually when people say that, the best advice is "Don't inhale." Enjoy the compliment, but don't inhale. Why did you inhale?

A. It is not only a compliment. I think that people genuinely felt that they, for whatever reason, feel that I am the individual that they would feel most comfortable with in bringing both elements of the party or perhaps even the province together and provide that balance.

Q. And at what point did you agree with that assessment? Because you disagreed, obviously, at the beginning.

A. Yes, I did, I did. And it took me, as I said, three weeks to get there, or two and a half years to get there, at least.

Q. Did John Laschinger's poll numbers help?

A. Well, polling information certainly was the first step, I guess. When people phoned me several weeks ago and asked me if they could put my name in a poll along with the other suggested leadership contenders, I said, "Well, it is a free country. I can't stop you from putting my name in a poll." So they did.

Q. Did you anticipate the big lead that you ended up having in this poll?

A. No, I didn't. It was quite flattering. They did a public poll first, and then they did a poll of party members. And the party members' poll was just about identical to the results of the public poll. So, I felt quite flattered by that and quite frankly humbled by the events of the last three weeks.

However, there are still lots of considerations, not just lifestyle, but the people around you. It is easy for an individual, or easier, let me put it that way, for an individual to say that he or she is interested in going into public life. Having been there for twenty years, I know the toll that it takes on family and those closest to you. So, the two people that I consulted the most, ultimately, were my daughter Natalie and Isabel [Bassett], my partner in life.

Q. Were they both immediately onside?

A. I would … well, I would say Natalie was. She has lived, you know, with politics, through no choice of her own. Having a father who has been involved for twenty years, and she has been with me every step of the way. And I must say that my former wife, Vicki, was with me every step of the way for a good part of that period of time, and she deserves a lot of credit, as well. And Isabel, of course, has been there; she knows what an onerous task it can be, how —

Q. Which is why I assume she tried to talk you out of it.

A. No, she didn't.

Q. She didn't?

A. She just said, "You know, you have to be happy with yourself at the end of the day. You have to make a decision that your inner self tells you is best for you." And we talked about it for a couple of weeks, I would say. And I think the real turning point in her mind, and she can speak for herself, I am sure, was when we went to the policy conference in London that Friday evening, and I think on the way home, in the car that weekend, she indicated to me, "Well, you know, perhaps this wouldn't be such a bad thing after all, and we could do this as a team." And that is the way we have approached most things in our life, as a team, and that is the way I plan to approach this.

Q. Why do you want to be premier?

A. I don't think it is a question of wanting to be premier as much as it is … I think I have something to offer at this particular point in time.

There are different people for different times; I firmly believe that. If you look through history of anywhere, that seems to be the case.

There is no doubt in my mind that Mike Harris was the right man for the time or the right person for the time in 1995 and 1999, again.

Q. What is different about you and different about these times?

A. But I think the events, first of all, of September 11 changed everybody's thinking. I think it changed everybody's world, especially in North America, dramatically. I think people are looking for experienced leadership. I think that they don't want to try something new at this particular juncture, untried. I think I do have a proven track record. Whether people agree with it or not is another debate for another day, but I think they do know what I stand for.

I think you can look at my five budgets that I introduced as the minister of finance, and there is always a measure, at least in my mind, in there, and I think you will find that to be true, of social justice, of a social conscience. And as I have said today, and as I have said many times before, a true conservative, by my definition, is somebody who is fiscally conservative with a large social conscience. I think that is a true conservative. That was Robert Stanfield's definition of a conservative, and it is certainly mine.

Q. I am trying to find out how many different people — we talked about your family before — that you asked for advice, for whom it would have been most meaningful, and I am assuming your friend Mike Harris would have been one of those people. What did he tell you when you asked him?

A. I talked to Mike a couple of times. Of course, Mike, being the premier, has to remain aloof from the race, but there is no doubt that we have been friends for many years. So, he is somebody that I talk to as a friend, not just … other people may see him as the premier. I see him as Mike. I have always addressed him that way.

Q. Your friend, Mike, didn't tell you that he was leaving early, though?

A. No, he didn't.

Q. Which might have changed your decision ten months ago [to retire from politics].

A. Quite frankly, I don't think Mike made that decision until, as he says, Thanksgiving weekend, and I take that for what it's worth. I had talked to him many times the week before, and he phoned me that Sunday evening before he made the announcement the following week to give me a heads-up.

Q. Did he tell you to go or not go?

A. No. No, he said, "You have to want to do this. I mean, it has to be something that you want to do, and if you want to do it, then go for it, but that is a decision that only you can make. We can all give you advice. You have been there. You have been close to the scene for twenty years. You know what it takes, so you have to decide whether you want to make that commitment or not."

Q. Were you concerned that that which you believe you have achieved over the last five or six years in public life on the government benches would somehow be at jeopardy if you are not there to see it through the next step of the way?

A. I don't think there is any doubt that I have a concern that the economic progress we have made in the province of Ontario I don't think should be wasted. It took a lot of effort and a lot of sweat and tears, and I don't mean by elected people now — I mean by the people of Ontario — to get us to the point where we are today. The economy is back on track in this province.

I understand that we are having difficulties now, especially after the events of September 11, but we do have the economic foundation now to deal with a lot of those issues, and I don't want to see that wasted. I don't want to go back to where we were before.

Q. Let's talk some policy. Is there anything in the recent economic statement by Jim Flaherty that you would not feel comfortable signing on to?

A. Everybody has their own style, Steve, of doing things. I mean, I am not about to start criticizing any decision that Mr. Flaherty made, because having done three budgets plus an economic statement in 1995 of my own, which some would argue was a mini-budget, having done that and having been through that process, I know how difficult it is, and I know the onerous decisions that you have to make. And I am not fully cognizant of all the options he had on the table when he made some of those decisions. I have to be guided that he used his best judgment to do the best job he could.

Q. Fair enough. But what about the $2.2 billion in corporate tax cuts that are on the table right now? Would you go ahead with those?

A. Well, I think corporate taxation, like personal income taxation, is an area of concern. I think we have to become competitive, and not just competitive within Canada, and not even just competitive within North America, but competitive with the rest of the world. And if you don't provide individuals and corporations who are legal entities, of course, under the law, with the opportunity to generate income and to generate employment, your economy is going nowhere.

Q. So, you would support that?

A. Well, I don't know what the options are. I mean, I would have to look at all the facts. Unfortunately, my legal training, I guess, and even my political and business training tells me not to make decisions until you have all the facts in front of you. But I have no aversion to reducing taxes. I have done it 166 times.

Q. As you constantly remind us. My impression is, and this is after having spoken to a number of your friends and colleagues over the last few days ... my impression is that you are not all that keen on the tax rebate for private-school tuitions, that you personally aren't that keen about it, but you are not about to start a food fight in the party trying to roll it back. Is that fair to say?

A. No, that's not the way I would characterize my feeling about it. I think choice is good in the education system, provided that we don't damage the excellent public education system we have in the process. If you can achieve that balance, then I think choice is a good thing. Many other jurisdictions have choice, and it has worked very well for them. But, as you know, quite often in these things, the devil is in the details. And I would have to see what regulation is being proposed, what options are on the table.

For example, I happen to personally believe that every student in this province should have a standard core Ontario curriculum. If you want to add on to that curriculum with other areas of education or endeavour, that is a fair comment. But I think if you are a student in the province of Ontario and your education is being paid for, in whole or in part, by taxpayers' dollars, then I think at least we have to look at having a basic core Ontario curriculum that is taught to our students.

Q. Let me ask you one last thing, and that is, you know one of your opponents, Tony Clement, has said that the Conservative Party has always done best when it makes generational change in its leaders: Leslie Frost to John Robarts, generational change; Robarts to [William] Davis, generational change; Davis to [Frank] Miller, not. You lost the next election. He is arguing Mike Harris to Ernie Eves is not generational change. It is the same generation, and that that could affect your party's prospects in the next election.

A. I think those are interesting coincidences of fact, but I don't think that they have anything to do with the real issues here at stake. The issues at stake in my mind are: What approach are you bringing to government? What ideas and new innovative things do you have to offer? And what choice do you have for the party and the electorate at large?

I am not knocking anybody in this. I don't know that a forty-year-old or a forty–some-year-old is a generational change. My daughter is twenty-five years old. I think Mr. Clement falls somewhere in between a generational change.

But all that nonsense aside, I think you are only as young as you think. I have the enthusiasm. I certainly have a renewed interest and vigour and perspective on the job, and I intend to fill it to the best of my ability.

Everything about Eves' answers suggested he was a confident, mature, serious, moderate Conservative — exactly what the province and the PC Party needed, as we all tried to recover from 9/11, which had taken place only six months earlier. And so, it was no surprise at all that when Tories gathered on March 23, 2002, Eves was the runaway choice for most party members. In a one-member, one-vote system, Landslide Ernie actually did win in a fashion reflecting his nickname. The contest required only two ballots, and the outcome was never in doubt. Eves claimed 55 percent of the votes, while his closest challenger, Jim Flaherty, took 38 percent. Lost in the shuffle of his relatively easy victory was this historical tidbit: Eves would become the first Ontario premier in eighty-two years to get the job without having a seat in the Legislature. And with his former riding (now called Parry Sound-Muskoka) taken by Norm Miller, the son of his former colleague and premier, Frank Miller, Eves would have to find a seat somewhere else.

But that problem would wait for another day. Job one was party unity. After every Progressive Conservative leadership convention, it's always an open question as to whether the party's two factions — the Red Tories and the small-c conservatives — can unite behind whoever wins. They did under Bill Davis. They didn't under Frank Miller or Larry Grossman. They did under Mike Harris. And for the most part they would under Ernie Eves, in large part because Eves did such a good job reaching out to his opponents after the convention. Every one of his challengers received a significant cabinet appointment.

Eves even went far beyond the call of duty to come up with something new and interesting for Jim Flaherty, lest his replacement at finance and leadership runner-up start causing too much fuss. Eves liked the idea of appointing a woman to his former finance portfolio, and so early supporter Janet Ecker would get that job and become the first female finance minister in Ontario history to bring in a budget (Bette Stephenson was actually the first woman treasurer in 1985, but the PCs lost power before she could bring in a budget). To placate Flaherty's supporters, he created the ministry of enterprise, opportunity, and innovation for Flaherty, who called it the "ministry of vowels."

Just before being sworn in as Ontario's twenty-third premier, Eves sat down for another interview.

STEVE PAIKIN INTRO: The transition out of the Mike Harris era continued today. Incoming premier Ernie Eves met with high-ranking PC Party officials, trying to gain a clearer sense of when Mr. Eves will choose his new cabinet, be sworn in as Ontario's twenty-third premier, and, of course, run in a by-election.

This morning, I had a chance to talk to the incoming premier about the importance of being earnest — Ernest Larry Eves, that is.

Q. Let me ask you this, Mr. Eves: If you asked Mike Harris in 1995, "How will Ontario be different after you have finished?" my suspicion is he would have said, "Your taxes would be lower, your budget will be balanced, your education system will be transformed." So, I want to ask the same kind of question: If you are successful in doing what you want to do with this job, how will Ontario be different when you are done?

PREMIER EVES: Well, I think we are going to continue to improve the economy and the economic situation, and taxes will continue to come down; we will continue to be competitive in the international marketplace.

But we have some real challenges ahead of us, in areas like health care, education, environment, infrastructure. And I think, hopefully, you will see in a few years' time a much more cooperative effort among all parties concerned in each one of those areas.

In the education front, I think we have to have cooperation and dynamic partnership, as I referred to on Saturday evening, among students, teachers, school-board trustees, parents. I think that that is all very achievable.

I think in health care we have to look for innovative solutions while protecting the single-tier aspect and accessibility of our health care system — make it more accessible, not less accessible. And I think with an aging demographic population, I think we can do that.

So, if we achieve all those things, I think we will have been successful.

Q. Do I infer from your suggestion that your government will be more cooperative and collaborative with partners, that you thought the last government was too in your face?

A. Well, I don't think the latter comment is a fair comment. I think that the Harris government in 1995 had a lot of things to do in a very short period of time, and if they hadn't have done them, they never would have turned the economy around, and we never would have turned the economy around. So, they had to be done, and I was part of that, and I don't have any regrets about what we did, because I think we had to do it.

Now that we have got there, though, and now that we have changed the fundamentals of the education system, for example, I think a more consultative approach is appropriate. I think that is what people want. I think the concern in education should be the student, not who has the most power — teachers union or the government.

Q. The true believers, though, in your party, and by those I mean the people who say the revolution is perpetual, the people who went to Mr. Flaherty on the second ballot, you say you were Dalton McGuinty's worst nightmare? They think *you* are their worst nightmare because you are going back to a kind of a more pragmatic, less ideological approach.

A. Well, I don't think those people have anything to worry about. First of all, I am the guy who lowered taxes 166 times, with all deference to Mr. Flaherty, in five budgets in six years. They don't have to preach to me about the need to continue to reduce taxation. I was there, long there, before anybody else was. I did most of them. So, that is not going to change. The economic and fiscal attitude of the government is going to be identical to what it was under Mike Harris' reign.

However, I do think that now that we have made significant changes in some other areas, I think it is time for a more consultative approach in those areas. And consultation, I don't think, should ever be depicted as a sign of weakness. As a matter of fact, I think that people that listen to people, who have the ability to listen to people, are stronger and more effective leaders as a result of the input they get from all different perspectives.

Q. Okay. Having said that, let me ask you a follow-up about Mr. Flaherty: The conventional wisdom on the day you win is that you are the big cheese. But the conventional wisdom on the day after you win is that, in a way, he is the big cheese because he decides whether or not the party is unified. He can either play along, or he can make a lot of trouble for you.

What do you intend to do to ensure that the one-third of party support that he got, that faction of the party, doesn't feel left out?

A. Well, first of all, I don't think it is an accurate thing to say that it rests with him or me. This isn't about two individual personalities here. There are a lot of people that voted for Mr. Flaherty, I am sure, that have all kinds of different points of view with respect to the party, as indeed people that voted for me have. I don't think there is any one issue or two issues that people support a candidate for. I think they support a candidate based on the overall direction they would like to see the party and the province go. And it is fair to have an exchange of those ideas.

Jim will play a very significant role in the government. He is a very bright guy. I worked with him very well before, and I am sure I can work with him well afterward.

Q. So, he will not be the parliamentary assistant to the minister for mines, as he has suggested?

A. No, no, he won't be. No, he won't be, unless he wants to be, although I doubt that very much. I think people play this up a lot more than it is. Sure, differences are heightened during a leadership contest. That's natural, because you are trying to appeal to a certain segment or group of voters, and you want them to see that you are different, whether it is Tony Clement or Jim Flaherty or Elizabeth Witmer or Chris Stockwell or myself. We are all different.

I have talked to Jim several times since Saturday night, and we have had great conversations — very positive.

Q. You talked one time on the stage, right after the results were announced. And if I was a good lip reader, and I am not sure I am, it looked like he was saying, "I want a job." And by that, I think he meant, "I want some big responsibility from you." Will he get it?

A. I don't think he said, "I want a job." He and the other three also indicated that they would like to play a significant role. He was no different than any one of the others. I have met with all the others, as well. I met with them earlier in the week, all very upbeat, all very positive. So we go forward from here.

Q. You are in an unusual situation here for a couple of reasons. Number one, I don't know if you know this, you are the first incoming premier in eighty-two years who doesn't have a seat. That is a long time.

The other thing is your significant other is somebody who has a job in the Ontario government, and I don't think that has ever happened either. So, I am getting a lot of questions about this, and I don't know the answer, so I thought I would just come out and ask you: Can Isabel Bassett, your life partner as you call her, continue to be the chairman of TVOntario? Or is there a conflict there?

A. I don't see a conflict, but that will be Isabel's decision, quite frankly. She usually is able to speak for herself, very well. I didn't appoint Isabel Bassett to TVO; that was done by Mike Harris. He chose, and I believe he made a wise choice. I think she has made a great improvement and a change in attitude at TVO, and taken it back to its educational roots, which is what the government decided two and a half or three years ago.

Her term expires, I believe, sometime in December of this year, and she will have to decide for herself what she wants to do.

Q. Could you reappoint her?

A. Well, I think that may be more difficult. I don't think this is an issue of me or my government appointing your significant other. I think this is a case of them already having a job and before I decided to run for premiership. Surely that wouldn't be fair to expect people to step aside, but Isabel will decide that for herself.

Q. Okay. And as I suggested, it has been more than eighty years since an incoming premier didn't have a seat. How quickly do you feel a need to announce where you are going to run and do it?

A. I think I am going to do that fairly shortly.

Q. This week?

A. I haven't got the week pinned down, but I think it is fair to say that I would prefer, and I think it is better, if the premier has a seat. There have been instances of leaders and premiers and prime ministers in the past who did not, but I still believe that you should be there if you can be while the Throne Speech is being read, while the budget is being read, and while your government starts off on a new chapter in party and in political history in the province of Ontario. So obviously my preference is to be there.

Q. I want, if I may, just to ask you a very personal question at the very end here, and that is, in 1990, in September, when Bob Rae won the premiership, I asked him whether or not there was a bittersweet aspect to it all because, as you remember, he lost his in-laws in a very tragic car accident and his brother to a fatal disease. And we talked a bit about that.

And I wanted to ask you the same kind of thing. Your son is not here, and your dad is not here, and you have had an amazing last fourteen months. How bittersweet was your win on Saturday?

A. Well, you certainly thought about those things; I thought about them after they announced the results on Saturday evening. Those are two people you certainly wish would have been there to share this with you. They were both very significant figures in my life, needless to say, and Justin in particular was my best friend as well as my son, and he worked very hard for me. He was quite effective, actually, a good campaigner in the 1995 election campaign. So, it is kind of bittersweet, as you say, that those two very significant ... my father, of course, was a great influence on me throughout my life growing up, and it is too bad they weren't there. But I am sure, perhaps, in some way they were there.

Q. Agreed. Thank you for your time, and best of luck in the new job.

A. Thanks, Steve.

You'll remember Ernie Eves talked in one of our interviews about being the right man for the times. Most people I spoke to at this time thought he was. But it didn't take long for some Tories to start expressing buyers' remorse. Some of it was Eves' fault. Some of it was simply the times.

In his relatively short time as premier, Eves had to deal with a Severe Acute Respiratory Syndrome (SARS) crisis that killed forty-four people in Toronto, a massive power outage of historic proportions that left millions without electricity, Ontario's first case of mad cow disease, an outbreak of the West Nile virus, and the budget going into deficit again because of a soft economy, in large part because of a persistent hangover from 9/11. Premiers obviously can't control events that are beyond their control. But the electorate does expect them to react appropriately. Eves' reaction to the new deficit was to break his own law. He decided he needed more revenues, so he raised taxes without asking the public's permission in a referendum, as the PC government's own Taxpayer Protection Act mandated. How that squared with Mike Harris' dogma that cutting taxes always brought in more revenue was left unexplained.

But the oddest moment of the Eves government was still to come. Despite his well-known appreciation for the trappings and tradition of Parliament, Eves agreed to have finance minister Janet Ecker bring down her 2003 budget, not in the Legislature, but rather in front of an invitation-only crowd at the Magna International auto-parts plant in Aurora. It's hard to know how this idea got green-lighted. No doubt, some well-intentioned staffer thought it was clever and fresh, and would associate the government with a profitable company that was part of Ontario's economic backbone.

But Ontarians didn't take it that way. Opposition politicians were furious because they weren't permitted onto the Magna site. How were they supposed to do their job, representing their constituents, if they couldn't be there to listen to and respond to the budget? If the Tories guessed that only opposition politicians and left-wing downtown Toronto types would be appalled by the PR stunt, they egregiously miscalculated. Critics appeared out of the woodwork to castigate the move. The speaker of the Legislature, Gary Carr, who was a Conservative MPP, ruled the move was a *prima facie* case of contempt. Even Ecker let slip that "It wasn't my idea." Weren't silly ideas such as the Magna budget exactly the kind of thing Eves' experience and judgment were supposed to prevent? The Magna budget was supposed to be the kickoff to a spring re-election campaign for the Tories. Instead, it was a black eye and forced the election call to be delayed.

There was another thing that became apparent as Eves' premiership continued and Ontario marched closer to a new election date. The premier really didn't have "his own people." Every successful leader has to have his own people, in whom he can have absolute and perfect trust. Those people have to have the premier's back and interests at the top of their agenda. For Bill Davis they were men such as John Tory, Hugh Segal, and Ed Stewart. For Mike Harris they were Debbie Hutton, Leslie Noble, and Tom Long.

Ernie Eves didn't have those kinds of people. He inherited Mike Harris' people. They were people who, quite frankly, were more devoted to the Harris legacy and the perpetuation of the Common Sense Revolution than they were to Ernie Eves. Once Eves called the election for October 2, 2003, not having "his own people" became problematic for a premier seeking his own mandate. The Ernie Eves who had won the leadership of his party by promising to be more consultative and more moderate was replaced by an Ernie Eves few recognized. He had Mike Harris' team running his campaign and, as a result, he ran on a platform Mike Harris would have been proud of, even though the words sounded somewhat inauthentic coming out of Eves' mouth.

I interviewed Premier Eves one week into the 2003 election campaign, in Belleville, Ontario.

STEVE: Premier, you are running as the candidate with experience. And I would like to start by asking you to give us an example of one policy decision that you have made as premier where the results turned out better than they otherwise would have because you were in the premier's chair and not somebody else?

PREMIER EVES: Well, I don't want to compare myself to somebody else. I just know that experience, certainly, has held me in twenty-two years of public life, and serving as finance minister of the province, and deputy premier for about six years. Every little bit of experience helps; there is no doubt about that.

Q. Give me an example, though.

A. Well, in the recent blackout, for example. I mean, being able to get a grasp of the issue, knowing immediately what to do in terms of calling the emergency operations centre and putting it together and being able to make decisions that were required to be made, especially in the first forty-eight hours, by how quickly we got different generators across the province back up and running, knowing that we were going to have to have a huge contribution, not just from industry and commerce, but by the people of the province of Ontario, to reduce consumption by 4,500 megawatts. And officials at the IMO, by the way, told us that was impossible. Nobody had ever done it, it couldn't be done.

Q. But it got done.

A. But it got done. And I go back to complimenting the people for that, because they all contributed. Sure, industry and commerce contributed a little bit more than consumers; nobody would have suggested that they wouldn't. But at the end of the day, the reality is all you had to do was look at eight o'clock at night and at 8:01 that peak demand went up by about 900 to a thousand megawatts. So, you knew that people of the province were paying attention, and that was very good.

Q. Okay. But, again, getting back to my question, though, what about your twenty-two years of experience in public life made that happen where it wouldn't have happened had somebody else been in the premier's chair?

A. I think you have to, a) be confident enough to be able to take control of the situation, and to chair those meetings, which I did every morning, and to make sure that even when some officials disagreed with you and suggested to you that that couldn't be done, that you knew instinctively that that is where you wanted to go, and you had to go there, and you had to do it right away. And that takes courage, sometimes, because when you have some people telling you that it can't be done, and you know instinctively and you believe that it can be done, you have to stick to your guns.

Q. Let's get into some of the issues. When you were running for the leadership of the party, you were, I believe, against banning teachers' strikes. Now you are promising to ban teachers' strikes if elected premier. Can you tell us how your thinking has evolved on that issue over the past couple of years?

A. Sure. Actually, my thinking on this issue, Steve, has evolved since about 1982, when I was first a member in Parry Sound. We had, I believe it is still the longest-standing teachers' strike in the history of the province, in the West Parry Sound Secondary Panel, and I will never forget the impact that had. A lot of young people lost their school years in that particular year, unfortunately.

I always believe that you should, if you can, resolve these issues by negotiation. But in the last couple of years — and during the leadership debate, by the way, which was in London, Ontario, I believe, where Mr. [Jim] Flaherty brought this idea up, I was the only one of the other leadership candidates, I believe, that said, "Good concept, but can you make it work from a fiscal point of view?"

Q. But you look skeptical.

A. Obviously, you are concerned about what effect it might have on the bottom line of the books of the province. Now, in the last two years, Elizabeth Witmer and I have given teachers across this province a 3 percent a year increase, which is $340 million a year. I think anybody in society would agree that that was a reasonable increase: 3 percent a year, 3 percent a year, $680 million. And yet we saw, like this past spring — in that case, it was the school board locking out teachers and 70,000 young students in the elementary separate panel in Toronto.

But I really don't care who is at fault. I don't think labour disputes in the education system should be resolved in the classroom, whether it is the teachers' union deciding to go on strike, or whether in that case it is a school board locking out not just teachers but also students, or whether it is work to rule, which seems to be a mini-strike within the classroom, flavour-of-the-month type of thing.

There are literally thousands of hours that are lost every year, or thousands of days, by young people in this province, due to labour disputes. Surely we can now devise a piece of legislation, a system that will allow teachers to be treated fairly and equitably, which I certainly believe they should be — I think my actions have demonstrated that in the last two years — but also remembering what comes first in the education system: keeping our students in the classroom every day. And I think we can do both.

Q. Okay. Another issue: When the Supreme Court of Ontario ruled that same-sex marriages were legal, you said, "If two people want to call themselves spouses to be at a union, why would I interfere with that?" That was your comment. "That is my personal view," you said.

Now, recently, you have said, "I have always believed that marriage was a union between two heterosexual people, a male and a female." Again, could you give us a sense of how your position has evolved on that issue?

A. Well, actually, my position hasn't changed. My personal belief of what is good for me, Ernie Eves, and how he was brought up — and everybody, I think every Ontarian, has personal life experiences as they were growing up as a child, their background, their religious belief, etc. All that moulds you into who you are and what your beliefs are as you become an adult.

I still believe that for me, that is what marriage means. But I don't have the right to impose that view on other people. As a matter of fact, I would go so far as to say as premier of the province, I have a responsibility to defend the rights of every citizen of this province.

Q. So you don't think your position has changed on this point?

A. No, it has not changed. I still believe that I am there to protect the rights of those people that might have different beliefs and different points of view on this issue than I do, and I will protect those rights.

Q. The reason I have asked about these issues in particular, and I hear your answers on them, but some people have asked me which Ernie Eves is it that is running for office? Is it the guy who had this position on banning teachers' strikes or that position? Is it the guy who said one thing on gay marriage and then appeared to say another, in their view? Is it the guy who is in favour of market opening on energy, but then came in and re-regulated with a vengeance?

And they are wondering which guy is running for office? Can you see why some people would have a problem understanding where you are on various days of the week on various issues?

A. Well, I don't happen to agree with the premise taken on each one of those issues. But putting that aside, I mean, I don't expect critics, and especially opposition critics, to give me glowing endorsements. That is not their job, and that is not what they are paid to do.

The reality is, it is a sad day when people can't learn from their experience, and it is a sad day when they can't evolve their thinking on some issues. But my basic principles or premises, I think, what drives me as to who I am, have never changed. I have often described myself as a fiscally responsible individual — I believe this is what a true conservative is, small-c or large-C conservative — but one who has a social conscience. I have always concerned myself about learning-disabled children, and, of course, I had a son who was learning disabled, and that was a thing that struck me very personally, and it was very near and dear to my heart. I have always had a concern about Native people, Aboriginal people. I have always had a concern about the less fortunate in society.

But at the same time, and this may sound like it is a contradiction but I believe it is not, if you don't have a solid economic base, you can't provide those things for the people of the province of Ontario.

Q. Fair enough, but if I heard it once, I have heard it a hundred times from Tories: "Ernie Eves got elected on a moderate, centrist, kinder, gentler platform, and now he is running on Jim Flaherty's harder-edged, wedge-issue driven, social conservative right-wing platform." And they think that is ironic as hell. Do you not see that?

A. I don't think that this is an extreme right-wing platform at all; I would beg to differ. Making our economy stronger, I am quite proud of my record as finance minister in this province. I don't think there is an individual in Canadian history that cut taxes as often as I did in the six years that I was finance minister of the province of Ontario, and it was a huge challenge.

And the people of this province responded to that challenge, and they responded to having us keep more of their own money.

And this is a very basic principle of mine, because I think governments from time to time of all three political stripes in this province have forgotten whose money it is. It is the people's money. Government doesn't have any money unless they take it away from you and I, the taxpayer, and they return it to us, as they should, in social programs such as health care and education. And we wouldn't have $28 billion to spend this year on health care or $15.3 billion on education, both up, I might add, substantially from 1995, if we didn't have an economy driven by the 225 tax cuts that is generating that $16.9 billion more a year in revenue. You can't have those things if you don't have the economy.

So I don't think our job of being competitive or cutting taxes, whether it is a tax cut for seniors and allowing them to live out their later years with dignity in their own homes, a property tax cut for them, or whether it is helping young families realize the Canadian dream of home ownership by allowing them to deduct some of the mortgage interest they pay off their Ontario income for their income tax for the province of Ontario, I believe that those are very important things to allow those people in our society who have contributed so much to our society to keep a little bit more of their own money. And that in turn has generated a climate here that has created over a million net new jobs in the last eight years.

Q. Let me ask about experience again. Do you think Mike Harris was a good premier?

A. Absolutely. Mike was a … first of all, I must say that Mike and I have been friends since about the late seventies, long before —

Q. Are you still?

A. We still are. We —

Q. When is the last time you talked to him?

A. Well, I talked to Mike about two and a half weeks ago, as a matter of fact.

Q. Did you ask him for some advice on how to campaign, given that he had been through three of these and you haven't been through any yet?

A. I think Michael smiled a lot, because he had had his experience first-hand, three times. And, you know, you can be close to something like that and still not know exactly what it is like if you are not in that chair yourself.

I must say that Michael is somewhat sympathetic because he has been there. He knows what it is like, he knows how difficult it is. And being premier is not an easy job. There is a difficult decision you have to make every day of the week, or several of them, usually, on most days.

Q. Yes. This is what I am getting to, because Mike Harris, as you know, had, I think, all of four or five months as natural resources minister in his hip pocket as the government experience he had when he became premier of Ontario, which is to say not very much governing experience.

You have said the premier's office is no place for on-the-job training. But he didn't have any on-the-job training, and you haven't had any on-the-job training so to speak. You haven't had any experience. There is no experience of being premier other than to be premier, right? So why can't [Liberal leader Dalton] McGuinty learn it on the job? Everybody learns it on the job, don't they?

A. Well, everybody can learn on the job, but are you going to make mistakes along the way that are going to potentially harm the people of the province of Ontario. I just happen to believe that everybody brings certain attributes and nobody is perfect in our society, no individual is. We all have strong points. We all have weak points. But at the end of the day, no matter what you are doing in your life, whether it is what occupation you have, what profession you have, the more experience you have certainly helps. There is no doubt about that in my mind.

Having been finance minister for this province, and taking it out of some very difficult times and putting it back on the right track economically, having been deputy premier, and had the occasion — and I agree it is not the same thing as being premier, but it is still a little closer to the premier's chair than not being deputy premier — having done that for six years certainly helped me quite a bit, and the fact that nowadays, in today's world, you have all these unexpected challenges. Who would have thought, two or three years ago, that this province was going to have to stare SARS in the face, that we are going to have to look out for mad cow disease, that we are going to have to deal with the West Nile virus and they were going to have to deal with a blackout created in the state of Ohio, but that impacted not just Ontario but seven other jurisdictions?

Now, you can't tell me that experience on the job, whether it was as finance minister or whatever, doesn't help you, put you in a mould where you are in decision-making mode every day, and you are able to respond in a calm, cool, collected manner to those unexpected challenges.

Q. I know you are a student of Ontario history, so I want to ask you a question about Ontario history.

A. [laughs] Uh-oh.

Q. In 1981 Tories win a majority; in 1985 the Liberals take over; in 1990 the NDP take over; in 1995 the Tories take over again. It looks like, if you follow the history of the last twenty years, that people want to throw the bums out after, you know, every five years or so. How heavily does that weigh on you?

A. I don't even think about it. What I think about is how important the vote on October 2 [2003] is to the future of this province. As you know, I left public life for about eight or nine months, and I came back when, unexpectedly to me, for sure, Mike decided that he was not going to seek re-election, and he was going to depart public life.

I think it is very important that this province continue on the economic road it is on. And we have enjoyed economic progress in this province in the last eight years that has surpassed all the G8 nations in the world. And it is not a coincidence. You don't do that eight years in a row by coincidence. You might do it one year in a row by coincidence, or even two — not eight.

And if we go back to the tax-and-spend policies of previous governments, and start digging ourselves a hole where the government was spending a million dollars an hour more than it was taking in, we are in a lot of trouble, and our future for our young people are in a lot of trouble, and I don't want to see that happen.

Q. But if that is so apparent and obvious, why are you, by different polls, ten to fifteen points behind the other guys?

A. Well, first of all, I don't believe that we are. But what I believe or don't believe is not really going to be relevant. In a democratic society, there is only one poll that counts. That is the poll —

Q. Let me guess which one that is: is that the poll on election day?

A. That is the poll on election day.

Q. Yes. Never heard that line before.

A. On October 2. And I am confident. Listen, all three parties, all three leaders, and the candidates for all three parties, we all have policies. And all I ask is that the people of Ontario look at the policies that we have put forward in the road ahead, compare them to those of the other two parties, that they compare leadership qualities of the three leaders and objectively ask themselves, "Which person do I think I would put my faith and trust in when the next challenge comes before the province of Ontario, and which party do I think best represents my principles, values, and beliefs which is most similar to mine?"

And I am confident that if the people of Ontario do this, and I do my job, and our candidates do their job that, on October the 2nd, they will re-elect our government.

Q. Are you predicting a third majority government for the Conservatives?

A. Yes, I am, absolutely.

Of course, the polls didn't rebound for Ernie Eves. For some reason, nothing seemed to work on that 2003 campaign. One press release went out accusing opposition leader Dalton McGuinty of being "an Evil Reptilian Kitten Eater from Another Planet." It was obviously intended as a joke, but critics spun it into something suggesting it was further evidence of the Eves' government's viciousness. Eves was forced to apologize. Repudiating some of the Harris government's more aggressive policies (such as on energy deregulation) didn't attract more moderate voters, and only served to tick off the party's right-wing core, which, frankly, had come to regard Eves with suspicion.

On election night, the Tories lost thirty-five seats and Eves' nineteen-month term as premier was done. Apparently, Ontarians disagreed that Dalton McGuinty wasn't "up to the job," as the PC campaign ads had blared for two consecutive elections.

Ernie Eves made history when he won the PC Party leadership, becoming the first premier in more than eight decades to win the job without a seat in the Legislature. He would also make history in the 2003 election, becoming the first Conservative premier of Ontario in seventy-three years to lose an election.

It was not the kind of history he wanted to make.

Eves took a risk coming back to public life. On the one hand, he got to become premier. On the other hand, he gave up a great job to do it. When he tried to return to the private sector as a premier who couldn't win an election, rather than as a triumphant finance minister, the welcome mat wasn't so bright. He didn't end up with one of the big Bay Street law firms or financial institutions.

Still and all, Queen's Park was happy to welcome Eves back into its midst in May 2012 on the occasion of the hanging of his official portrait.

The public may not have seen much of it, but Eves has a well-earned reputation for having an extremely sharp tongue. When he saw Mike Harris in the audience, he couldn't help but tease his predecessor for working at the same law firm, first of Bob Rae (Goodmans), and then David Peterson (Cassels, Brock & Blackwell).

"For a guy who cursed Liberals at virtually every cabinet meeting we attended, it sure is strange to see who his law partners have been," Eves cracked.

Sitting three feet away from Premier McGuinty at the foot of the Grand Staircase in the Legislature's foyer, Eves then took a shot at all three party leaders.

"That last budget that was brought in was one of the most tepid I've ever seen," he started. "Then my party voted against it without even reading it. And the NDP didn't even show up to vote for it even though they negotiated 'improvements' to it. Things sure have changed since I left here."

Lots of nervous laughter and people staring at their shoes after that one.

Eves then took a long walk down memory lane, including sharing a story about attending former U.S. president Gerald Ford's annual golf tournament. "And I paid my own way to get there," he clarified. "We didn't fly down in any ORNGE helicopters." Another zinger, referencing the air ambulance scandal which was engulfing the McGuinty government at that moment, and suddenly the smile was completely gone from Eves' successor's face.

Eves admitted "getting hung in front of 300 people isn't necessarily my idea of a good time." But it was left to the guy who defeated him in the 2003 election to point out the obvious.

"Every day, I walk out of my office and see portraits of my predecessors," Dalton McGuinty said. "And it's a constant reminder that we'll all be hanged someday."

Dalton James Patrick McGuinty, Jr.
(2003–2013)

At the time, it seemed as if the 1990 Ontario election was a disaster in every way for the provincial Liberals. The party was crushed in an election it should have won. Fifty-nine Liberal members of the Legislature lost their seats, including the premier, David Peterson, who went down to defeat in his own London Centre riding.

But with a couple of decades of hindsight, we can now re-evaluate that initial analysis. Maybe 1990 wasn't a disaster in every way after all. In fact, although no one knew it at the time, the seeds for a Liberal renaissance were planted in that election debacle.

Yes, it may have been the worst election night ever for the Ontario Liberals (and the second-worst loss ever for a governing party), but amidst all the carnage the Liberals did manage to elect one new MPP.

His name was Dalton McGuinty.

Strangely enough, if things had gone the way they should have in life, McGuinty wouldn't even have stood for office in that 1990 election campaign. But in March of that year the family's patriarch, Dalton McGuinty Sr., was shovelling snow in his driveway when he was felled by a fatal heart attack. He was sixty-three years old. Not only did his death leave a chasm in the McGuinty family, but it also left a vacancy at Queen's Park, since the senior McGuinty was also the MPP for Ottawa South.

As the story goes, the McGuintys held a family meeting to determine what should happen next. Someone pointed out that since the name

"Dalton McGuinty" was already on a garage full of lawn signs, perhaps it made sense for Dalton Jr., a thirty-five-year-old lawyer, and the oldest male offspring of the McGuintys' ten children, to be the candidate.

And thus, the decision was made that Dalton Jr. would attempt to win the Liberal nomination and contest Ottawa South whenever the next opportunity arose. Since the Liberals were only two-and-a-half years into a massive majority government, conventional wisdom suggested the next contest would likely be a by-election, called within a few months. Instead, Premier Peterson announced in July he was sending the entire province off to the polls on September 6, 1990, so McGuinty found himself in the thick of a general election.

With Liberal fortunes falling all around him, it was no slam dunk that McGuinty would keep the seat in the red column. After all, his father was the first Liberal *ever* to win Ottawa South, which had been reliably Conservative in every election since 1926. But the younger McGuinty bucked the province-wide trend, and while he didn't win the margin of victory his father had (Dalton Sr. took 51 percent of the votes in 1987), he earned a very respectable 46 percent of the votes cast, a full twenty points ahead of his second-place NDP challenger.

Dalton McGuinty in the studio.

There's not a chance in Hades that the newly minted MPP would remember this next story. But I do. As the Queen's Park correspondent for CBC-TV at this time, I invited McGuinty out for lunch. There were fifty-five new NDP members, three new Conservatives, but just one new Grit. I wanted to know more about this MPP who managed to survive in the face of an awful night for Liberals almost everywhere.

The one thing I remember about that lunch was how openly ambitious McGuinty was. This was the first time we'd ever met. He didn't know me from Adam. And yet at some point in our conversation, McGuinty mused aloud about running for the party leadership some day.

Frankly, I was incredulous. True, given David Peterson's personal defeat, the leadership was vacant. But all the scuttlebutt centred on which former senior cabinet ministers would vie for the job of opposition leader, not some rookie greenhorn who barely knew where the bathrooms at the Legislature were. And yet, there he was putting it out there.

Before long the attention focused on the six candidates who actually did throw their hats into the ring in February 1992 to replace Peterson (Lyn McLeod, Murray Elston, Greg Sorbara, Charles Beer, Steve Mahoney, and David Ramsay). Dalton McGuinty's name wasn't on that list and I didn't give his musings another thought. At least, not for four more years.

The February 1992 Ontario Liberal leadership contest at Hamilton's Copps Coliseum was one for the ages. Thanks to five ballots and plenty of vote-counting screw-ups, the convention lasted more than twelve hours before Thunder Bay's Lyn McLeod claimed victory over Murray Elston by just nine votes out of more than 2,300 cast. As often happens in these things, the future first couple of Ontario politics were on opposite sides of this one. Dalton McGuinty approached Elston very early in the piece and told him he'd support Elston if he sought the leadership. Elston said he wasn't running, and took the interim leadership of the party on the condition that he not run. So McGuinty supported McLeod instead. Then Elston changed his mind, got into the race, and got an endorsement from none other than Dalton's wife, Terri McGuinty, who had held her powder dry, waiting for the entire field to declare.

I was anchoring CBC-TV's live coverage that night with former-Pierre Trudeau press secretary Patrick Gossage, and had never attended a political event that was as dramatic as that one. Elston led on the first two ballots, McLeod narrowly passed him on the third and managed to barely hang on for the win at about 1:00 a.m. the next day.

But four years later, after Mike Harris had crushed McLeod in the 1995 election, the Liberals were looking for a new leader yet again. This time, against all odds, the Grits managed to put on an even wackier and more thrilling event. Liberal delegates gathered toward the end of November 1996 at Maple Leaf Gardens, site of William Davis' four-ballot, forty-four-vote squeaker in 1971. The conventional wisdom going into the contest was that it was Gerard Kennedy's to lose, and if he did, who knew who could win it. The outcome was totally up in the air.

Kennedy was a charismatic newcomer to politics. He'd won a high profile for himself by making the Daily Bread Food Bank a household name in Toronto. When he opted to run for the Liberal leadership at age thirty-six, despite never having been elected to anything ever before, longtime Liberals were surprised at how much support Kennedy's candidacy attracted. In fact, when the four-time Liberal party leader and former treasurer Robert Nixon came out for Kennedy, some clever PR type got a bunch of buttons stamped saying "Kennedy and Nixon: Together at Last," playing off the enmity between the 1960 U.S. presidential election combatants.

Kennedy despised the seamier side of politics. After all, his profile came from doing good works in social justice circles. When he put an "ask" out in the past, it was to help feed Toronto's poor. He always found it tough to ask people for money just to fund his political operation. He wasn't a fan of backroom deals either. But he did bring a ton of cachet to the race, and a lot of heavy hitters lined up behind him.

To show you how much Ontario had changed in just four short years, the biggest threat to Kennedy's claiming the crown was the eleven-year MPP for Lawrence, Joe Cordiano. Four years earlier many Liberals had marginalized Greg Sorbara as "the ethnic candidate" or "the Italian candidate" during his leadership bid. This time, while there was no mistaking the thirty-nine-year-old Cordiano's ethnicity, it didn't prevent plenty of people from supporting him. His cousin, future Liberal MP Tony Ianno, ran an elbows-up, machinelike operation that delivered more support for Cordiano than, frankly, his candidacy may have merited.

Also capturing attention was thirty-seven-year-old Dwight Duncan, the MPP from Windsor-Walkerville who had only just been elected for the first time eight months earlier.

Those young guns were considered the top tier of candidates. Probably Kennedy or Cordiano would win. Maybe Duncan had an outside shot, if the "Joe Clark Scenario" presented itself. (Clark came up the middle in the 1976 federal PC leadership race as the compromise candidate, after Claude Wagner's and Brian Mulroney's forces tore each other to bits.) Oh yes, there were four others in the '96 race, but they were definitely considered faint hopers: two more rookie MPPs in John Gerretson and Annamarie Castrilli, an Ottawa businessman named Greg Kells, oh, and one more: the guy who told me six years earlier at lunch he'd like to be leader, the now forty-year-old Dalton McGuinty.

The seven candidates gave their speeches on Friday night, November 29, 1996. It was the first time the delegates had a chance to compare and contrast all the candidates in person. Seventeen years later, the only speech I can remember is McGuinty's. And not because of any particular turn of phrase he used. Unlike all the other candidates, I remember noticing how he drew the audience in by speaking more softly, eschewing the typical partisan fire-and-brimstone convention speech. Yes, there was some personal awkwardness. He certainly wasn't completely comfortable in his own skin. But I do remember saying to myself on the floor of the convention, *there's more to this guy than I had previously thought.* He was connecting with the crowd in a way the others weren't. But numbers speak louder than hunches and I was convinced McGuinty didn't have the numbers. In fact, a look at the convention floor boxes showed caucus support overflowing for Kennedy, and just four caucus members supporting McGuinty: Gilles Morin, Ben Grandmaître, Bob Chiarelli, and Tony Ruprecht. The first three were backing him because they were fellow eastern Ontarians, so it was no doubt mostly the geography speaking. Ruprecht, the only MPP not from the Ottawa area supporting McGuinty, was considered a master of handing out plaques to ethnic groups, but otherwise not the kind of guy who would inspire others to say, "Hey, Tony Ruprecht is supporting Dalton so we should too."

Still, there was that hunch …

The next morning I had an appointment with my physiotherapist, whose office, coincidentally, was right next door to Maple Leaf Gardens.

She asked me what I thought would transpire in just a few hours, just a few steps away. Not that I expect anyone to believe this next story, but it is the God's honest truth.

"I'm hearing so much negative stuff about the top tier of candidates, I'm starting to wonder whether any of them can win it," I told my physio. "In which case, look for a compromise candidate." Recalling how long it took Liberals to elect their last leader in 1992, and the impressive speech I'd heard the night before, I tossed this out: "I'm betting McGuinty on the fifth ballot."

I know. I know. You don't believe me. And as I type these words, I'm not sure I'd have bet anything more than five bucks on that prediction. But I know I said it. And so does Anita Lorelli, my physiotherapist. (Whether she'd remember I said it seventeen years later is another question.)

In any event, off to the Gardens I went. It was Saturday, November 30, 1996. And the Liberals did not disappoint. What followed was the worst run, most incredible, most thrilling convention I had and probably ever will attend. My "McGuinty on the fifth" prediction seemed dead in the water after the first ballot results were announced. As expected, Kennedy led with 770 votes, but that represented only 30 percent of the delegates' support — a long way from the finish line. Cordiano came second with 557 votes (just 21 percent support). And Duncan placed third with 464 votes or just 18 percent. But in fourth place was McGuinty with 17.6 percent, just fourteen votes behind Duncan. The other three candidates were well back of the front four.

So McGuinty's campaign was over. It was simply impossible to win from fourth place. It had never happened before. Joe Clark's winning from third place was improbable enough. But fourth? Cannot be done. Mind you, I thought, the top three candidates really are miles away from the finish line. Their support is quite fragmented and the antipathy among them and their supporters suggests it's going to be a cold day in Hell before one of them walks over to the other.

By rule, the last place candidate had to drop out before the second ballot. That meant Greg Kells' twenty-four votes were up for grabs. Strangely enough, despite having almost no support at all, John Gerretson (6 percent) and Annamarie Castrilli (5.5 percent) stayed on for the second ballot. (Actually, Castrilli first announced she was dropping out, then changed her mind and stayed on for another ballot. Her dithering contributed to a three-hour delay before the next ballot results were announced.)

The second ballot did nothing to bring the convention to a more decisive conclusion. Kennedy remained in first place, but only managed to pick up five extra delegates. His 775 votes now represented 31 percent support. Cordiano actually showed some decent momentum, relatively speaking, picking up thirteen new supporters for a total of 570 (23 percent), nudging him closer to Kennedy. Duncan picked up ten new votes for 474 total votes (19 percent).

What happened to McGuinty? Yes, he was still in fourth place but, believe it or not, it was a *worse* fourth. The man actually *lost* ten delegates, dropping to 440 votes, good for only 17.5 percent support. If winning from fourth place on the first ballot was impossible, then surely the notion of winning from a *worse* fourth place on the second ballot was completely ridiculous.

But then two very strange things happened. By rule, the last-place Castrilli had to drop out, and Gerretson, only eleven votes ahead of her, chose to withdraw at the same time. Of course the smart, conventional play for both of them would have been to support one of the top two candidates. But for reasons that seemed completely inexplicable at the time, they both moved to the guy who had just demonstrated less popularity on the second ballot than on the first. That's right: the sixth and fifth place candidates dropped out to support the guy in fourth.

Suddenly, a whole new buzz took over this convention. McGuinty had The Big Mo. The top three candidates may have had more strengths than McGuinty, but they also clearly had significant weaknesses as well. Kennedy had zero political experience and many feared he was a *prima donna*. Cordiano didn't seem to have the intellectual heft many wanted to see in a leader. Duncan was a fire-and-brimstone speaker, but was a short, pudgy guy from Windsor who'd only just been elected. Those weaknesses prevented Gerretson and Castrilli from supporting them.

Also, like the dog in the Sherlock Holmes novel that didn't bark, this moment at the convention became famous for what *didn't* happen. There were rumours all over the convention floor that Duncan and McGuinty had a deal. Whoever was behind would drop out and endorse the other. But McGuinty didn't move. Duncan, who wore a wire for CPAC's documentary coverage of the convention, was notoriously captured on camera pointing across the floor of the Gardens at McGuinty's box saying: "Come on, come to Papa." Over the years, many people have insisted there was no deal, but if there wasn't, it's hard to know what Duncan's "come to Papa" line could have meant. If there had been a deal, it was clearly off. The member for Ottawa South had the momentum. But still ... fourth place ...

The third ballot results didn't arrive until after 12:30 a.m. on December 1, meaning this was probably the first leadership convention in history that took place in two separate months. The results vindicated McGuinty's decision to stick it out, despite his inferior standing after two ballots. Kennedy held his first-place position with 803 votes, but, as feared, he had virtually no momentum or growth potential at all. He was now up to just 32 percent support. Cordiano seemed to have some wind in his sails, moving up to 601 votes (24 percent). But the compromise candidate — Dalton McGuinty — continued to show the most growth, moving into an exact tie with Cordiano for second place. That's right: out of 2,514 ballots cast, both McGuinty and Cordiano snagged an identical 601 votes.

As the last-place candidate, Duncan and his 509 votes had to drop off before the fourth ballot. It was here that Duncan made a decision that infuriated most of his supporters. Throughout much of the campaign, he and his supporters had railed against the two Toronto candidates, Kennedy and Cordiano, for a host of reasons, not the least of which was the need for the party to recognize that there were important voices outside of the capital city that also needed listening to. But at the juncture of this convention, when McGuinty, another non-Torontonian, had all the momentum and Kennedy and Cordiano had almost none, Duncan inexplicably cast his lot with Kennedy.

The CPAC cameras caught Duncan trying to explain his decision to supporters, but one by one they ignored him. They were furious. Duncan had almost no coattails. So when the fourth ballot results were announced at 2:30 a.m., yes, Kennedy was still in first place with 968 votes, but still a shade below 40 percent support. McGuinty's extraordinary momentum continued as he blew past Cordiano and clocked in at 760 votes (31 percent). Cordiano placed third with 696 votes (29 percent). Cordiano would have to drop off the ballot and decide whether he would play kingmaker or free up his delegates to support whom they pleased.

Kennedy had led on every ballot. He still had a substantial lead on McGuinty, but the antipathy between the Kennedy and Cordiano camps was just too intense. Cordiano walked over to Dalton McGuinty and endorsed him. And unlike when Duncan moved to Kennedy, he brought more than 80 percent of his delegates with him.

The fifth and final ballot results put the finishing touches on what was simply an impossible-to-believe outcome:

> Dalton McGuinty 1,205
> Gerard Kennedy 1,065

McGuinty had gone from 31 percent to 53 percent support on just one ballot. He was at 17.5 percent support on the second ballot. I saw Joe Cordiano wandering aimlessly on the floor of the Gardens after the results were announced at 4:30 a.m. I said something that I hoped would make him feel better, since he looked completely exhausted and crestfallen at the outcome.

"Imagine that, Joe," I said, "you're the kingmaker."

I'll never forget his reply: "Yeah, it's 4:30 in the morning and I'm the kingmaker. Big fucking deal."

For a guy who would go on to become one of the winningest premiers ever, McGuinty's term as opposition leader started badly. His first move was to hire his brother Brendan to be his chief advisor. Being good Irish-Catholics, it was a move reminiscent of President John F. Kennedy hiring his brother Bobby to be attorney-general. In both cases, both men wanted someone at their side they could trust implicitly. But the hiring got portrayed as the new leader offering a patronage plum to a family member. Rather than stare down the critics, McGuinty first stuck by his brother, then backed down, then fired his brother, and looked indecisive and weak in the process.

Two-and-a-half years later, Mike Harris called an election for June 3, 1999, and the PCs mounted a series of devastating ads against the rookie opposition leader. Up came a not particularly flattering picture of McGuinty, followed by a series of question marks over his picture. The narrator asked a series of probing questions, which by the end had the viewer wondering whether McGuinty was even capable of walking your dog, let alone being premier of Ontario.

And then came the kicker: "Dalton McGuinty: Not Up to the Job."

The worst part of the commercial was it was true. McGuinty *wasn't* ready and his performance frequently indicated it. During the leaders' debate, Mike Harris caught a break and had the centre podium. He spent almost the entire night with his back turned away from the Liberal leader, marginalizing him with his body language and playing to NDP leader Howard Hampton. McGuinty couldn't break through and was irrelevant most of the night.

But he got lucky in the dying days of the campaign. Much of the anti-Harris government sentiment that had parked itself with the NDP abandoned Hampton's party with just a few days to go, recognizing that only one party could stop a second Harris landslide, and that was McGuinty's. They may not have liked the Liberal leader much, but they could count. That 5 to 8 percent of the electorate that shifted from the NDP to the Liberals saved Dalton McGuinty's job. On election night, Harris was re-elected with the same 45 percent of the vote he got in 1995. But McGuinty's 40 percent was well above expectations (in fact, the second best showing for the Grits over the past half century, even if it was in a losing cause). His thirty-five seats were five more than in 1995, despite a smaller Legislature with twenty-seven fewer seats. (The Conservatives lost twenty-three seats, the NDP eight.)

McGuinty's better-than-expected showing put the "Dump Dalton" forces back on their heels. The fact was, he was starting to get better. He started to find his voice. Then Harris retired, Ernie Eves took over and turned out not to be "Dalton McGuinty's worst nightmare" as he boasted he would be during his run for the PC leadership.

By the time the 2003 election campaign was underway, there was a palpable desire for change in the Ontario air. Inexplicably, the Tories ran virtually the same ads in this campaign as they had in 1999. Except this time, the ads just didn't ring true. When the announcer came to the tag line ("Dalton McGuinty: *still* not up to the job"), too much of the public had seen for themselves that the guy was infinitely more capable this time 'round. He was now forty-eight years old, more comfortable in his own skin, a better speaker, and promising to rebuild the public services he felt were devastated under eight years of harsh conservative revolution.

Perhaps the key moment in the 2003 campaign for McGuinty happened on September 11. With all the flair of President George H.W. Bush's "read my lips, no new taxes," McGuinty promised to fulfill his campaign commitments to improve health care and education *without raising taxes.* Flanked by much of his caucus, McGuinty signed the Canadian Taxpayers Federation's taxpayer protection pledge, promising never to raise taxes. The Liberals felt they needed to sign the pledge and get that organization's gold star, to erase the stigma of the party as a bunch of tax-happy spendthrifts. It would also be the first of many promises McGuinty would simply jettison once he became premier.

Election night, October 2, could scarcely have gone better for the Ontario Liberals. The man who "wasn't up to the job" picked up thirty-seven more seats for a total of seventy-two, on the strength of more than 46 percent of the total vote. The Tory campaign showed the revolution was clearly over, losing thirty-five seats and reduced to a total of just twenty-four, one of their worst showings ever. The NDP picked up a couple of more points of support to 14.7 percent, but still lost two seats, from nine to seven. Officially, they were no longer an official party.

It was the first Liberal majority government in Ontario in sixteen years, and McGuinty would become just the second Roman Catholic premier in Ontario history (the first was John Sandfield Macdonald, the province's first ever premier in 1867).

When the McGuintyites took over, they took a play out of a familiar playbook. They claimed the cupboard was empty, the previous guys had left a $5.6-billion deficit, and one of two things was going to have to happen: either all those promises to rebuild Ontario's public services would have to wait, or taxes would have to be raised, pledges to the CTF notwithstanding.

McGuinty opted for the tax increases and left it up to his finance minister, Greg Sorbara, to figure out how to do it. The solution, unveiled in the May 18, 2004, budget, was the Ontario Health Premium. The new tax had three immediate effects: it raised billions of dollars to pay for health-care improvements, it firmly established the McGuinty government in the public's mind as promise-breakers, and it probably had a significant negative impact on Paul Martin's efforts to win a renewed majority government for the federal Liberals in the June 2004 election. All over Ontario, federal Liberal candidates got an earful from constituents about the new health premium, and no amount of explaining "that was Premier McGuinty's doing, not Prime Minister Martin's" seemed to help.

Around this time, I interviewed Premier McGuinty to get his side of things:

PAIKIN INTRODUCTION: It has been a rough couple of months for Dalton McGuinty. The Ontario premier has been accused of breaking his promises, hiking our taxes, and saddling Paul Martin with an unpopular budget during a closely fought federal election. But McGuinty says he is at peace, that he has done the right thing, and that the public will soon understand that. I sat down with the premier a few hours ago in the halls at Queen's Park.

Q. Premier, the honeymoon does seem to be over. In hindsight, is there anything you might have done differently?

A. Well, it has been a rough start, no doubt about it. I have had to make some tough calls given the financial circumstances we found ourselves in, but I think one of the things that I can do for Ontarians is ensure that this kind of a surprise is never sprung on them again in the future.

That is why, together with this challenging budget, we have introduced this new law, the Fiscal Transparency and Accountability Act, that will require that before the next election and every election after that, the state of the books, the state of our finances, have to be made public, so everybody knows, going into the election, what we are going to come out on the other side with.

Q. People are so cynical, though. Do you think they will believe it even if they hear it from a neutral third party?

A. I think that once they see it, and once we institutionalize this, it will be something that they will begin to believe in. Yes.

Q. I must tell you, most of the feedback I have received to your budget has not been focusing as much on the broken promises of no tax increases and no deficit, but on the notion that you, they say, perpetuated the fiction that everything was going to be tickety-boo, and then suddenly budget day comes and new health premium, new taxes, big deficit, and so on. Is that a fair comment?

A. I think it is fair to say that we engaged Ontarians in a most extensive pre-budget consultation exercise ever, far beyond meeting with the usual interest groups, who have a kind of an ongoing and abiding interest in budget-related matters. We went to town halls in the evenings. We had a citizen's dialogue conducted during weekends where we had people from six to eight hours. We got a very strong sense of where it is that they wanted it to go, while they did not want to pay additional taxes.

Q. They did say that.

A. They did say that. They also said they didn't want any cuts to their services. Steve, I had a pretty stark choice facing me, all right? Remember, now, three weeks before the election, the government released its official quarterly financial update, and in that update they said the books were balanced, there would be no deficit. Our best estimate was that they were hiding a $2-billion deficit, and that was approved by the chief economist for Scotiabank and some other senior economists.

We come out on the other side of the election. We bring in the provincial auditor, and he says, "No, they weren't hiding $2 billion. They were hiding close to $6 billion." So, I got a couple of choices. Choice number one was to honour my commitments. What did that mean? Balance the budget this year and hold the line on taxes. I got a $6-billion deficit. I turned to my minister of education, [Gerard] Kennedy. I said, "What can you do for me? How can you get me $1 billion?" He said, "Well, we will fire 16,500 teachers."

I went to [George] Smitherman over at health. "What do you do?" He said, "Well, if you kick 30,000 seniors out of their beds in the nursing homes, that will save you $1 billion."

Q. These were obviously not options.

A. You know, I could shut down ten hospitals; you know, that is another billion dollars. That was option number one.

Option number two was to take the time to balance the budget over the course of our mandate, and call upon the people of Ontario and ask for their help.

Q. But should you have sign-posted that decision-making process better? You knew, before budget day, that you were going to have to bring in these tax increases. Should you not have indicated that earlier?

A. Well, you know, in hindsight, maybe we could have done a better job at dropping broader hints about where it is we were going to go, and about the nature of the challenge before us. And ... I have done some canvassing door to door in this federal election, and there is no doubt about it, people are upset with the fact that I changed my mind.

During the course of the campaign, I looked people directly in the eye through their television sets. They were watching me in the living room, or maybe they had a little TV on the kitchen counter, and I told them, "I am going to fix your schools, I am going to improve your health care, and I won't raise your taxes." Then I get this tough choice. People are thinking, "Well, McGuinty is not going to raise my taxes," but the alternative is to cut their services dramatically.

Steve, this was the toughest decision I have ever made in my life, let alone my fourteen years in politics — the toughest decision I made in my life. You don't grow up with nine brothers and sisters and not get some kind of an understanding of how hard families work just to make ends meet, and I have just imposed, unilaterally, an additional burden on Ontario families. I certainly didn't want to do that, but I felt that given the circumstances, this was the best option available to us.

Q. This sounds strange to say it this way, but there is a sense of you made them believe, in the fall election campaign, and now they feel, in a sense, like jilted lovers. Is it accurate to say that? I have had so many people come up and say that to me, "I actually believed in this guy, and now I feel like he has broken my heart."

A. Yes, I have encountered some disappointment at the doors. There is no doubt about it. But when I do explain to people what our circumstances were, the choices that we faced, what it is that we are getting as a result of this budget, and I think most importantly my motivation, this budget isn't about boosting my short-term popularity.

Q. Because goodness knows it didn't do that, right?

A. It sure as heck did not do that. I could have put up my feet for four years and said, "Folks, there is nothing left in the till. All I can do is proceed with more dramatic cuts to public services." That way, I honour my commitment, I get to say I kept my promises, and you people suffer the consequences as a result. I decided that I should do what is in the interests of Ontarians, and I am hopeful, very hopeful that at the time of the next election, October 4, 2007, people will look back and say, "McGuinty made a tough call. I am not particularly enamoured with the idea of paying more by way of taxes. But you know what? We have got shorter waiting periods, we have got better home care for my mom. We have got smaller classes in the early years. We have got higher student achievement."

Q. You think all of this will be measurable in three and a half years?

A. Yes.

Q. That is not very much time to turn around the *Titanic*, if you know what I mean.

A. It is ambitious, but it is essential.

Q. Okay. Don't misunderstand this next question; I am delighted that you have decided to sit down and talk to us. However, with less than a week to go in the federal campaign, and the verdict on your budget is pretty much in, do you think giving interviews right now is the wisest way to help Paul Martin win the federal election?

A. My responsibility, at the end of the day, is to advance the cause, the interests of the people of Ontario. That is what this budget is all about. As I said a few moments ago, it is not about boosting my popularity. And for that matter, it is not about boosting Paul Martin's popularity —

Q. But you would prefer Martin wins, presumably?

A. There is no doubt about that whatsoever. I think he has got the more responsible plan. And my strongest caution that I am offering to the people of Ontario is, just listen. We have got another guy who is telling us that he can cut our taxes dramatically, that he can balance the budget, and he can improve the quality of our public services. He is telling us we can have our cake and eat it too. The last guy that said that here in the province of Ontario has left me in the position of being the bearer of bad tidings; I have got to clean up a $6-billion deficit. I have placed an additional burden upon the people of Ontario when it comes to helping us so that they all work together to improve the quality of our health care. Think about that for a moment, when somebody else says you can have it all.

Q. Do you think the Paul Martin forces have run a coherent national campaign?

A. I think they are working as hard as they can.

Q. That's not what I asked.

A. Yes, I know, I hear you. You get to ask the questions, and I get to give the answers. But I can tell you that I have spent some time knocking on doors, and I think people are … my sense is that people are becoming a bit more thoughtful as the campaign has been wearing on. I think there was no doubt about it, there was some anger, and some of that connected with my budget, and me having broken a promise — no doubt about that, I take full responsibility for that. My job is to work us out of this difficult situation.

Q. Your brother, as everybody knows, is a candidate in the same riding that you are in. Could you let us in on a bit of the private conversations that no doubt took place between you and him just days after your provincial budget?

A. Right. I can tell you that I am very, very proud that my brother has decided to participate in public service. He has got four kids. He had a great job. He has got a mortgage. He gave up that job and doesn't want to do anything more than serve the people of his riding. And when my budget came out, he phoned me when it first came out and said, "Listen, I am proud of you."

Q. He said that?

A. Yes, it took a lot of courage, and "Good luck." So, you know, from time to time, I am sure we are going to have some disagreements when it comes to policy. But, for the time being, we are very supportive of one another.

Paul Martin's Liberals were reduced to a minority government the following month, in no small part because of the loss of twenty-five Ontario seats. But David McGuinty did keep Ottawa South in the Liberal column.

McGuinty at an announcement at St. Michael's Hospital in November 2012.

In the years that followed, McGuinty focused laser-like on improving health care and education, suspecting the electorate would forgive his *volt face* on taxation if he could demonstrate that their services had improved. So, where the Harris government was constantly at war with teacher unions, McGuinty invited them into the tent, gave them darned near everything they wanted, and essentially bought peace with them. The government also successfully concluded negotiations with the doctors and the public service employees' union. Gone were the days of the perpetual revolution. Now, Ontario had a kinder, gentler premier.

But the image of promise-breaker was a hard one for McGuinty to kill. He ran into it again when he had to acknowledge that he couldn't close all the coal-fired generating stations by the end of 2007, as promised, but rather would need a couple of more years. (In fact, he'd miss that deadline too.)

In the summer of 2007, Ontarians were preparing to render their verdict on McGuinty's first mandate. The PCs had replaced Ernie Eves with John Tory, Premier William Davis' former principal secretary, and an even more moderate leader than either Harris or Eves. Tory had captured considerable public respect when he ran for mayor of Toronto, moving from 3 percent support at the beginning of the 2003 mayor's race to 38 percent on election night. He came second to David Miller, but raised his profile immeasurably. He was now pledging to lead Conservatives to an urban renaissance. At the moment the party was nothing but a rural rump.

In June 2007 McGuinty's Liberals and Tory's Tories were tied at 35 percent apiece in the polls. But then, McGuinty once again demonstrated the luck of the Irish. During his run for the PC Party leadership in September 2004, Tory was frequently confronted by party members who wanted him to do something on the inequality in Ontario's education system. Part of the grand bargain of Confederation was that Ontario had to promise to fund a parallel school system for the province's Catholic minority. In exchange, Quebecers would do the same for their Protestant minority.

But Quebec passed a constitutional amendment in 1999 changing its public funding of education from religion to language. So here were Ontario taxpayers, at the dawn of the twenty-first century, still funding separate schools for Catholics but not for any other religious minorities. The Harris government saw an unfairness in that and went some distance to levelling the playing field by offering an "equity in education tax credit" to parents who wanted to send their children to private schools of other religions. But McGuinty scrapped the tax credit when the Liberals took over in 2003, saying it diverted much-needed funds from the public school system.

Tory pledged to do something about the unfairness of a province where Catholics had their choice of two publicly funded school systems — a secular and a religious one — but adherents of other religions didn't. The solution he offered was a gift from heaven for the Ontario Liberals.

Tory said the way to start to end the unfairness was to offer some public funding to *all* religious schools: Jewish ones, evangelical Christian ones, Seventh Day Adventist ones, Muslim ones — whoever wanted to adhere to the province's curriculum. He demonstrated that the costs would be relatively insignificant, but it would go some distance to making things fairer. The policy also had what backroom PC types thought was a neat additive. Tory was leaving behind his safe Dufferin-Peel-Wellington-Grey seat (the same one Ernie Eves held) to contest Don Valley West against Kathleen Wynne, a popular Liberal cabinet minister. But Don Valley West had the highest concentration of Muslims of any riding in Ontario. Surely, Tory's people thought, that policy would not only make Ontario fairer, but also help their guy win that seat.

It was a huge miscalculation. The 97 percent of Ontarians who weren't Muslim were frantic at the notion that "madrassas" would get public funding, thereby using tax dollars to make those students even more fiercely anti-Western than they already were. There seems little question much of the antipathy to Tory's policy was rooted in Islamophobia. Particularly problematic for him was that the Conservative heartland universally opposed the plan. Frankly, most people seemed to prefer defunding the Catholic system, rather than giving money to other religions.

For a guy who claimed to be all about bringing Ontarians together, McGuinty then did a very un-McGuinty-like thing: he poured gasoline all over the burning Tory campaign. He waxed eloquent in his campaign speeches about creating an Ontario public school system where the "Christian kids sit beside the Jewish kids, who sit beside the Buddhist kids, who sit beside the Muslim kids." Of course, absent on McGuinty's list were the Catholic kids who were overwhelmingly hived off into a whole system of their own. In fact, the premier himself is a product of the separate school system, and his wife taught in it.

During the leaders' debate during that 2007 campaign, I kept waiting for John Tory to put that bit of hypocrisy to McGuinty (as I did, during a pre-2007 election interview), but he never did. He later told me he and his team had discussed it, but decided against it, fearing it would further inflame religious sensibilities.

The public funding for religious schools policy completely consumed this campaign. Wherever Tory went, he was asked about it. It made it impossible for him to hold McGuinty to account on the premier's own broken promises. The result was a status-quo election: McGuinty was re-elected with seventy-one seats (down just one), while Tory's first effort as leader saw the PCs pick up two seats, even though they lost 3 percent of the total vote. Sadly for Tory, he went down to personal defeat in Don Valley West, tried to make a comeback in a by-election seventeen months later, but lost that too.

For the premier, it was an historic victory. He became the first Liberal leader since Mitchell Hepburn seventy years earlier to win back-to-back majority governments. And as he told his caucus in their first meeting after a successful re-election campaign, "We've proven you can raise taxes and still get re-elected!"

In fact, that was a trick McGuinty would manage to pull off not once, but twice. If creating the health premium was the taxation highlight of his first time, he surpassed even that piece of *chutzpah* in his second term.

There seems to be two truisms about consumption tax policy reform no matter where you go in the world. First, once implemented no succeeding government would repeal it, despite promises to do so, because it made sense and worked. But second, no government that had tried to bring in meaningful consumption tax reform ever won the ensuing election. Just think about the Goods and Services Tax in Canada. Brian Mulroney's government brought it in. Jean Chrétien's government pledged to scrap it if elected. They didn't. But the federal Tories had to spend so much political capital to get the GST through, it was one of the many reasons they were a spent force after. They got blown out next time they went to the polls. And that pattern repeats itself all over the world.

So it seemed another political suicide mission when Dalton McGuinty decided he wanted to harmonize the Ontario retail sales tax (which applied to a fairly narrow base of products) along with the federal GST (which was on almost all goods and services). Despite some generous rebates and income tax cuts for the Ontario public, in the long run the Harmonized Sales Tax (HST) should prove to be a revenue bonanza for the province (if the economy ever gets truly back on track), and many people were incredulous that once again, after pledging in 2007 not to raise taxes, McGuinty would do it again. But he did.

He handed the file to one of the steadiest hands in his cabinet, Revenue Minister John Wilkinson, who barnstormed the province and successfully — in his inimitable cheery, competent, and plain-spoken way — sold the HST to Ontarians. However, the Liberals got lucky on this one too. The federal Conservative government of Stephen Harper was in favour of harmonizing the sales taxes and even gave the Liberal government more than $4 billion to ease the transition. So the new Ontario opposition leader, Tim Hudak, found himself railing against a policy that his mentor, the federal finance minister Jim Flaherty, was championing. And it got even stickier. Flaherty's wife, MPP Christine Elliott, was Hudak's deputy leader. The pro-business Ontario Conservatives' opposition to tax harmonization just didn't feel authentic. The McGuinty government put it through and there was nary a protest.

Just a couple of months before the HST was set to go into effect in July 2010, we had another visit from the member for Ottawa South.

STEVE PAIKIN: And joining us now, the twenty-fourth premier of the province of Ontario, Dalton McGuinty. It is good to have you back in that chair.

PREMIER MCGUINTY: Thanks for having me, Steve.

Q. You were abroad very recently. You went to the Middle East, you went to the West Bank, Israel, Lebanon. And why don't I ask you what is the most significant thing you learned in perhaps the most troubled part of the world, having left there?

A. It is complicated. Very little geography and a lot of history. And we deliberately chose to visit Israel. We were drawn there because of the masterful way they have created an innovation-based economy. On a per capita basis, Steve, I don't think anybody has got more patents and copyrights and start-ups and Nobel Prize winners and the like.

Q. And violinists and poets, too, apparently.

A. Yes, they are. Necessity being the mother of invention, they are really successful in a number of areas. But we also visited the West Bank to get an understanding of some of the challenges associated with people living there. And we also, beyond that, went to Lebanon, as well, to get a better sense. So, it is complicated.

Q. What is the biggest challenge of living in the West Bank today?

A. I think it is economic. I think most families, Steve, the more I travel, I always get briefed on how different everybody else is. You can't talk about this, you have got to be careful about this, using your sense of humour there and all that stuff. I ignore that completely.

Here is what I have discovered: people are the same everywhere. If you knock on a hundred doors on the West Bank, if you knock on a hundred doors inside Israel and you ask those people with the greatest stake in the future, parents, what their greatest priorities are, they will all tell you the same thing: "We want good schools for our kids. We want good health care for everybody in the family. We want a strong economy that supports good jobs. We want a safe and clean environment, and we want to live in a world of peace."

And if you begin with that understanding, I think there is a lot that we can bring to the table as Ontarians and Canadians in trying to build on that common ground.

Q. Provincial politicians don't normally talk international affairs, but it is a small world now, and you have always talked about trying to make Ontario more open to the world. Are their problems over there, things that we need to know about over here?

A. Yes, they are. We no longer enjoy the luxury of saying we are a sub-national government, and we will let all international issues and complexities of the global economy, we will let those remain the province, so to speak, of the federal government.

Q. So, when you are over there, do you talk terrorism to Palestinian leaders, and do you talk respect for human rights to Israeli leaders?

A. No, I didn't get into that with them. This was a first visit. I have been to China and India a number of times, and so that gives you greater moral authority to weigh in on different issues. But this is my first time over and, as a guest, so to speak, I think my responsibility is to build that strong, initial relationship, and that gives you authority over time to broach more sensitive subjects.

Q. Now that you have been there, would you say that this is the most impossible international relations crisis anywhere in the world?

A. It is. You know, the interesting thing, Steve, that I learned when I was over in Israel, and this is kind of noteworthy, is what I heard from businesses who have now become proponents of peace, because —

Q. It's good for business.

A. — instability and conflict is something that business recoils from. They want stability and predictability.

Q. Well, on the issue of business, let's move to the economy here. And I don't know if you know this, but the new harmonized sales tax is coming in July 1 [2010].

A. I heard something about it.

Q. You have heard something about it? Here is my first helpful question on that. I am sitting here today, I thought, what am I going to ask him that he hasn't been asked a thousand times before on the HST. So let me try this: when Tim Hudak beats you in the next election, do you think he will reverse the HST?

A. No, he won't. And the opposition have done their job, and I think a fairly effective job. I spent a number of years there, and it is an important responsibility, pointing out some of the challenges associated with the HST. But they won't withdraw it. They won't rescind it. No place has ever done that. The 140 countries and the four other provinces — four other provinces of all political stripes, by the way — because it is good, sound, economic policy. And it is part of our comprehensive plan to make of Ontario one of the most competitive places in the world so that we can compete for and win new investment and new jobs.

Q. Work with me here on the windup, because this has got a couple of premises going into it: Before the 2003 election, which you won, that was your first win, you promised not to raise taxes, and then, of course, you did. You brought in that new Ontario health tax, and you explained why you thought you had to do that.

Before your second election victory, 2007, when you were asked, "Will you raise taxes?" you said, "You know I won't." And eventually, we now know that the harmonized sales tax will take more out of people's pockets. I know there are rebates coming up initially, but eventually it will take more out of people's pockets. Are you concerned you have a credibility problem with voters on the issue of taxes?

A. We worked really hard to ensure that the HST is minimally intrusive on family budgets. There is this transition payment. There are a number of new sales and property and energy tax credits. There is a permanent personal income tax cut. But here is the story on this: there are kind of two questions that loom large every single day in my line of work. One is a very simple one; it is always put to voters by pollsters, and the question is simple: what do you people want?

Here is the more important question. It is the one that is put by voters to me every single day — sometimes you have got to listen very carefully for it, but that question is what do we need to do to grow stronger? We lost 250,000 jobs in this recession. What do we need to do to ensure that there are more jobs for me today and my kids tomorrow? What do we need to do to make sure we have the capacity to support good schools and good health care and environmental protections, and supports for our vulnerable?

We need to grow stronger, Steve. Some people maintain if there is nothing that we need do, that the old world is somehow going to magically reappear. Our world has changed. The old world is not coming back.

I wish I could say to Ontarians, there are no efforts that we have got to make. Nothing of any kind. We will just sit here and it will all come back. And I am very reluctant to ask of Ontarians, but especially to ask of families ... I understand how hard they work, and how they count their pennies, and how you want to save up a bit of money so you can have a vacation with the kids. You want to make sure you have got enough money for tuition. You want to make sure that you have enough money to retire on.

But I have never met a mom or dad or a grandmother or grandfather who is not prepared to do what we need to do to make sure that there are jobs for us today and jobs for our kids tomorrow.

Q. But the question is about your credibility with those very people you have just described. Do you think you still have it?

A. I think I do. And you know what? The great thing about the line of work I am in, people get to make that judgment call.

Q. Only once every four years, though.

A. They get to make that judgment call, but it is a pretty important judgment. And I will work as hard as I can, I will do the best that I can, always trying to find ways to ensure that we grow stronger as a province. Some of those ways aren't easy. I understand that.

Q. Here is my next helpful question, which is yes, there are new taxes, and there was a billion dollars wasted on eHealth, and there are public sector employees who admittedly, in the last budget, got their wages frozen, but before that saw increases in both the number of jobs and in their salaries the people in the private sector sure did not experience.

And I wonder whether you are concerned that there is a perception out there that your government is not careful enough with the public's money.

A. Well, you know, we got elected, originally in 2003, on a mandate which I think was pretty clear. People said you need to restore vitality to and confidence in our public services. So, we have hired many more teachers, and we have hired many more nurses, water inspectors, and meat inspectors, Crown attorneys and judges and the like. But those are all essential contributors to the quality of our public services, and by extension the quality of our life. So, yes, we have invested in more public services, but what I am asking of our public servants now is, I am saying that I need your help. We have been confronted by this terrible global economic recession, and we need to find a way to deal with some of our expenses. So, I am asking you to freeze your pay for two years.

We will lead by example. We in government will take a three-year pay freeze, but for everybody else who is within the employ of the public sector and the broader public sector, I am asking them to take a two-year pay freeze.

Q. Okay. But, again, on the question, are you concerned there is a perception out there that you are not careful enough with the public's money?

A. People are always concerned about their governments and their accountability, and whether they are using the money wisely. On the matter of eHealth, for example, I take responsibility for insufficient oversight. Governments have become so big and so complicated, we have so many agencies working for us. This was an agency that is working beyond government, and we have to bring the same kind of scrupulous oversight to agencies outside of government as we have brought to bear inside government.

Having said that, Steve, it is unfair to say that it has cost us a billion dollars. In fact, there has been a significant investment in infrastructure, the highway, so to speak, when it comes to this electronic records system. The complaint was, and it is a legitimate one, we haven't done enough to put money on to the vehicles back and forth that carry the information. And some people who were working with the system got carried away, and they lost sight of who they are working for, ultimately. And it is not me. It is not the cabinet. It is not my caucus. It is Ontario families.

Q. Well, I want to take you up north, because we take this program on the road a few times a year, and we were in Timmins earlier this year. One of the things that we heard over and over again in Timmins was, "This guy has got billions of dollars to buy up car companies in order to save good-paying auto manufacturing jobs. He has got hundreds of millions of dollars to lure videogame producers here, or to keep film and television production in the big cities in the south here. Where is the investment in the north that could help, for example, keep the Kidd Creek smelter open, the mining smelter up in Timmins? Where is the money to help subsidize power?"

I know you did some of that in your last budget, but they would say not very much. They are wondering, "When do we get that kind of a deal?" What's the answer?

A. I think that the last budget clearly demonstrated our commitment to the north. There was a number of things that we did there, whether it was an energy tax credit for Northern Ontario families, an electricity rebate program for our businesses up there. I sat down and met with the folks that came to that, the mining operation and smelting operation in Timmins, and we asked ourselves what it is that we might do, if anything, to turn that around. But there are some global forces here. Sometimes we just aren't strong enough to contain them.

Q. We are a little bit more than a year away from the next Ontario election, and let me put this thesis to you: governments often get defeated, not over big dumb things, but little dumb things. For example, 1990, David Peterson's early election call. He didn't have to go that early. He did. He lost. Paul Martin called a public inquiry into the Quebec sponsorship scandal. It got out of control. They didn't have to do it. We know he lost the next election after that.

What is there out there that may be a minor irritant, but could be something bigger that could be of concern in a year's time?

A. You know, it is very tough for me to predict those kinds of things. And if I was to awake every morning and go to bed every night thinking about those kinds of things, I would be overcome by paralysis, because every day is fraught with risk and uncertainty. So, notwithstanding the fact that it is a really complicated and a much more transparent world today for political leadership because of you guys and the job that you do, it is kind of a simple line of work. You do the best that you can. You try to do the right thing. If you screw up, and I will screw up from time to time, I think it is important to own up to that, and put the kind of measures in place that correct that and ensure it doesn't happen again. That is really what it is all about, and you try as hard as you can to stay connected to families with their hopes, their aspirations, and their dreams for themselves and their kids, and as they get later on in life, too.

Q. I want to follow up on that, because I think that is very interesting. You have been premier for ... since 2003 now?

A. Yes.

Q. Seven years almost. And you have been in politics for ...

A. Twenty.

Q. ... twenty.

A. Right.

Q. Leader of your party for fourteen?

A. Yes.

Q. I mean, that is a long time to be, you will forgive me, living in a bubble, which it is a bit of a bubble, you will admit. You don't have a normal life. You are premier of Ontario. You've got people, you have got OPP guys who follow you around. How do you stay in touch with Mr. and Mrs. Everyday Ontario, leading this abnormal life?

A. Well, you have got to work against that, because it can be a little bit unusual. And every once in a while, you get through something completely normal. I had a son who graduated and was called to the bar a couple of days ago.

Q. Congratulations.

A. Thank you very much. And I sat beside a lovely couple in front of us, who didn't know who I was, and we had a lovely chat, just as parents, and talked about what the future might hold for our kids. So having a family keeps you grounded. Having nine brothers and sisters and staying in touch with my mom, and doing whatever I can to not lose my sense of who I am and where I come from.

At some point, Steve, I am not going to have this job anymore. And it is a wonderful honour to serve, but I am going to go back to who I was, and I don't want that to be some kind of quantum leap. So, I work hard to try and just be the same guy that I always was.

Q. How do you know they didn't know who you were?

A. All because we had a nice chat.

Q. Who doesn't know who you are?

A. Some lucky people who don't pay a lot of attention to politics.

Q. Tim Hudak, as you know, the Conservative leader, is kind of test driving this notion right now that Dalton McGuinty wants to tell you what you can do in your car, where you can smoke, what kind of dog you can buy, where you are allowed to text message people, all that kind of stuff. One columnist, I guess, felt the need to remind you that you are the premier, not our dad. Do you have your nose in too much of our business?

A. I certainly hope not. I try not to do that. I like to think of myself as kind of a small-l Liberal in that sense, and I believe that my job and the job of government is to create the conditions that allow people to flourish in so many different ways. So, we have done a few things that could be categorized as being restrictive. Using the cellphone when you are driving, I think that is just sensible. I think most people understand, if they give it some thought, that is probably not a safe thing to do. We have been restrictive when it comes to smoking, but I think most parents would tell you they don't want their kids to take up smoking and the like.

So we have done a few things, but I think, as well, that I hope that people will come to understand, our much bigger focus has been on the quality of our schools and the quality of educational opportunities for young people, and health care, environmental protections, and those kinds of things.

Q. You are soon going to be asking us not to re-elect you for the first time, but for the second time, for your third mandate. How do we know there is still enough gas left in the tank?

A. Well, it is funny you mention that. You know, my kids would say "seven years may not seem like a long time to you, Dad, but that is twenty-one iPod generations." It is a long time. The world has changed a lot. But I think the test that I kind of hold myself up against is, do I still have a sense of idealism?

The environment in which I work can be corrosive. There can be a tremendous amount of cynicism. A lot of people will tell you that they have seen it all, know it all, have done it all, and that there is nothing more that we can do. But I still have a strong sense of idealism, a strong sense of purpose and determination and drive and energy.

I am very ambitious for Ontarians. We enjoy a tremendous quality of life, and we are really lucky, you and I, Steve, to be raising our kids here. But there is still so much more that we can and should do together.

Q. Who is going to be — oh, I shouldn't say this — who is going to be ballsy enough to tell the premier of Ontario, "You know what? You have lost that sparkle. You have lost that sense of wonder"?

A. Hopefully, there will be people who will be strong enough when the time comes.

Q. *Strong.* That was a better word. I should have said *strong.*

A. Yes. But, you know, my wife is a really good judge of it. I wouldn't do this job unless I was enjoying it, and I wouldn't enjoy this work unless I felt that I could continue to make a difference. It is not a place to just hang your hat and put your feet up and bide your time, especially now in a just-in-time world with so many changes taking place in a global economy. With the advent of globalization, there has never been a more exciting time to be a premier in Canada. There have never been more opportunities to find ways to go stronger.

Q. Mr. McGuinty, we appreciate your being here tonight. Thanks so much.

A. Thanks for having me.

There was one thing that constantly amazed me about Dalton McGuinty, and I wasn't alone in this observation. The guy seemed not to age at all. I remember what five years in the premier's chair did to David Peterson and Bob Rae. They visibly aged. Their hair turned white. They looked quite a bit beaten up by the job. So did Mike Harris. But not McGuinty. Even eight years into the job, at age fifty-six, he still barely had any flecks of gray in his hair and hadn't put any weight on at all. Politics is a great business if you want to get prematurely fat and old. Getting out of politics is a great way to look healthier and younger. His friends tell me McGuinty leads a remarkably disciplined life, and only rarely indulges in the kind of junk food that can give you a spare tire.

Good health notwithstanding, the premier found himself in tough during the summer before the 2011 election campaign. He was fifteen points behind PC Party leader Tim Hudak and it looked very much as if his lucky streak was coming to an end. But there is a reason why no rookie leader has won an election since 1971. It's extremely hard to do. The experience of having a province-wide campaign under your belt is an enormous advantage.

Having said that, one night that summer I found myself out for dinner with a group of small-c conservatives, all of whom were adamant that McGuinty was toast.

"No premier in history has come back from this far behind this close to an election," one of them told me. "His right track/wrong track numbers are also horrible. We've got this one in the bag."

This was from people who have run campaigns. They know politics inside and out. Nevertheless, I meekly suggested the following: "You guys all know more about this than I do," I started. "But I'm not convinced this guy is done. Furthermore, every single time in Ontario history a two-time winner went to the polls seeking a third mandate, he got it. So you don't mind if I just watch this play itself out, do you?"

I am the first guy to admit I am probably overly influenced by historical trends. But trends are trends for a reason. And while I was happy to be the butt of jokes that night for refusing to crown Tim Hudak three months before the election even started, I began to feel better about my open-mindedness when I went out on the hustings. When I asked Conservative MPPs how they were feeling during the campaign, the reply I got back more often than not was "nervous."

Why would any of these folks be nervous? Wasn't their victory a sure thing?

The 2011 Ontario election campaign began two days after Labour Day, when Dalton McGuinty visited Lieutenant-Governor David Onley's office, asking the Legislature to be dissolved and the writs to be drawn up to elect a fortieth Parliament. The previous day, McGuinty visited our studios for a sit-down interview on *The Agenda*:

STEVE: And joining us now here in studio, the twenty-fourth premier of the province of Ontario, and the MPP for Ottawa South, here is Dalton McGuinty. Premier, welcome.

PREMIER MCGUINTY: Steve, it is always good to be back.

Q. No, it is a pleasure to have you in, because I know you tend to make this one of your very early stops in the last couple of election campaigns, and we are grateful for that.

So, let's start with this, something you know well: No Ontario premier in fifty-two years has won three consecutive majority governments.

So, why should Ontarians give you a third term as premier?

A. Well, it is an interesting historical fact, but I think at the end of the day it is what motivates you deep down inside. And as far as I am concerned, Steve, we have done a lot of great things, made a lot of progress, but the job is half done. I want to deliver now fully on full-day kindergarten. I want to exploit every possible opportunity when it comes to building a strong, clean energy sector in Ontario. I want to make sure that every single young person in Ontario, regardless of their family background or income, has got access to the best possible post-secondary education. I want to do more for seniors. I want to do more to ensure that they can stay in their homes and grow older safely, and getting the best possible health care.

Q. If the job is only half done, so you are going to run for two more terms then, is that right? If I got my math right? I am only being half-facetious here. Most leaders ... I must confess, I am very fascinated by this decision to go again, because most leaders, if they are lucky enough to get back-to-back majority governments, they say, "Thank you, and now I will go on and do something else." At what point did you consider, "That is not for me. I am going again."

A. Probably, you know, eighteen months to two years ago, and I had kind of a heart-to-heart conversation with my wife, Terri. And I am cursed or blessed, depending on how you look at it, with a strong sense of respon-sibility, and these are uncertain economic times. If you take a look at the global economy — it is challenging times for our families — that news about that uncertainty pours into our homes, tweet by tweet. We used to say daily, we used to say hourly; now, it is instantaneously. And there is a lot of great things that we have done, and lots more that we can, and I feel that we should do.

I have asked Ontarians to do some difficult things. I take responsibility for that. But I also take responsibility for moving this province forward, helping families, helping us ensure that we have got that certainty in our lives that has been lacking, certainty that comes from knowing that schools are getting better, health care is getting better, the economy is getting stronger. We are exploiting new opportunities in the global economy.

Q. It is a gutsy move, I can say, because it has been half a century since anybody did what you are trying to do. You mentioned you talked to your wife. Did you talk to anybody else, in terms of getting advice on whether to do this?

A. Well, there is kind of the personal dimension to it, but then there are young moms who talk to me and say, "You are not going to walk away from full-day kindergarten, right?" You brought that —

Q. No, but your successor could bring that in.

A. Yes, no, no … yes. "But you brought that forward, you are not going to walk away from that, right?" And I am not going to let them down. There are the tens of thousands of people who have now got a job in the green-energy sector, and I have met with some of those folks in the manufacturing centres, and they say to me, "You are not going to walk away from this, right? We can't count on the other guys to keep driving this." And I said, "Don't worry, I won't let you down."

So, there is a sense of when you apply yourself, when you engage, when you invest yourself in better public services and in exciting new economic opportunities, Steve, it is not an easy thing to walk away. There are, obviously, other things that might attract you, but I feel a strong sense of responsibility, and these aren't the best of times, right? This isn't late 1980s. It is a time of uncertainty. I feel a sense of responsibility to help us continue to move forward.

Q. You are going to forgive me trying to get inside your head here a little bit because I am interested in this, and that is, I presume at some point you had to look down at your cabinet or your backbench, and you had to make the calculation that "You know what? Either I can lead this team to a third consecutive majority, or one of them can do it. And as I look at them, I think I am actually better to do it than they are." Did you make that calculation?

A. No, that is not the way I saw it. I've got lots of bench strength. I think I have been blessed more so than probably any other Ontario premier in terms of capable, committed, hard-working, successful public servants. At the end of the day you've got to ask yourself, do you want this, with all its wonderful privileges and opportunities that it creates for you, and all of the challenges, and with the public accountability that characterizes a leadership at the beginning of the twenty-first century? And do I still want to do it? Yes, I do want. Do I think I can still do more for the people of Ontario? Absolutely.

Q. Tony Blair, did you read his autobiography, by any chance?

A. I sure did. Yes.

Q. I thought of you, actually, when I read this line in it. He said, "You've got to get out of public life before people stop listening to you." And for him, I mean, he did get three terms. Can you tell whether people are still listening to you?

A. Yes, you can. You can and this is not just a function of the science, the data collection, and the polling. I speak to people by the thousands, and people can become fairly good judges of speakers, and speakers can become fairly good judges of audiences, through body language, their sense of engagement, their receptivity, their desire to listen, to learn a bit and, of course, to follow. And I still have a strong sense that while I have asked Ontarians to do some tough things, there is, if not a warm embrace, an acceptance that this guy's heart is in the right place, he is doing these things for the right reasons. And the fact of the matter is at the end of the day there is measurable progress, whether you are talking test scores, graduation rates, wait times, access to doctors, economic growth — measurable, solid improvement.

Q. You smiled when you said it, because you know; you have looked at the polls, too. You know you are the second-most unpopular premier in the country, and even in your ads, your most recent ad, you come out and you say, "Look, I know I am not Mr. Popularity." Do you —

A. But, you know, you can't just run on the basis of how you think you are going to be perceived in any immediate sense.

Q. Well, when you are running for re-election, it is good to be popular.

A. It's good, it doesn't hurt. But I have a tremendous confidence in Ontarians and their desire to bring a thoughtful approach to judgment when it comes to comparing the three options before them. And I think they are going to take a look at the big picture, not just my tax initiatives, but also our achievements in schools, health care, economic growth, and the like.

Q. I guess, you would suggest that the people take a good, logical, thoughtful look at the *four* platforms, I will say, because the Greens would want to be in that, as well —

A. Being fair, yes.

Q. — and all the others, as well, that are out there, and make a decision.

A. Right.

Q. And you were very much on fire this morning at your event in Markham where you said, "The Conservative Party has turned into a Tea Party. They have become," I think you said, "resentful and bitter and angry and mean, and they don't represent Ontario values." But the people in this city were in the mood for a Tea Party last October, when they voted for mayor [Rob Ford]. How concerned are you that people are in the mood for a Tea Party right now, and if they are, that is not you?

A. Well, you know, people are going to do what they are going to do, and my responsibility as a leader, at least, this is my understanding of leadership, is to find ways to appeal to our best. My responsibility is to be you on your best day. On our worst days, we can be selfish and shallow and shortsighted, and at our worst mean spirited. On our best days, we are kind, caring, considerate, thoughtful, responsible, determined, resolute, and successful. That is what I am supposed to reflect of Ontarians every day.

Q. But you are all running negative ads, which suggests there are some bad times ahead.

A. We may not express that at all times because of who we are as human beings, but I believe, and one of the important reasons that I got into this line of work and stay in this line of work is that people … I think there is a fundamental yearning. We long to be a little bit bigger and better than ourselves. We long to do something of lasting value. We yearn to do something good for the next generation and the one after that, and that is a tough thing to kind of … to give expression to every single day. But the fact of the matter is we are always at our best when we work together.

Q. Does that suggest, if you lose, that we were probably in a small-minded, less generous point of view?

A. People are never wrong. When it comes to these big decisions, they are never wrong, and I will accept whatever outcome they determine is fitting, but I will work as hard as I can between now and election day to convince them; we have done a lot of great things together, and we need to keep going together.

Q. The history nerd in me is going to ask you another question here: Do you remember what happened twenty-one years ago today?

A. You bet. I was there. Not now, today. Was today the actual election day?

Q. Yes.

A. Yes, I remember that, then, yes, very well.

Q. For those who don't remember, it was a disaster for your party, but you were the one new MPP elected for the Liberals on September 6, 1990, twenty-one years ago. I raise it because some people may not know that you have actually been around this province, at Queen's Park, for a hell of a long time. Leader since '96, premier since '03, and they may be asking themselves, "Has this guy got any gas left in the tank? This is a long time to be around." How would you prove to people that you are still on the job?

A. Well, take a look at the platform, take a look at our plan. This is hardly a case of resting on our laurels, whatever those might be. The plan is ambitious and it is bold. It is the single biggest investment in post-secondary education, in terms of making tuition affordable for families. We are going to redesign and reform health care so it is going to help us cope with a real challenge, which is an aging demographic, and we are pursuing with zeal and aggressivity a clean-energy economy.

So, you know, we are the … you know, they have told us that our schools now, Steve, are the best in the English-speaking world. They are telling us that in our health care, we've got —

Q. Wait a sec, who is they, and what are they saying?

A. McKinsey … McKinsey International, right?

Q. … are saying we have the best schools when measured by?

A. Best school system. They took a look at the fastest … the schools that are improving the fastest in the world, and they put out an independent report and said that we are the best. Of course, there is the program for international students, the PISA results, that show us that we have cracked the top ten. When it comes to our health care …

I mean, these are achievements. The point I am making, these are achievements that we are making, because I have been quietly presiding over the evolution of government at the beginning of the twenty-first century. It is because I am an activist, and I have been driving change in our schools and health care. We didn't even measure wait times in Ontario, before. Now we measure them, and we have got the shortest time. We had nine wind turbines when I got the job. We've got hundreds up around the province now.

Q. Not everyone is happy about that, I don't have to tell you.

A. Not everyone is happy about that, but you know what? That is picking a lane. It is saying, "Folks, you know, I would love to be able to say that we don't have to put up any more gas plants or we don't have to replace nuclear, and we can all conserve." But that is not reality. We've got to come up with some way to generate new electricity. And I prefer to do it in a way that is clean and that creates jobs here in Ontario for our people. We started by cutting the price of electricity, 10 percent. We have started by cutting income taxes, $355 for the average family. And now, going forward, we can do even more for families: cutting tuition and helping seniors stay in their home.

Q. I am giving you a chance to get all that out …

A. Good.

Q. … because I want to come back at you with: My suspicion is that people think you have got a good story to tell on things like health and education. My other suspicion is, I am not sure you have sold them on your trustworthiness on the issue of taxes, because you have raised taxes twice when you said you wouldn't. Do you have a credibility gap on taxes?

A. Well, you know what? Being premier means you have got to make calls on a daily basis. And every four years, voters get to make a call on what I have been doing. So, I will be asking voters to take into account what I have done on taxes. I am not asking them to pretend that it did not happen, but I will also be asking them to look at the big picture. What has happened to our schools, what has happened to our health care? What has happened to our economy? What has happened to our clean-energy future, how much closer it is to us now in Ontario as a result of the steps that we have taken together — what has happened in the province generally?

I would like to think that, quite apart from distinct policies and pro-grams and economic growth, there is a stronger sense that we are in this together in this province, that we are still the most powerful driver of growth in the country. I have always felt that we have been commissioned by history to lead. We don't enjoy any options in this regard. I like to think that Ontarians are a bit more plugged in to what it means to be an Ontarian, a bit more proud of the great work that we have been doing together.

Q. It has been your belief, I think it is fair to say, that in order to attract the best jobs to this province, you are prepared to lay out some pretty significant government subsidies, investments, call them what you will — $250 million to get a videogame manufacturer here, $48 million for Magna, the other day, to spur on infrastructure for electric cars. Would we get those jobs if we didn't offer those subsidies?

A. No, we wouldn't.

Q. Are you sure about that?

A. Positive.

Q. How do you know?

A. Because I like to think I have a pretty good understanding of how competition works in the global economy. And the most successful jurisdictions have … are characterized by a few things: number one, they invest heavily in the skills and educational levels of their people. Number two, they drive hard on the innovation file, so that they are looking for ways to constantly reinvent themselves into prosperity, always looking for what's next.

The other thing is that … and this is a great lesson I learned growing up in a big family … you are always at your best together. Always. So, governments … you know, if you take a look at China, for example, right? This is not a government that just quietly removes itself from the day-to-day activities of business. Every once in a while, it puts its considerable muscle behind an effort. China is a little bit different, all right, in terms of its political system, but if you take a look at Germany, for example, if you take a look at a number of U.S. states, you don't even have to go that far, it is one thing for the private sector to do its shtick in the global economy, and to be supportive in that with a capable workforce. But if you get the private sector and a capable workforce and a government in sync, well, now you are talking an unbeatable combination.

And then all you have got to do is pick a lane. You can't be best at everything. So, for example, we have decided in Ontario that, notwithstanding the uncertainty that prevails in the global economy, there are a couple of things of which we are absolutely certain. One is the price of oil and gas, Steve. It is only going one way, and that is up, and there is something we knew about and we know about technologies in general and renewable-energy technologies, in specific, they are coming down. Flat-screen TVs came down in price. Cellphones came down in price. Renewable technologies are coming down in price. We want to be at the head of that curve.

What we have done for auto in Ontario … we are the number one producer in North America. I want us to become the number one producer of renewable technologies in North America. At some point in time, American moms and dads are going to say, "We've got to stop burning coal. It is not good for our kids' health. There has got to be a better way."

And we want to say, "You know the folks up north who make all those great cars for you, we are really good at making renewable technologies? So, let us produce those for you," and let's create jobs here for ourselves.

Q. Premier, as always, good of you to join us here at TVO. And as I will say to all the candidates, good luck out there on the hustings.

A. Thanks so much, Steve. Always a pleasure.

Oftentimes when my interviews with premiers are over, they've got to scram so quickly to their next event, their press secretary bounces into the studio, grabs him, and off they go. For some reason, that wasn't the case on this day. The bright studio klieg lights went out, the camera operators left the studio, no one rushed in to grab the premier, so suddenly it was just McGuinty and me. I took advantage of the moment to follow up on something I raised during the interview. While the polls had tightened somewhat over the past couple of months, Hudak's Conservatives were still in the lead. And not too many people were yet betting that the Liberals could mount a comeback.

"I hear you when you say, as Lincoln did, that you want to appeal to the better angels in all of us," I began. "But what if the electorate isn't interested in our better angels? What if we are in a crankier, harsher mood? Maybe Ontarians aren't who you think they are?"

"No, I don't accept that," the premier said in a quiet voice. "If I lose, it won't be because Ontarians are a mean-spirited people who want a Tea Party. It'll be because I failed to adequately articulate the differences between us and the other guys. It would be my fault, not theirs."

History, it turns out, was not a bad guide at all in determining what would happen one month later on election night, October 6, 2011. Yet again, a two-term premier sought a third term and the electorate gave it to him, as they did for Bill Davis, Leslie Frost, George Drew, G. Howard Ferguson, James Whitney, and Oliver Mowat. It also turns out the Conservatives I spoke to during the campaign were right to be nervous. Tim Hudak wasn't ready for prime time, something even he himself acknowledged after the election was over.

What was astonishing about the 2011 election campaign was that almost everywhere you went, people who claimed to know about politics told us that the Liberals' green-energy policy was a turkey. McGuinty had "picked a lane" all right, and that lane was trying to make Ontario the greenest jurisdiction in North America. The premier determined that to accomplish that meant offering significant subsidies to this nascent industry. As a result, when power was available on the open market for five or six cents per kilowatt hour, Ontario taxpayers were offering, at one point, eighty cents per kilowatt hour to help get solar power generators off and running. We similarly "overpaid" for wind power as well, not to mention that the government also infuriated tons of its former supporters in rural Ontario, who didn't like seeing all those wind turbines McGuinty bragged about dotting their landscape, ruining their view, making so much noise, making them sick, or reducing their property values.

So what did McGuinty do about this controversial green-energy plan during the campaign? Did he low bridge it? Keep it hidden in his back pocket and focus on something else? Not one iota. In fact, he doubled down on it. He visited solar panel manufacturing plants. He constantly met with workers whose jobs depended on his subsidies. As the Liberal leader's critics wondered why in heaven's name he was devoting so much campaign time to such a loser of an issue, McGuinty just kept his head down, stayed in his lane, and kept trumpeting the virtues of his green power plans as part of an overall economic renewal.

Amazingly, it worked. Not perfectly, but considering where he'd started, well enough. McGuinty's Liberals ended up one seat short of a majority government with fifty-three seats. Yes, it was a drop of seventeen seats, almost all of them in rural Ontario, but it was, as the premier called it, "a major minority." McGuinty also became the first Liberal leader in 128 years to win three consecutive elections. No Liberal had done that since Oliver Mowat won his third of six elections in 1883.

Announcing a cabinet shuffle, 2011.

Both other rookie leaders improved their party's fortunes. Hudak got almost as many votes as McGuinty (35.4 percent, compared to the Liberals' 37.6 percent) and the PCs won twelve new seats. Andrea Horwath, the NDP leader, also had a good night, winning seven more seats for a total of seventeen, the best result for the party since 1995.

There was another historical trend that was at play that election night. For some reason, Ontarians have been in the habit of hedging their bets in elections for more than a hundred years. If one party is in power federally, chances are a different one will be in power provincially. There's something about handing the keys to Parliament and Queen's Park to one party that Ontarians find discomforting.

And so, when Stephen Harper's Conservative Party won a majority government on May 2, 2011, strategists in the provincial Liberal backrooms were secretly thrilled. I'm not sure they wanted to see the federal Liberals embarrassed by coming third behind the NDP. But they knew two things. First, the Canadian electorate wasn't punishing the federal Conservatives for the poor state of the economy. If anything, voters wanted the devil they knew in power. It was not time for a change. And second, that could only mean good news for the provincial Liberals and bad news for the provincial Conservatives five months later.

True on all accounts.

No one knew it at the time, but the 2011 election would be Dalton McGuinty's last campaign. Although just one seat short of a majority, everything was now different at the Legislature. The opposition smelled blood in the water. The headlines were constantly filled with government scandals such as eHealth, ORNGE, and hundreds of millions of dollars in contract cancellation fees relating to two gas-fired generating stations in Oakville and Mississauga.

And the province's books were still in horrendous shape. The Liberals acknowledged they couldn't balance the budget until 2018, and even then, their plans for getting there looked more like budget science fiction than budget science.

Then came one political showdown after another: the doctors, workers in the broader public service, and the granddaddy of all political nightmares: a confrontation with the teacher unions that had previously been so instrumental in the government's educational and political success.

This moment in history has often been portrayed as the Liberals "turning against" the teachers in an effort to look tough in advance of the Kitchener-Waterloo by-election in September 2012. In fact, McGuinty did try reaching out to the teachers well before things went south. The government set up a conference call with large numbers of union representatives and school-board heads. They all expected to hear only from the education minister, Laurel Broten. But McGuinty surprised them by joining the call, telling them "we're going to ask some hard things from you," but that at the end of the day, protecting the classroom experience was Job One. Then, feeling the pressure of the deficit, McGuinty went on YouTube to tell the teachers they'd need to freeze their wages for two years and give back half their sick days. And in the ensuing spring 2012 budget came the other shoe: if the unions refused, the government would legislate a deal and forbid them from striking. So strike they did, at first only rotating one-day strikes, but those were the first school days missed due to a labour disruption in McGuinty's entire premiership.

Everything looked as if it was closing in on the Grits. The opposition was "ringing the bells" on every vote, causing interminable delays. And so McGuinty shocked the political world on October 15, 2012, by calling a last-second, end-of-the-day caucus meeting and announcing two things: first, he would prorogue Parliament to see whether that might lower the temperature, and second, he would resign as premier.

Eight days later, he gave his first sit-down interview about those decisions to us at TVO.

STEVE: Twenty-two years as an MPP, sixteen years as Ontario Liberal leader, nine years as premier: that's a long time by any measure. And yet, Ontario's twenty-fourth premier surprised everyone with his decision to step down.

Joining us now to explain why he is leaving, why he is proroguing, and what his ultimate legacy in this province will be, Dalton James Patrick McGuinty Jr., the premier of Ontario and member for Ottawa South.

Welcome back to TVO.

DALTON: Always good to be here.

Q. Okay, let's get into this. The proroguing: Remind us why you decided to do it.

A. Things were getting a little heated, and they are in danger of seizing up. The place has become overly partisan. One of the most astute observers of affairs at Queen's Park is a cameraman by the name of George.

Q. He works for CTV.

A. Absolutely. And he said in his forty years of observing activities at Queen's Park, the place has never been more partisan — just one example.

On forty-five separate occasions, the opposition has moved a motion to adjourn the debate. That causes the bells to ring for thirty minutes; they did that forty-five separate times.

Most recently, the most important priority that we are seized with today being the economy, we would like to move ahead with a bill that freezes public sector wages. Both opposition leaders have told us in writing they are not prepared to support that.

We need an opportunity to cool off. We will use this time productively.

Something else to keep in mind, Steve: we are going to sit this year … we were scheduled to sit for ninety-six days. The average in the rest of the country is fifty-one days; we sit a lot more than everybody else. At the end of the year, as a result of prorogation, and having sat extra days already, we will lose a grand total of the Ontario legislative calendar of eighteen days. Not eight-zero — one-eight.

Now what are we going to do with those eighteen days? We are going to use them very productively. We are going to be reaching out to the labour community to see if we can land agreements that freeze public sector wages and, at the same time, we will continue to work with our opposition partners to see if we can secure an agreement to a bill which they would support that would have the same effect.

Q. You know, just because I am who I am, I want to find out how you made that decision. Did you consult your caucus on proroguing?

A. No, I did not.

Q. Did you consult cabinet?

A. Yes, I did.

Q. Who in cabinet? At a cabinet meeting?

A. No, it wasn't, it wasn't at a full cabinet meeting. But I feel it's incumbent upon the premier to use his or her judgment and make a determination as to when and whether the Legislature is still functioning in the public interest. So I made that call. Things were getting overheated …

Q. Did anybody tell you not to make that call?

A. There are always people on both sides of these kinds of things, I appreciate that. But my job is to figure out when the water is getting a little too rough. You blow the whistle, "All right, everybody out of the pool, everybody out of the pool. Let's allow things to settle."

A surprise departure: McGuinty stuns everyone by announcing his retirement from politics on October 15, 2012, then gets a hug from wife Terri.

Q. Okay, but it's different this time, you acknowledge, because you are leaving.

A. Right, eighteen days.

Q. It makes it different.

A. Eighteen days. Now, during the previous government, when they prorogued for the purpose of a leadership, they prorogued for five months, right? So I am saying eighteen days. And let's use those days, very productively, which we are. And we have already got good results to report in terms of new agreements that we have already struck with the labour community.

Q. When you went to David Onley, the lieutenant governor, and you asked him for prorogation, did he make you sit and cool your heels a bit while he thought about it, or what happened?

A. No. I gave him a heads-up, phoned him first thing in the morning, told him of my intention; I let him know why I thought it was the appropriate thing to do in the circumstances. And when I met with him he agreed to it.

Q. Right away?

A. Yes.

Q. No questions?

A. No questions.

Q. You saw your *Globe and Mail* this morning, I suspect. The lead editorial in the *Globe and Mail* reads, thus: "The Ontario Liberals have a good record in government, but that record has been tarnished by the strategy to shut down the Legislature and is at risk of being overtaken entirely in the next campaign."
Are they right?

A. No. I appreciate the advice that all of our editorialists offer on an ongoing basis —

Q. You did not say that with much sincerity, yes, but anyway, I hear you.

A. — from the comfort and convenience of the sidelines. But I am in the game, and I've got to make a call. And I believe I made the right call.

Q. I hear you, and we have talked about that on this program, how the fact that just because the Legislature isn't sitting doesn't mean government comes to a grinding halt. However, I think fair-minded people look at this and they see that the reaction has pretty much universally been negative, certainly among your opponents, but even among some people who like you.

You look at letters to the editor, you look at online forums, you include the blog that we do here at TVO; you know, I can't find anybody who thinks this was a good idea. Some of your cabinet ministers have already started to distance themselves from this.

So what is the response to them?

A. Well, you may know we have prorogued five times already. You may know that in the previous PC government, I believe they prorogued six times. I believe the previous government to that prorogued a number of times. The last government prorogued for a total of one year. We will have prorogued over the course of nine years — they were there for eight years, they prorogued for one year. We have been there for nine years; we are going to prorogue for a total of seven months.

So, again, we sit longer than any other Legislature in the country. We have even passed a law mandating the attendance of the premier and cabinet ministers at our question period; nobody does more question periods than me and my cabinet in the country, in comparison to our provincial and territorial counterparts.

Q. I grant you all that. However, in my experience, governments in the past prorogued because they wanted to put a fresh coat of paint on things or they wanted to reboot, or a fresh start, that kind of a thing. It feels as if this prorogation has more to do with shutting down legislative committees that are looking into contempt motions against your government, shutting down question period so you don't have to answer uncomfortable questions about moving gas plants and the compensation you are going to have to pay to private companies to deal with that. And I want to play a clip; you can watch it on the monitor over me, here. Here is Peter Russell, whom you know, the professor emeritus at the University of Toronto; he knows a thing or two about constitutional affairs, and he is not happy. Roll tape, please.

> Peter Russell Clip: "The principles of parliamentary democracy, they are not in the written constitution. The prime minister is not even mentioned in the written constitution. The principles of parliamentary democracy have been worked out informally in a part of our constitution that is not legally enforceable, and a fundamental principle is the responsibility of government to the elected Legislature. That is the principle that is violated here."

That is the principle that is violated, he said. This is different. It's not like a typical prorogation; he thinks you are kind of going around democracy here.

A. Well, I appreciate that opinion from on high, but I am on the frontlines. I work in a contact sport, and my responsibility is to make a call as to when things are getting out of hand. For example, the opposition also had a week consumed by a spurious, phony contempt motion. And you will know that in the 220 years' history of the Ontario Legislature, no member has ever been found to be in contempt of the Legislature, okay? This is partisan games; I understand that. But we've got a responsibility that we owe to Ontarians.

So I have come to the conclusion we can actually do more work for Ontarians during this dissolved eighteen-day period outside of the Legislature, than we could —

Q. How long is it, again?

A. I think we've got that now.

Q. Okay, yes.

A. — than we can do inside the Legislature.

Q. Okay. Moving on — your resignation. You caught everybody by surprise. I want to know when you first started thinking about stepping down.

A. Well, I think seriously it was brought home to me as a result of two recent events. Now, it is always somewhere there in the back of your mind, and let me just preface this by saying, just as it is really hard to get in, it is really hard to get out. After my dad had passed away, I said to Terri, "Hon, I think I am going to have to do this." And she reminded me that we had four kids under the age of eight, and I said, "I think I still have to do it." And then she didn't talk to me for a week. And then I decided I was going to seek the leadership of the party. I had a first mortgage on the home, a second mortgage so we could put a tenant in the basement and have a bit of extra income and make a few renovations so Terri could run a daycare on the ground floor, and that is how we were getting ahead in life. And there was my law practice on top of that. And I was seriously considering at the time putting a third mortgage on the house, and I said to myself, "What are you doing to your family?" So what … I didn't end up doing that, by the way. So it is hard to get in, and it is very hard to get out because when it comes to getting out you are thinking, "Man, the next thing that I can do in education is so exciting. Transforming health care — there are all kinds of opportunities there. And there are a lot of people who count on me. And then there is my immediate staff."

So it is really hard to get out. Timing is always a challenge as well, but it is especially challenging in the context of minority government. When can you do it so that the opposition don't seize on a moment of vulnerability and cause an election at a point in time when the government lacks a leader?

So I came to the conclusion that, after my daughter's wedding, which was three or four weeks ago, we had an opportunity to be visited once again by those things that are most important in life, the family that I love and the friends who support me. And then the party annual general meeting, I came to the conclusion there, Steve, that we have achieved a level of maturity and sophistication that allows us to cope with the internal stresses and strains that are about to be placed upon the party as a result of an internal competition for leadership.

Q. But you got a good number; you got 87 percent approval.

A. I got a great number.

Q. Which suggests, hang around, don't go.

A. Well, look, that means they've got my back. But what I owe them is to look to the future, and this is not the Dalton McGuinty party, it is the Ontario Liberal Party, and we have never had a stronger stable of potential successors than we have right now. So it is going to be a very exciting race; we've got a bright future.

Q. Now let me hold off on that; I am going to come back to that.

But when the results of the election came in a year ago this month, and you discovered you were just short of a majority government, did it dawn on you at that moment that this is going to be harder and maybe … "Maybe I've got to start thinking about exit"?

A. It certainly dawned on me that it was going to be harder. And I was immediately consumed by, "Oh, so how do we make this work?" Because it's a different animal. I never experienced that before. I had never observed that before in all of my years at Queen's Park; everybody has had a majority.

So we are trying to figure out how that works and then, of course, you know, Terri and I would have the occasional conversation and she would say, "So, doesn't this make it more complicated when it's time for you to get out?" And I said, "Yes, it does, but we'll worry about that later."

Q. Okay. Somebody called me, a mutual friend, after you made your announcement, and said all of these pointy heads who are trying to come up with theories and explanations and analysis of why he is doing it,

"Look, he is resigning because he's had enough." Is that it, at the end of the day, really what it's all about?

A. I think it's a combination of things, and it's hard to put your finger on any one thing. But I think in particular I do actually want to spend a bit more time with my family.

Q. Are you sure they want to spend more time with you?

A. Steve, they have endured this, all the ups and downs, with a quiet nobility. And there is always some chatter about a political figure. So there are my four kids. Then there are my nine siblings. Then there are all the in-laws, then there are the twenty nephews and nieces. They have always been there, had my back, been there for me. So whenever I launch myself into something, I actually have a lot of people in tow. So I give some serious consideration to what I put them through.

But I also thought it is really important that I put in place a succession plan. We've got a great team of people here and, as I said a moment ago, it is hard to get out because I see so many more opportunities to build on a strong foundation that we have put in place.

Q. How do you know when it's actually time?

A. First of all, I can tell you it's not a matter of science; you cannot put this into a textbook. You'll know it when it's in front of you, you'll see it —

Q. Could you feel it in your gut?

A. Yes, yes. Yes.

Q. A loss of buzz or energy or something?

A. No, no, not so much a loss of buzz and energy. I love the job. I was saying a moment ago to you, off-camera, I am convinced I will never get a job anything like this, that gives you so much opportunity to make a difference. And I think fundamentally, in life, that's what we all want to do.

First, we are consumed by our needs and then we go after the wants but, at the end of our days, what we all want to know is that we made a difference for others. And there is no better way to make a difference for others than to serve in a leadership position in government.

Q. When you first got elected as premier in 2003, you got elected, I think it's fair to say, on a promise of rebuilding health and education. You thought our public services were degraded during the Conservative years; you wanted to get in and fix those, and I think there is lots of independent evidence around that you did that.

You now find yourself in a situation where conquering the deficit is Job One. That has never been an animating feature of your premiership in the past, or probably why you got into public life to begin with. Can I conclude from that, that this job, now, has less appeal than the job did because of that different focus?

A. It's different, and you know you've got to take the job as you find it. A few years ago, Terri and I were excited because we were going to finish the basement. We had all kinds of interesting plans, kind of a vision for the basement. Then the basement started to leak. We had to dig up the outside, go to the bottom of the foundation, wrap it in a plastic blanket, an expensive proposition. That we set out to do, not as glamorous or as exotic as the vision that we had in mind to finish the basement …

Q. But there you are …

A. … but there you are. You've got to do what you've got to do. And I think the exciting part of this mandate is that, yes, we've got to eliminate the deficit, but we've got to do in a way that protects the gains that we've made in health care and education and we've got to use it as a catalyst to transform the way that we do some things in government so there is lots of room for creativity and innovation and activism, even though there is this fiscal constraint in place.

Q. Is there a part of you that when you actually look at the numbers, you say to yourself, "Oh my God, I've doubled the debt. Now I know there were extraordinary circumstances, and the Great Recession and all of that, and I helped save General Motors and Chrysler, but I have doubled the debt." And all those kids out there that you are sort of going to bat for every day as premier, they are going to be paying it off.

A. Well, let's see what we've done here. Here's a quick run-through: So we got into government, discovered the hidden PC $5.6-billion deficit. We quickly passed a law saying that that can't happen again in the future. We got to work, eliminated the deficit, and then we balanced the budget three years in a row, right? Then the recession came. Then we made a deliberate decision to help Ontarians get through that: invest billions in infrastructure. You had to borrow that, but that created jobs and we have lasting infrastructure ... invested in job retraining, invested in the auto sector to save some 400,000 jobs. Those assembly plants? They are just the tip of the iceberg when it comes to the auto sector.

So now, where do we find ourselves? We find ourselves in a position where we've got a deficit, but we also have a very competitive tax environment. We've got the HST and lower capital taxes; we have eliminated capital taxes, lower corporate taxes. We have a highly sophisticated and educated workforce, the best trained among the thirty-four OECD countries. We are renewing our infrastructure and, in terms of jobs, since the recession we have regained all the jobs, plus another 34 percent, for a total of 134 percent. Compare that to the U.S. — they are at 49 percent.

So we have made difficult decisions, but they are the right decisions. And I haven't even touched on health care and education. The best schools in the English-speaking world; they used to struggle. We had the longest [hospital] wait times in the country; now we've got the shortest.

So people have got a good return on that investment. We are better positioned than we ever have been in the last decade, for the coming decades.

Q. To govern, of course, is to choose and to choose is to please some people and upset other people. And if you look at the polls today, and I appreciate it is only a snapshot, you appear to have upset more people than you appear to have made happy. And my question is, are you concerned that through the natural course of governing, where you get some right and you get some wrong, you have left a poisoned chalice to your successor?

A. Absolutely not. First of all, for those who disagree with me, I respect that and I would request of them that they give my successor a fresh opportunity, and see them with a fresh set of eyes and give them a fair chance. But I have always tried to do what I thought was right. I don't pretend that I brought perfection to the responsibilities, but some of the things were not easy, some of the things were not popular. The HST was not popular, our health premium was not popular. The fact that we are going to phase out our subsidies for horseracing is unpopular in some quarters. Our green-energy agenda is unpopular in some quarters.

But, at the end of the day, if you are looking to please everybody, you will do nothing. So that is not why you're hired on. You're hired on to make decisions, do the best that you can, listen to as many people as you can, but, ultimately, you've got to come to a conclusion; you've got to decide.

And I am proud of the decisions that we have made and proud of the results that we've gotten, whether you are talking about the progress in our schools, health care, environmental protections, or our strengthening economy.

Q. Eight days ago, when you announced your resignation as premier of Ontario, you were asked kind of facetiously as you were walking out the door, "What advice do you have for your successor?" And do you remember what you said?

A. [laughs]

Q. "Don't screw it up."

A. Yes.

Q. That's what you said.

A. Yes.

Q. I am going to invite you to answer that question a second time, now, perhaps with a little more thought. What is the most important thing for your successor to know?

A. At some point in time you have to stop listening and you've got to make a decision. And I think that's maybe the toughest thing to come to grips with as a premier or as the mayor or as the prime minister. The head of a government, at some point in time they've got to say, "You know what? I have heard enough."

And here is the other thing that you are going to have to reconcile yourself to: it is not all black and white. So you've got to decide on this side or that side. Well, now there are some things on this side that draw you to that. But you can only make one choice, and people are counting on you to make one choice and, ideally, it's the right choice.

So it's not often clear cut; it becomes a preponderance of right versus wrong. Most positions adopted by the opposition have a little bit of right in them. And you need to find a way to recognize that and, ideally, to marry it up with what it is that you want to do. But ultimately, I think the danger that leaders have got to confront every day is that they are overcome by paralysis because they can't make the call and, more than anything else, you are there to make the call.

Q. Forgive me, I am going to ask some touchy-feely questions, if you don't mind.

Is being premier a lonely job?

A. It can be a little bit lonely. First of all, it consumes pretty well all your time, even when you are on holidays, even when you are with time with the family, there is going to be a part of your brain that is devoted to some particular challenge, or something might just happen, Steve, and you've got to remove yourself from that setting and apply yourself to your responsibilities. So it can be a little bit lonely in that regard.

But that is offset by the number of supporters that you are going to develop over time, people who are in earnest, and want to help you and want to see you through difficult challenges.

You know, I have had the great and good fortune of being able to travel on behalf of Ontarians on many occasions. I have been to China, on trade missions to India, I have been to parts of Europe, the U.S., Mexico. And, as you get to know counterparts, and as they better understand what it is that we have got going for us here, both our challenges and opportunities, they all want my job. They all want my job.

I know that there is still work to be done, there are still challenges to be overcome. But it doesn't get any better. And people ask me, "So what does it feel at the end of … at the end of your … your … your twenty-two years in politics?" I just feel lucky.

First of all, I was born in Canada; it doesn't get any better. I was born to a mom and dad who loved me, supported me, encouraged me, and inspired me with their work ethic.

Then I married my high school sweetheart who, for some reason known only to heaven above, still loves me; this was never in the cards. I was going to be a doctor and be home every weekend — a family doctor, right?

Then we had these four great kids who helped me understand a complicated, fast-changing world; and they still talk to me. Then I have acquired supporters along the way in politics.

I know politics has got its ups and downs and if there are some people who are little less than enthusiastic about my leadership, I accept that and I respect that. But I have got to say, all in, it doesn't get any better than serving Ontarians as their premier.

Q. Well, this dovetails nicely to my last question, which is, are you yet prepared for the emotional reality that, at age fifty-seven, you are never for however many years you live going to have a job as interesting, fascinating, meaningful, impactful as the job you've now got?

A. Yes. You know, it's interesting that you raise that because I have spoken with other premiers as well, and they have all said the same thing. And it's going to call for an adjustment. And there will be other opportunities; they will have their own kinds of rewards and excitements associated with them.

But I think I've got just a few quotations under the glass of my very old desk at Queen's Park. One of those comes from the most performed American play ever, *Our Town*. And the quotation is: "Does anybody ever realize life while they live it, every minute?"

So what I have tried to do is, yes, you've got to work hard in this job. And sometimes it can seem overwhelming. But there is no better job in the world. I have tried to realize that as I have lived it so that I won't regret later on not having squeezed out as much of the joy of the job as I could.

Q. You squeezed every drop out of the lemon?

A. [laughs] Yes.

Q. Premier McGuinty, it is awfully good of you to visit us at TVO. We always appreciate it when you drop by, and we will look forward to seeing what comes next.

A. Steve, it has been a pleasure, always. Thank you.

Q. We know it's not going to be the federal Liberal leadership, right?

A. No.

Q. You took yourself out of that.

A. It's not.

Q. Okay. We'll see what comes next. Dalton McGuinty, the twenty-fourth premier of Ontario.

On January 25, 2013, thousands of Liberals gathered at Maple Leaf Gardens in Toronto to pay tribute to Dalton McGuinty and thank him for his twenty-two years of public service. The location was appropriate: the same venue where McGuinty won his own improbable leadership race in 1996. There were video tributes, speeches, and musical performances including Matt Dusk singing "I Wouldn't Change a Thing," although McGuinty surely would have. For half a century, Liberals won one election in Ontario until the man from Ottawa South "won, and then won, and then won," as he described the party's *threepeat* in his farewell address. But the last year was rough. After an eight-year love-in, relations with the teachers hit rock bottom. The gas plant cancellation in Mississauga, which cost taxpayers $585 million in penalties, turned into an absolute fiasco. The deficit and debt are scary big. The ORNGE air helicopter scandal isn't gone. Proroguing the Legislature as he resigned added more barnacles to the ship of state. (And the information and privacy commissioner's expressing alarm at the practice of former McGuinty staffers deleting emails had yet to transpire). At the moment, Dalton McGuinty is not the popular guy he once was, which might explain the less than frenzied mood in the arena that night.

But down the road, with the advantage of more hindsight, a list of the McGuinty government's achievements may look more impressive: full-day kindergarten, the Ontario Child Benefit, eight years of labour peace in elementary and secondary education, independent studies showing Ontario's education system the best in the English-speaking world, major re-investments in the post-secondary sector, reducing pollution-belching coal-fired generation by 90 percent, the attempt to create a home-grown green-energy sector, a harmonized sales tax, a reborn auto sector, and so on.

Giving a speech in 2012.

McGuinty is not an outwardly emotional guy. Although much less personally awkward than when he first got the job, he still holds his emotional cards pretty close to his chest. So the one lovely moment in his farewell address that will stay with me was when he suggested "I have only one regret: that my dad never saw me enter public life."

Of course, it took the death of McGuinty's father, Dalton Sr., for the son to enter public life. And, although he leaves politics as the second-longest-serving Liberal premier in Ontario history, the party was concerned enough about its prospects going forward that they elected, as McGuinty's replacement, someone who on paper couldn't have been more different than the stiff, male, Catholic, Ottawa-based twenty-fourth premier of Ontario.

KATHLEEN O'DAY WYNNE
(2013-)

~

Some of the most exciting moments of my job have been at political leadership conventions. I haven't been to all of them over the past three decades, but I've seen my share. Brian Mulroney winning on the fourth ballot over Joe Clark in 1983; John Turner over Jean Chrétien in 1984; Frank Miller over Larry Grossman in 1985; Larry Grossman over Dennis Timbrell by nineteen votes less than a year later; Mike Harris over Dianne Cunningham in 1990; Lyn McLeod over Murray Elston by nine votes in 1992; Kim Campbell over Jean Charest in 1993; Howard Hampton over Frances Lankin in 1996; Dalton McGuinty over Gerard Kennedy in 1996; Ernie Eves beating Jim Flaherty in 2002; John Tory over Jim Flaherty in 2004; Stephen Harper over Belinda Stronach in 2004; Andrea Horwath over Peter Tabuns in 2009; Tim Hudak over Frank Klees in 2009; and Tom Mulcair over Brian Topp in 2012.

If you add up all the candidates who've participated in these events, I've probably heard close to a hundred speeches. And truth be told, there are precious few that stay with you. But ask me which one was *the most memorable*, hands down, no questions asked, and that's easy: the speech that Kathleen Wynne gave on January 26, 2013, that simply dazzled everyone at Maple Leaf Gardens that morning. Speeches are almost never good enough to actually sway votes at a leadership convention.

This one did. I'm convinced of it.

Kathleen O'Day Wynne's personal story is utterly unlike any of her twenty-four predecessors. In fact, if you went to Central Casting and told them to send over someone with a backstory that would inevitably lead to the premier's office, it's a pretty good bet they wouldn't send you a fifty-nine-year-old lesbian from Toronto, who has three children from an earlier marriage to a man, who's a Harvard-trained mediator, and although charming and personable in her own way, never really seemed to lift a speech off the page.

But that gives you some insight into what Ontario Liberals felt they needed to remain competitive after Dalton McGuinty. And it also gives you a ton of insight into how remarkable and special Kathleen Wynne is as a politician.

For an MPP who was told she couldn't win the leadership because she was simply "too Toronto, and everyone hates Toronto," Wynne's life actually began north of the city in the sleepy, conservative suburb of Richmond Hill. She seemed to have a blessedly normal life (wife, mom, engaged citizen) until Premier Mike Harris decided he wanted to radically reform two things: Toronto's system of municipal governance by creating the MegaCity, and Ontario's education system. Wynne thought the changes were completely wrong-headed, and so she got involved, first with Citizens for Local Democracy (C4LD), and then got herself elected as a Toronto school board trustee in 2000.

Not satisfied to stop there, she ran provincially in 2003 in Don Valley West, defeating PC Cabinet Minister David Turnbull by more than 5,000 votes. Wynne has come so far in a relatively brief political career that it's easy to forget Dalton McGuinty left her out of cabinet during her first three years at Queen's Park. She was, however, the parliamentary assistant to two ministers of education: Sandra Pupatello and Gerard Kennedy, both of whom she would challenge for the leadership of the party in 2013.

But sometimes politics is a funny business. Kennedy unexpectedly left Queen's Park to run for the federal Liberal leadership, which required a cabinet shuffle. Pupatello got the education portfolio for half a year, and then, in the fall of 2006, McGuinty gave Wynne the job she seemed destined to have. Oh, and the only Ontario MPP who supported Kennedy's federal leadership bid was Wynne.

As it happened, it was a great time to be education minister. McGuinty wanted to be "the education premier," and with Wynne they were determined to transform the government's toxic relationship with the education sector. Wage settlements were generous, although not ridiculously so. The government wanted to show Ontario's teachers they were respected and admired, and paid them accordingly. Only once did Wynne get into a smackdown with a union leader, but the poor bugger didn't stand a chance.

The country's first openly gay premier addresses an Ontario Public Service Pride Week event in June 2013.

Wynne was offering three-year contracts at 3 percent a year. Take it now, she told the unions, and we're good. Miss my deadline, and all bets are off. David Clegg of the elementary teachers union challenged Wynne, saying his members were determined to "catch up" to the secondary teachers who were better paid. He ignored the deadline, figuring he'd still get the three-year, 3-percent deal anyway. He miscalculated. Wynne stared him down, Clegg capitulated, the elementary teachers had to settle for less, and Clegg found himself out of a job the next time his members voted.

The Wynne legend took another giant step forward in the fall of 2007, when Ontarians went back to the polls to render their verdict on the McGuinty government. PC leader John Tory hoped to lead his party back to respectability in Ontario's cities, where the party was almost non-existent. (Since 1999 the Conservatives have won one seat in the city of Toronto, Doug Holyday took Etobicoke-Lakeshore in a 2013 by-election.) And so, rather than stay in his very safe exurban Dufferin-Peel-Wellington-Grey riding, he decided to challenge Wynne in Don Valley West, where he grew up.

Turns out, it wasn't such a good decision. Wynne got more than 50 percent of the votes again, and bested Tory by nearly 5,000.

Wynne kept the education ministry for another couple of years, but then McGuinty shuffled his cabinet in January 2010, a shuffle that had Wynne-watchers scratching their heads. Wynne was getting rave notices in education. One day after school, I was shooting the breeze with one of my daughter's teachers. I asked her what she thought of Dalton McGuinty and his government's changes to education.

"Oh, we like him," the teacher said.

"And what about the minister, Kathleen Wynne?" I followed up.

"Oh, we *love* her."

Wynne seemed to do such a good job in education, even former Progressive Conservative premier Bill Davis jokingly called her "the second-best education minister Ontario has ever had." (Who was the best? Well, Davis himself, of course.)

And yet, McGuinty shuffled Wynne out of education, moving her to transportation. In public, Wynne claimed to be thrilled with the move, thanking the premier for giving her an "economic portfolio." However, at Queen's Park, where the number of zeroes in your budget often determines how much power you have, Wynne was moving from a ministry with a $21-billion budget to one with a $2.1-billion budget. Decimal points matter. To the outside world, it sure looked like an inexplicable demotion.

Wynne would get two more portfolios before McGuinty's departure — Aboriginal affairs, and municipal affairs and housing — again, perfectly respectable stuff, but hardly ministries such as health, finance, or energy, much higher profile and prestige portfolios.

Wynne couldn't have known it at the time, but as it turns out, she was incredibly lucky to be in a lower-profile ministry. The health ministry turned into a minefield. David Caplan resigned over the eHealth scandal, even though most of it happened on his predecessor's watch. Deb Matthews took over, tried to clean up the mess, then got hit with another scandal: ORNGE air ambulance helicopters. Matthews was at the top of many Liberals' lists to replace McGuinty, but not after ORNGE broke.

But that was kid's stuff compared to what happened to the minister of energy. In a desperate bid to save seats in Etobicoke and Mississauga during the 2011 election campaign, Premier McGuinty cancelled a contract for a gas-fired energy plant in Mississuaga in the dying days of the campaign. The Liberals went on to hold all the seats in question. But the hundreds of millions of dollars in penalties to be paid to the company building the plant put the energy minister, Chris Bentley, in the midst of a political firestorm. Bentley, who had been planning to run for leader, instead announced he'd had it with Queen's Park.

Finally, when finance minister Dwight Duncan opted to pack 'em up as well, suddenly the field for the 2013 Ontario Liberal leadership was decidedly less competitive than it might have been. Wynne, who'd simply kept her head down, done her job, and avoided any of the minefields the premier's office planted, was suddenly one of the frontrunners to replace the retiring McGuinty. The other favourite was the woman Wynne replaced as minister of education, Sandra Pupatello, who had been working on Bay Street in the year since declining to run for re-election in 2011.

Pupatello's strengths as a leadership candidate were formidable. Her retail political skills were phenomenal. She lit up every room she entered, made people feel great about being part of what was now a beleaguered political party, and reminded people that her time spent in opposition (1995–2003) would be crucial in a minority Parliament, where the opposition were constantly laying traps for the government.

Wynne's campaign team couldn't outmatch Pupatello on personality, so it decided to showcase its candidate as being the best prepared for high office. The candidate could speak confidently, without notes, on a wide range of policy issues. She had great facility, as befits a Harvard-trained mediator, at bringing disparate groups together and finding solutions that worked. She listened well, a skill often lost in today's bumper-sticker world of politics. She had a refreshing, personable authenticity when discussing issues with people. But in attending many of her speeches to larger audiences, as likeable as Wynne was, I had to conclude she didn't exactly light up the crowd. In fact, her delivery bordered on technocratic. People listened, but they never interrupted with applause. Conversely, Pupatello would sprinkle her speeches with ad-lib references to people in the room. You had to pay attention, lest the candidate point at you, remind you of something you worked on together, then tell a joke about it. Pupatello was entertaining as hell. Wynne was competent, but as I tweeted after one of her speeches "didn't sizzle."

That word would come back to haunt me.

Later that night, all seven Liberal candidates gathered at the Old Mill in west-end Toronto for their final leadership debate. Wynne and I accidentally encountered each other before the debate. The first words out of her mouth were: "So, I don't sizzle, eh?" She wasn't smiling. I tried to remind her I also said a lot of nice things about her too. But the criticism rankled. Clearly, Wynne and her team saw her as a shining star. And while she may have been good at a lot of things, the theatre of politics — so crucial in a leadership bid — wasn't one of them. Wynne then went out and mailed in a thoroughly forgettable appearance at the all-candidates debate.

Less than a week later, she visited us at TVO for a feature interview:

STEVE: She's had a lot of big jobs in Dalton McGuinty's government: education, transportation, municipal affairs and housing, and Aboriginal affairs. But, of course, the job she now wants is premier, and the numbers suggest she is one of the favourites to get it. Let's find out more about Kathleen Wynne, the MPP for Don Valley West, whom we welcome back to TVO. Nice to see you again.

MS WYNNE: Pleasure to be here.

Q. I am asking the six of you the same first question off the top, so here we go: what particular skill set do you offer that would make you the best choice of the six [candidates] to be premier of Ontario at this particular moment in our history?

A. At this particular moment, we need a premier who is going to be able to reach out to people who have different views of how to move forward, who have differing opinions, be able to bring them together and find common ground. And it is what I have done in my career. I mean, I am a trained mediator, so in the decade before I came into office, that's the work that I did. But more than that, working in community, working as a minister, I have brought people together and been able to find common ground. I think that's what we need right now; that's the skill I have.

Q. How did the portfolios that you have had prepare you to be premier?

A. The portfolios allowed me to learn about Ontario. You know, I made it my business to travel around the province, to understand the regions of the province, whether we were talking about small schools — I mean, I always talk about the school of six students in Sioux Narrows, outside of Kenora. You know, six kids. And then in downtown Toronto, an elementary school in my riding that has 2,000 kids in it. So those ... the continuum of difference across the province is huge.

So it has allowed me the opportunity to do that, and I have learned about the interconnectedness of portfolios and of the endeavours in the province. So when I was minister of transportation, I was learning about infrastructure. But learning about infrastructure is to learn about the economic pulse of the province because if you don't have good infrastructure you don't have a strong economy. So it's allowed me to learn those lessons of how everything is connected.

Q. Let me pick up on that economic piece of the puzzle because, strictly speaking, you haven't had one of those so-called finance or economic development — one of those economic portfolios.

A. Well, I would argue that transportation actually is an economic portfolio.

Q. Okay. Argue away, because the critics will say Job One is fixing the economy —

A. Yes.

Q. — and here is a woman who hasn't had, strictly speaking, an economic portfolio. To which you say what?

A. To which I say that my experience across government has allowed me to see what makes a strong economy, you know? And really understand that the conditions that we have to put in place as a province for business to thrive has everything to do with great education, great health care, great infrastructure.

It also has to do with having the right tax regime, making sure that small business gets access to capital, and those are things that are in my economic plan as well.

But honestly, Steve, my economic plan is my plan for the province, you know? It's about social justice and fiscal responsibility going hand in hand, being one and the same thing.

Q. You mention taxes; let me pick up on that. Can we balance a $14.4-billion deficit without a tax increase?

A. What I have said is that we are going to need revenue streams. So if I go back to infrastructure for a moment, we are not going to be able to balance the budget and provide the amount of new infrastructure — transit in particular, if we talk about the GTHA — but roads and bridges in Northern Ontario and small municipalities, we are not going to be able to do those things without revenue streams.

So I am going to be very clear with the people of Ontario about how we are going to have to pay for that infrastructure that we need. So that is the kind of policy that I will put in place.

Q. Okay. So to be clear here: What does that mean? Tolls?

A. It means that there will have to be a choice among a number of tools and, you know, road tolls is one, parking levies is another, payroll taxes are another. So there is a whole range of tools and the Toronto Board of Trade and Civic Action in Toronto are talking about the GTHA, and the kinds of tools that we need here. But I think we need to make sure that we have a revenue stream across the province.

Q. But income taxes, harmonized sales tax increase, you think those are...?

A. No plans to change those, you know? The reality is that we are going to have to work together. I mean, you have had Glen Murray on the show and he is now working with me *[Murray dropped out of the race and endorsed Wynne]*. And we are looking at his economic ideas in terms of restructuring within the tax system and, if there are good ideas there, I will draw on those.

Q. Let me ask you about your favourite subject, which is education. You were a pretty successful education minister for three years when you had the portfolio, but I am wondering if you can kind of peel the curtain back a bit and give us some insight into some of the presumably private conversations you had with either the premier or your cabinet colleagues or caucus colleagues. When they put Bill 115 on the table and said, "Here's what we need to do in order to achieve these savings and get these contracts ... I's dotted, T's crossed," I am wondering if the woman who had such good relationships with the teacher unions at any point said, "Are you guys out of your mind? You are going to screw up my legacy on this file." Did you say that?

A. Just like that?

Q. In those words, exactly.

A. No. No. I have been pretty clear and I have been pretty public about the reality that there is a range of opinion about many subjects in caucus and cabinet, and there was a range of opinions about this strategy as well.

The premier's been clear that the process as it evolved was not what it should have been, and I certainly agree with that.

Never in my wildest dreams, Steve, did I think we were going to have to impose contracts. I knew that we had said in the budget last year that we would put legislation in place, if necessary, because we had to constrain those compensation packages. But it was always my belief and my expectation that because our relationships were as good as they were with our education partners, that we would be able to reach negotiated settlements.

Q. So why didn't it happen in your view?

A. Well, in my view, it went wrong early on, and got positional very early. It was a combination of the process not being as clear as it should have been, and, you know, the reality is that Gerard Kennedy had started a process when he was minister of education. I refined that process; it became somewhat more formal, but nothing was written down. It wasn't a formal statutory process. And then, when we came to this round of negotiations, there really was a lack of clarity about what was the role of the school boards, what was the role of the local bargaining in this process.

So the process was not clear, there were no extra resources on the table. We were looking for constraint obviously, and I honestly believe that there were the wrong people at the table. I think there was not a good engagement.

Q. The wrong people on which side?

A. I can only speak from the government's side. You know, I think that there probably should have been some other people at the table but, again, I didn't get to choose those people; that was another process. But I can't speak for the other side of the table.

Q. I get that you established good relationships with the people on the other side of the table while you were the minister. But if you win the leadership and become premier and try to reach out to the other side to get this thing done, I mean, you have said it yourself — you have said the reality is we have no more money.

A. Right, right.

Q. So we are still looking at zero and zero.

A. Right.

Q. And they are still looking at a year of being disrespected, in their view. How does any of that change that?

A. Well, so here is the thing: I believe we have two groups of people who want to get along. I mean, remember, this impasse at the moment, this conflict at the moment is not borne of a long-term, deep-seated hostile relationship. We had had a very good relationship, and so it is very different than the government before us, if I may say, where there were two terms of really bad blood between the Conservative government and the education sector. That hasn't been the case. So we want to get along and we know how to get along.

The other piece of that is that teachers want to deliver extracurriculars, they want to be engaged with their schools, and they want schools to do well. So we are natural allies. There has been a very bad process and I am absolutely willing to say that and open to it.

But we don't have any choice about trying to repair the relationship. We have to repair it; in the interests of students we have to repair it. That is what we have to put at the centre of the conversation.

Q. Well, there is a choice: they can say "You know what? You guys messed with us and now we are going to get rid of you and put somebody else in."

A. Well, I don't think … that is not a long-term strategy that is going to work.

Q. It is a strategy they have pursued for twenty-five years, frankly.

A. Well, from my perspective, there have been ups and downs in that strategy, you know? And there have been long periods of getting along with the government and working with the government and we have had one of those long periods, and that is when the improvements get made. That is when we move ahead in education.

And so, when I say there is no choice, there is no choice. If we are going to continue to improve the education system, there is no choice about the government getting along with the education sector; it has to happen. And I said to teachers: I will stay in the room until we figure out how we are going to re-engage. That is how committed I am to this. I just need to say, I just need to be clear that I do not intend to rip up the contracts. And I just need to be clear about that because there is no more money. What we have to talk about is how we go forward and how we put a better process in place.

Q. Okay. Let's talk some politics in our remaining moments here. And this is the part of the interview where I say, "Here is what I am hearing." Because I am out there and I am attending stuff and talking to people, and here is what I am hearing: Kathleen Wynne is terrific, great integrity, knows her brief, she knows so much about so many different levers in the government, brings people together. However, she has never been in opposition, we have a minority Parliament right now which is fractious. We may need somebody who has got an outward appearance of being more aggressive and tougher in the premier's chair in order to deal with the opposition, and that is Pupatello, it is not her. What is your response to that?

A. So, let me just tackle the first part, the opposition part, and then I will come to the what's needed. I think if you ask some of the members of Mike Harris' cabinet and government whether I know how to act in opposition, they would probably say indeed, she does. I wasn't in the Legislature; that is absolutely true. I was a public-school trustee, I was a community activist.

But my skills at opposing and clarifying issues and making sure the people understand where I stand and where we differ are pretty finely tuned. And, you know, I have demonstrated that I can win elections. So from my perspective, that is not an issue for me. I believe that I can build a team and we can launch a very strong campaign. And we will do that, if necessary.

But to the second part of your question, I am not sure that *that* is what is needed right now. I think what's needed right now is someone who is going to be able to work with the opposition, someone who is going to be able to reach across the floor and say, "Look, we had an election a year and a bit ago, and we need to govern now. The people of Ontario have asked us as a minority government to work together and govern."

So that is what I am going to do. But if we have to, if we have to go into an election, I am ready to do that. Absolutely.

Q. You did a scrum a few hours ago, after your speech to the Board of Trade, where you were cockier than I have ever seen you before. And I wonder if that is because Sandra Pupatello is out there, and her people are out there saying, "I am the one to win the election. She is the one to bring people together but, when we are into a campaign and at a leaders' debate, when you've got to be in somebody's face, Pupatello is your person, not Kathleen Wynne."

That is what's out there.

A. Yes. No, I hear you. It's just so interesting to me that that's being said, given my history as a feisty community activist, you know? That's why ...

Q. So this is not a new thing for you.

A. That's why I got into provincial politics.

Q. Okay. Here's the other thing I am hearing: Some people have said to me, if we vote for Sandra Pupatello as leader, we get Kathleen Wynne, too, because she will stick around and they will be a good team. If we vote for Kathleen Wynne for leader, we don't necessarily get Pupatello because she probably won't come back from private life where she is, right now, and she won't come back into public life. Pupatello, we get two; Wynne, we only get one.

A. Well, I ... you know, I haven't ... I haven't heard Sandra say whether she is going to run or not; I guess I assumed that she would run for office. Whether she is the leader or not.

Q. I asked her about it, and she gave me a bit of a ... well, I will tell you what she said: What she said was, "I can't commit 100 percent to coming back because whoever wins, the new leader would have to sign my nomination papers and I don't know if the new leader would want me back or welcome me back, so I can't commit."

A. I will sign Sandra's nomination papers.

Q. You will sign the papers?

A. Absolutely, absolutely.

Q. Okay. So that excuse is off the table.

A. Happy to have her. You know, it would be great to have Sandra as part of my team, absolutely, and I am happy to sign her nomination papers, and happy to find the rest of the people that she needs to sign the nomination papers.

Q. What about the other though that, if she decides not to come back, you get both if you get her, you get one if you get you?

A. Well, you know, people have to make that decision, Steve; the members of the party have to make that decision. They have to decide what is needed right now. And I have put myself forward as someone who's got experience, I've got the energy and the enthusiasm, and, you know, I understand how to win and I understand how to collaborate and work together. So that is the skill set that I have and I hope that will be seen by the party and that I will have an opportunity to lead.

Q. Is she a riskier choice because she doesn't have a seat in the Legislature and, therefore, if she stays true to what she said, she doesn't want to bring the House back until she has a seat, so that wouldn't be the day after Family Day; that would be, presumably, later, maybe March. Who knows? Is that a problem for her?

A. So I am not going to pass judgment on Sandra or —

Q. Why not?

A. — or her situation.

Q. Pass judgment. Why not?

A. I am not going to do that. What I am going to say, and you can extrapolate from what I say, I think we need to get back to the Legislature right away. I think the fact that I have a seat is an advantage; I think it's important to get back to the Legislature. No one is comfortable with prorogation. You know, the reality is that we have lost 18 days in the House. It is enough; we need to get back and we need to get at it. So I think that February [2013] is the date we need to go back.

Q. Have you or any of your people had any conversations, either officially or unofficially — I am trying to cover every base here in asking this question — with anyone on the NDP side of the equation on how your parties could work together if you win, once the House is back?

A. No.

Q. Really?

A. No.

Q. Nothing?

A. To the best ... now, there are a lot of people working on my campaign so I can't vouch for every single conversation that every single member of my team has had. But I can tell you that I have had none of those conversations, my senior team has had none of those conversations. And, you know, I think that there have been signals sent in public, certainly by me, to both leaders of the opposition that I want to work with them. But, beyond that, there haven't been any private conversations that I am aware of.

Q. Because people are, I think, entitled to know whether or not you are considering a variety of options for working with one of the other two opposition parties such as a possible coalition, such as a possible formally written-out accord, such as a … I don't know, we will go bill-by-bill and just see how we go. What's your thinking on that?

A. So, honestly, I haven't talked about coalition; that is something that has come at me from the media. I haven't heard anybody else talking about coalition. But what I am clear about is that it is going to be up to me and to Tim Hudak and to Andrea Horwath to have a conversation about how we can or cannot work together. I am willing to work with one or both of them.

But the nature of that conversation and what it will lead to has got to be with all of us; it is not for me to say, "This is what I want to do," you know? "This is how I see it." That is not the kind of leadership that I bring. It is not the kind of leader that I am.

I want us to work collaboratively, and I want us to co-create whatever that go-forward position is going to be.

Q. Understood. That is our time and, as I say —

A. Thank you.

Q. — to all the candidates, good luck on the 26th of January at Maple Leaf Gardens.

A. Thank you, very much.

You'll notice during that entire twenty-minute interview for *The Agenda*, there wasn't one question about Wynne's sexual orientation, about which there had been plenty of whispering among party members. My preference in doing interviews is to avoid talking about peoples' private lives because I think they're entitled to a private life, as long as whatever happens there doesn't affect their ability to do their jobs.

But potentially being the first openly gay premier in Canadian history was a big deal and couldn't be entirely avoided. So Wynne and I did a separate, brief interview, for *The Agenda* website on that issue:

STEVE: I am going to start by saying get comfortable, because this is going to take a bit of setting up here. Your first interview on *The Agenda* was just after you became the minister of education; we had you in for sort of, "Here she is, here's who she is." That was back in 2006.

And we had a heck of a debate in this studio among the producers about how much we should ask you about your private life, because I actually believe private lives are entitled to be private. And we had a discussion about it, and we decided no, we weren't going to ask you about your sexual orientation.

Five years later, we are doing another program on something related to a gay theme. You were a guest on the program, and out of the blue — it was not on our question sheet — you and I ended up having a very spontaneous conversation about that first interview and whether I should have asked the question. And let's play the clip of what you said at that time and place. Roll clip, please, control room:

> *MS WYNNE: Yes, I wish you had asked and probably what we should have done is had a conversation before. I should have had that conversation with your producer and they could have asked me, "Is it okay to talk about this?"*

> *Q. I was even too nervous to do that.*

> *MS WYNNE: Really ... okay.*

> *Q. I was too nervous to bring it up with you personally, ahead of time, as I always do, chat with a guest before the program. Because I just thought, if the answer is no, then I am going to ... it's going to be in the back of her head and it is going to screw up the whole interview. So I didn't do it. But I should have done it?*

A. Well, it would ... yes, and it would have been fine and I would have appreciated the opportunity.

Q. Okay. So that's the set up. Having established it's okay to now talk about this subject, let me raise it, since all twenty-four premiers from now going back to 1867 have been, as far as we know, straight, white men, how big a deal would it be to have a premier who is an out-of-the-closet lesbian?

A. Well, I think it's a question that is being asked because it's been raised by the newspapers and it's a question that actually is circling among Liberals; there is a sort of, how will this work? But my experience is, and I have been around the province as the education minister, transportation, all the portfolios that I have held, and now as a leadership candidate and, to a group, Steve, people have said to me, it doesn't matter. And I have raised it.

Q. You have raised it?

A. I have raised it. I say to them, look, this is one of the things that is being talked about and I need to raise it with you because here I am in rural Ontario; you are Liberals, I am a Liberal. I want to make sure you know that I am comfortable with this, that I am able to deal with this, and that I can win an election working with you.

Q. And are they?

A. They are, they are.

Q. You haven't had any feed ... like, brush-back, on this?

A. I haven't. And, in fact, there is an element of, you know, it's kind of a point of pride among us, I think, as Ontarians; I don't think it is just Liberals, but it is a point of pride that we are inclusive people. And everybody, Steve, has a cousin or an aunt or an uncle or they know a child who lives in the community who's struggling. Everybody knows somebody who is gay. So it's not like this is a foreign subject to people.

And I think over the last five years, because there has been much more discussion about it, people are more and more sensitized to it. So I have been so gratified in having conversations with Liberals around the province, and I believe that it is not going to be an issue.

I believe that we will, as a party, we will choose the leader on his or her merits. I honestly believe that.

Q. It is almost unprecedented how well you and your colleagues are getting along in this leadership fight, so far. It is amazing to me how there has been an absence of rancor among the actual candidates.

But that often doesn't extend to the candidates' staffs. And I wonder whether you are hearing anything from any of them through your people, presumably, that they are torquing it or using it or trying to stir something up with that?

A. And I haven't heard that; I hope it is not happening. But that is how homophobia works, you know? And people can use homophobia as a tool. But it backfires. I mean, I represent one of the most diverse ridings in the province, in the country. And I have people who support me and have supported me for nine years who are devout Muslims, who are devout Catholics. I have people from all walks of life who support me.

Q. And they know who you are.

A. And they know who I am. They know I am "out," they know I live with a woman, and we coexist, and they know that the Charter of Rights and Freedoms protects them as much as it protects me.

A week and a half before the day Liberals would gather at Maple Leaf Gardens to pick their new leader, Kathleen Wynne spoke to the Toronto Board of Trade. The speech was classic Wynne: she covered the landscape on policy, demonstrating a breadth and depth on so many issues that Sandra Pupatello could never do, and she was never interrupted by applause.

But then something interesting happened in the "scrum" with reporters after her speech. After Wynne reminded us for the umpteenth time that she thought she could make the Legislature work because she could find common cause with Tim Hudak on fiscal management issues, and Andrea Horwath on social justice issues, one reporter asked, "What happens when it stops working?"

Without missing a beat, Wynne said, "Well, we'll go to an election and I'll beat Tim and Andrea, but until then, I'm going to try to make it work." A rare moment of cockiness for the member for Don Valley West. It made me wonder where that burst of personality had been hiding for the past three months. I wouldn't have to wait long for an answer to that question.

Saturday morning, January 26, 2013, at Maple Leaf Gardens. Leadership hopeful Harinder Takhar was the first scheduled speaker on the day when more than two thousand Liberal delegates would choose Dalton McGuinty's successor. Then came Gerard Kennedy, who sixteen years earlier had been in the same arena asking delegates then to make him their leader. He led on every ballot except the last one.

Then came Kathleen Wynne. What came next was the most extraordinary speech at a leadership convention I've ever seen.

It started with the fabulous up-tempo music of the song "Take a Chance," followed by a group of Wynne supporters taking the stage to dance and rev up the crowd. Even her co-chairs Deb Matthews and John Wilkinson were boogieing up there. The Wynne campaign looked like the fun campaign.

But after the dancing, the campaign played a video which was serious and thoughtful. I remember thinking, you've just worked the crowd up into an enthusiastic frenzy and now you cool everybody down? How does that make sense? But the video picked up near the end, the crowd returned to its enthusiastic former self, and then the candidate came on stage to a thunderous cheer. The first words out of her mouth: "So, which team has sizzle!" There was that word again. Except this time, unlike every other time, it actually was Wynne who was sizzling.

Wynne began her speech by recognizing that we were all gathered on the territory of the Mississaugas of the New Credit — a nice touch. Yes, there were the policy pronouncements you'd expect from this candidate. And yes, she told delegates she'd been all over Ontario listening to their concerns and "taking notes. And you've told me economic growth is our top job." In other words, I am not ceding the "jobs and the economy" issue to Pupatello.

But there was also an authenticity in the speech that was uncommon. It didn't feel as if she was reading it off a teleprompter as so many do. She was *saying* the speech, as if she were having a conversation with each individual member of the audience. It was working well. Maybe too well. Her supporters cheered and cheered so much, Wynne told them, "I love you all, but I'm watching the clock and I'm going to finish this speech!" So fewer interruptions for applause please.

Rather than revisiting old, tired partisan platitudes, Wynne dispensed with that schtick and spoke directly to Hudak and Horwath *by name*, urging them to join her in a quest to make Ontario more governable.

"Tim. Andrea. I'm sure you're watching. Tim, let's talk about fiscal responsibility. You care about that. So do I. And Andrea, you care about creating a fair society. Well, so do I."

This was a different speech. It was about getting along. It was about collaboration. But no one doubted Wynne possessed those skills. What they wondered was whether she could be a juggernaut like Pupatello. So there was this: "If they choose to trigger another election, I will fight them for every seat, every poll, and every vote.... And we will win!" That line brought the house down.

Of course, the big question was, how would Wynne handle the issues only whispered about in the corridors, that she was too Toronto and too gay for too much of Ontario? The answer came next: she went after those whispers head on.

"I want to put something on the table," she began, the audience not exactly sure where she was going. "Is Ontario ready for a gay premier? Can a gay woman win?"

The Wynne supporters at the base of the stage were on fire. Their candidate continued. "There was a time, not that long ago, when most of us in this leadership race would not have been deemed suitable. A Portuguese-Canadian. An Indo-Canadian. An Italian-Canadian. Female. Gay. Catholic. I do not believe that the people of Ontario judge their leaders on the basis of race, sexual orientation, colour, or gender. I don't believe they hold that prejudice in their hearts."

The hall exploded. Wynne was putting "the issue" out there with astonishing guts. This is who I am, she was saying. If you don't want this, I'm okay with that. But if you do want me, you'd better know this is what you're getting.

At the risk of overdoing it, I believe when historians write about the great political milestone speeches of all time, Kathleen Wynne's leadership address will be on that list. John F. Kennedy challenged America to look beyond his Catholicism when he ran for president in 1960. It wasn't just a campaign speech, it was an historic challenge to Americans. Barack Obama urged his fellow countrymen to deal with race in a memorable campaign address in 2008. That one, too, was for the history books, not just another stump speech. I believe Kathleen Wynne's speech demanding that Liberal delegates face their concerns about her sexual orientation belongs right up there. It was bold. It was honest. And in the end, I'm convinced it moved delegates, who had their doubts, to support her.

As Wynne tried to wrap up her speech echoing Dalton McGuinty's well-worn tag line — "Ontario: the best province, in the best country in the world" — she botched it. She mixed up some of the words. But she was so genuine in screwing up, laughing at herself, then trying again, it didn't matter. By then, much of the room was eating out of her hands.

You know the rest of the story. Sandra Pupatello spoke half an hour later, and while her speech was fine it simply couldn't compare. When the first ballot results were announced and Pupatello was clinging to a mere two-vote lead, it felt like a done deal. Eric Hoskins, the last-place candidate, dropped off the ballot and went to Wynne. Takhar dropped off and went to Pupatello. After the second ballot, Pupatello extended her lead to sixty-seven votes, but it wasn't nearly enough to overcome the Gerard Kennedy and Charles Sousa supporters, the vast majority of whom went to Wynne for the third ballot. In the end, Wynne won by 284 votes, a veritable landslide in a race that was allegedly too close to call.

But if convention-goers thought they'd already seen all the great speeches they could expect in one day, they were mistaken. Sandra Pupatello took to the stage, and paraded the victorious Wynne from side to side, pointing to her, raising her arm aloft, then delivering the best and classiest concession speech I've ever heard. Somehow, amidst the heartbreak of losing and seeing some of her fellow candidates break what she thought were agreements to support her, Pupatello summoned the strength to urge all party members to get behind their new leader, even managing a joke about how the two female front-runners "sure gave those guys a run for their money, eh?"

Later that night, about fourteen hours after arriving at Maple Leaf Gardens, I sat down with the new leader of the Liberal Party of Ontario.

STEVE: How did you get the news that you had won? How do they tell you?

MS WYNNE: The scrutineer comes into the backroom and gives you a piece of paper about two minutes before it's announced.

Q. So you had the heads-up?

A. Two minutes, yes.

Q. And was Sandra Pupatello with you backstage …

A. Yes.

Q. … getting the news all at the same time?

A. We were both in a room; her person was giving her the information, and mine was giving me the information. And, you know, then we both had it and we acknowledged each other and then we basically went out on the stage.

Q. So that's not much time to get your game face on, is it?

A. No, no. It's not. It's not a lot of time. And she did a great job, you know, and I hope I did, too.

Q. The first question is pretty simple: Can you believe this?

A. No! No, there's a surreal quality to it, you know? You just sort of can't really believe. And the thing about a campaign is that it is so focused. You are focusing on every day, performing, and of course you are thinking about the end goal but, for me, it's getting through each day and keeping my energy up and saying the things I need to say and meeting the people I need to meet, and then when you have done everything you can do, then you wait for the results.

But there isn't really a lot of reflection time during the campaign. The only thing I did … I did write my speech. About three weeks ago I wrote the speech that I was going to give here and then I gave it to the people who were going to edit it and change it and do all of that, but I really wanted to get the framework of what I was going to say down on paper, because I kept waking up at three o'clock in the morning thinking, I am going to say this, and I thought, okay, I am just going to get up and write the thing. So I did.

And so that actually took a load off my mind, thinking about what I was going to be doing here today.

Q. A couple of quotes I want to share with you in the lead-up to this question: Bobby Kennedy used to say, "If you've got a problem, shine a lantern on it." David Peterson was in that chair a few hours … well, more than a few hours ago, now … when he said that his wife, Shelley, has an expression that "if you've got a skeleton in the closet," as he called it, "drag it out and dance with it."

You took a big risk in your speech to absolutely go face on on the issue that I guess a lot of people have been whispering about, namely your sexual orientation, and I want to know why you decided to hit that so hard?

A. Because I wanted everybody in the province to know, I wanted every member of the Liberal Party to know who I am and how I am going to deal with issues. And it had been raised so many times in the press and it just was something that, even though people knew, it didn't seem to go away, it didn't seem to be something that everybody could just say, "Oh, well, we can set that aside." It kept coming up.

And so I thought, you know, I am going to come into the convention and I am going to lay it on the table and make it so clear that people have to make a decision about whether they are ready to accept that or not.

Q. Anybody in your campaign tell you not to do it?

A. No. No. They knew better than to do that.

Q. How do you think the speech went?

A. I was very happy with it. I felt that I did it exactly the way I wanted to. Of course, there had been lots of practice and you never quite know how it is going to go.

Q. Lots of practice, and you flubbed the kick-off line.

A. I know, I know.

Q. Yes. The kicker at the end, there.

A. You see, you just never know what's going to happen.

Q. Although you recovered so nicely and so authentically that it went over —

A. Actually, somebody asked me if … if that was planned.

Q. To blow the last line?

A. Yes. I said, "No, not really."

Q. No. Consensus in the room, obviously you have heard: it was the best speech of the day by far. Do you think that helped in subsequent ballots?

A. What some people said to me was that for folks who didn't know me, the speech really helped them to see that side of me. There has been this kind of talk about, "Well, is she feisty enough, is she able to confront issues? Is she able to speak out and be strong?" And I really wanted to show people my version of that. You know, I am different than the other candidates; we all have our own styles. But I have my own version of feistiness and my own version of strength, and I wanted people to see that because I think that that inner resolve is what I bring to this job.

Q. The first line out of your mouth for the speech — I am not sure it was scripted and I don't even know if you remember saying it — was, after the big dance show ...

A. Yes.

Q. ... "how is that for sizzle?"

A. Right.

Q. Why did you say that?

A. I said that because there was a journalist who said that ... wasn't sure I had the sizzle.

Q. Who would say such a silly thing?

A. I don't know who said that. *[Author's note: it was me.]*

Q. When you were two votes behind on the first ballot, I looked over at one of the guys here, and I said, "It's over, she's won," meaning you. Did you know that, too?

A. We were very excited because it meant we had momentum; we had gotten more of the ex-officio vote than we had expected, and so we were pretty excited about that. I mean, there were lots of nervous moments after that, let me tell you, but that was an indicator that, you know what? This was within our reach, for sure.

Q. Not necessarily a huge shock that Eric Hoskins went to you. Yes, a bit of a shock that Charles Sousa went to you. How did that happen?

A. Well, Charles and I have had lots of conversations over the last three months, you know? And our value system is not very far apart, and I think that, again, in the same way that rumours and characterizations grow up during these things, the characterization of him that wasn't necessarily accurate had been created. So, when he and I talked, it was like, you know, is it the centre-right thing? You're centre-left, I am centre-right. You know, is that really where we are? And I think there is much more commonality.

But the other side of it is, he gets how important it is and I get how important it is that we have a balance, that we have people who have slightly different views of the world. So I think it's a good ... it was a good moment for us, for sure.

Q. And do you actually know before he walks across the room that he is coming over to you?

A. Actually, we didn't know exactly what was happening. And, in fact, when he started to ... people in the box and I were saying, "He's moving. Okay, Charles is moving." And I would look over and he was standing perfectly still; so I had no idea what they were talking about.

And then he came out and went around and we weren't sure exactly where he was going, so it was one of the moments that was very important because we needed Charles to come to us and we just weren't exactly sure. And then when he started to move, it was terrific.

Q. And [Gerard] Kennedy moved, I guess, about twenty minutes later and ...

A. Kennedy came right over.

Q. ... did you know that was coming?

A. So Gerard and I did have a conversation just before that happened, so he gave me a heads-up that they were coming.

Q. Okay, the job ahead.

A. Yes.

Q. Who's your first phone call to, tomorrow?

A. Well, actually, I just had a conversation with Tim Hudak.

Q. Already?

A. He reached out. Yes, he called. And I had said I was going to call both Tim and Andrea Horwath, tomorrow, but Tim already called me and we are going to try to get together on Monday; he is around on Monday.

Q. Was it anything more than kind of congrats, courtesy call, that type of thing?

A. Well, we both agreed that he and I … actually, Tim has lived in the neighbourhood that I live in, in North Toronto, for awhile. So every now and then when I am running I will see him out walking his dog, so …

Q. And when you say running, you don't mean for office; you mean actually with your legs?

A. I mean actually jogging. Yes, jogging, yes. So we have had casual interactions. And we acknowledged that we both have had good conversations in the past. So, who knows? We will have a conversation on Monday and I hope to talk to Andrea Horwath, either tonight or tomorrow.

Q. What do you do about Sandra Pupatello, now?

A. Before I meet with the leaders of the opposition, I am going to be meeting with all of my colleague candidates, and just finding out where they are at and taking stock of that situation, because I don't know exactly what they all want to do, I don't know what Sandra and Gerard are going to do, for example, but I look forward to talking to them.

Q. If she were to say, yes, sure I will run in a by-election and come back to public life if you make me finance minister, what would you say to her?

A. Well, I am not going to play that version of let's make a deal. But I hope she will run. It would be great if she would run.

Q. And would she have the senior-most job in your cabinet if she were to run?

A. You know what? I have to build a cabinet, Steve, and you know — you have studied politics, you know that is the hardest job that a premier has to do, and it has to be done with care and consideration. And so I need to find out where everybody's at, and I need to move the pieces of paper on the wall and figure out who fits where, based on what their talents are, what their experience is, and what they are interested in doing.

Q. You have to, in relatively short order, bring the House back, have a Throne Speech, you've got a budget coming, presumably a couple of months later. You're in a minority Parliament, you've got a really hard job to build a cabinet because you have obviously got leadership candidate considerations, supporter considerations. I mean, you've got a mountain of work ahead of you and you have said you want to be the agriculture minister as well. How are you going to do all this?

A. So I have said that and I believe that it is the right thing to do. There will be a strong parliamentary assistant, there is a strong deputy minister in the ministry of agriculture, and I will take that guiding role because I think it is very important, as Dalton McGuinty took research and innovation when we first came to office, I think it is very important to shine a light on that file.

I said I would take it for up to a year, Steve, so this is not a forever proposition, whatever number of months that I think it is necessary to make sure that files like the wind turbine sitings, the horseracing industry, at least getting on a path to making sure that the regulations that are getting in the way of our agriculture, whatever those are — our agrifood industry — I want to make sure that we are at least examining those things, and I want that directed from the premier's office.

Q. How is it going to feel the first time somebody calls you premier?

A. I probably won't turn my head.

Q. You'll be looking for Dalton.

A. I'll be looking for Dalton. Exactly, exactly.

Q. The candidate you were on Day One and the candidate you are today, those are two different people; I don't know if you appreciate that or know that, but —

A. Well, thank you.

Q. — you all improved considerably, and you did, too.

A. Somebody said to me that a leader is forged through a process like this, and I do feel that … I do feel that confidence. It is not arrogance, it is just a sort of solid belief in what I can do, and so I am really happy to be able to bring that to the province.

Q. That's Kathleen Wynne, incoming premier, twenty-fifth premier in the history of the province of Ontario and — need we say it? — the first woman to ever have the job. Thanks so much for stopping by.

A. Thank you. Thanks, Steve.

The history-making nature of Wynne's victory continued two weeks later when she was sworn in as premier. "I'm here to accept the profound honour of this office," she told the overflow galleries in the legislative chamber. "And it has not escaped my notice that I'm the first woman to have this job." But Wynne wasn't finished. She went on to thank her partner Jane — "the woman I love" — before swearing in Deb Matthews as deputy premier and health minister, and Liz Sandals as education minister. In other words, four of the top five jobs in Wynne's government (not to mention $67 billion in program spending) were staffed by women, and that was unprecedented too.

Jaime Watt, an original member of Mike Harris' *Common Sense Revolution* and himself an openly gay man, was watching from one of the public galleries. He tweeted, "Just watched Premier Wynne and her partner, Jane, walk into the Ont Leg with the LG. Never let anyone say it isn't a big deal."

People just couldn't say it. Because it was. Actually, it was a very big deal.

But of course, despite the historic nature of Wynne's achievement to get to that day, the *really* hard work was just beginning.

THE EX-PREMIERS
David Peterson, Bob Rae,
Mike Harris, Ernie Eves
October 11, 2006

O ne of the programs I'd always had a hankering to do was one with all the living ex-premiers of Ontario on at once. Yes, I'd been told numerous times it could never happen, and for perfectly good reasons. These were some of the busiest men in the country, they sat on numerous boards, were constantly travelling, and the demands on their time were already outrageous.

Still, I thought a program that could share the collective wisdom of the five ex-premiers (at the time) about their very different experiences in the premier's chair could be very useful to our viewers. So I set out to try to make it happen.

Much to my delight, most of them were quite open to doing it. That surprised me because one could scarcely find a group of former politicians who seemed to like each other less than these ex-premiers. And they all had perfectly legitimate reasons not to want to spend any time together. David Peterson and Bob Rae fought three elections against each other (1985, 1987, 1990). They found common cause to sign an "Accord" after the first, Peterson romped to victory in the second, but Rae got his revenge with an historic upset in the third. They'd gone after each other hammer and tong across the floor of the Legislature for too many years to be friends. Even Bob Rae's switch to the Liberal Party of Canada and his plans to get back into politics didn't ameliorate the rough edges there.

Then there was the Bob Rae–Mike Harris relationship. Rae beat Harris in 1990, but Harris took the next election in 1995, then spent the next eight years trying to undo everything Rae accomplished. In his first few months in office, Harris rolled back Rae's welfare rates by 22 percent, eliminated Bill 40 (the anti-scab legislation), cancelled photo radar on the major highways, and started filling in the tunnels in Toronto that Rae's government had hoped to put subways in. Much of question period is show biz, but the antipathy between these two wasn't.

And then, interestingly enough, there was the Mike Harris–Ernie Eves relationship. Despite the fact they were great pals and colleagues for more than two decades in public life, there was now considerable frost on the friendship. Harris thought Eves repudiated too much of the *Common Sense Revolution*. Harris was particularly miffed that Eves reversed his energy deregulation policies.

Also, Eves had developed quite a tart tongue while in public life. It made for some wonderfully outrageous speeches, but also alienated him from those who were the target. One night at what was supposed to be a celebratory dinner in Harris' honour at the Royal Ontario Museum, Eves

Peterson, Paikin, and Rae, March 2004.

(who was premier at the time) got into the middle of a stem-winder of a speech and let 'er rip. He roasted Harris quite viciously, even teasing his predecessor that he'd have to pay his own legal bills if he found himself testifying at a public inquiry into Ipperwash. (In September 1995, just three months after Harris became premier, Dudley George was killed in the Ipperwash Provincial Park, after a protest between First-Nations and the Ontario Provincial Police went horribly wrong.) Much of the audience was horrified but sloughed it off as "Ernie being Ernie."

Finally, William Davis required the most convincing to appear. He had done precious few television interviews about politics since leaving public life more than two decades earlier. And despite two trips to his office to try to convince him to come on with his colleagues, I wasn't making much headway. Ironically, Davis and Rae got on famously (and still have a warm relationship). He got on with Eves well enough. He disliked Peterson because of how tough Peterson was on Rae. But the greatest antipathy he had was for Harris, whom Davis thought was outside the mainstream of past moderate Progressive Conservative leaders. The feeling was mutual. Harris thought Davis' conservatism was squishy and too tolerant of special interests.

But to their great credit, despite all that tension percolating just under the surface, four of the ex-premiers showed up to our TVO studios on October 11, 2006, to talk about a life in politics. Davis had actually agreed to do it, then took sick the night before and had to cancel. (At age seventy-seven and fighting numerous battles with ill health over the years, we all understood and no one thought he was bailing for any other reason.)

There's a tradition at television stations that what happens in the "green room" — the room where guests wait before going on the air — is off the record. And while I will respect that tradition here, let me simply say I was struck by how cordial the four ex-premiers were to each other while waiting for the taping to begin. These four men had almost never been in the same place at the same time (unless it was a political function, in which case there'd be hundreds of other people there too and they could easily avoid one another). But they all made small talk quite effortlessly, inquired about each other's careers and families, and cracked the odd joke too.

Behind the scenes, there were two items of business that concerned our editorial team at TVO. First, on the set, who would sit beside whom?

Given all the intricacies described above, could we really put Peterson beside Rae? Or Eves beside Harris? Or Rae beside Harris? Believe it or not, a lot of consideration goes into guest placement. Get it right and you can add just the right energy and excitement to a discussion. Get it wrong and your guests can shut down and completely ruin a show. So we had to figure that out.

In addition, how should we introduce the former premiers, and in what order? Should we indicate what elections they'd won or lost? Should we introduce them in order of most success to least success (Harris and Peterson had both won two, lost one; Rae was 1–3; Eves was 0–1). If we did that, would we get Eves off to an uncomfortable start because unlike all the others, he'd never won an election as leader?

This may seem silly, but these are all things one has to consider every night on *The Agenda*, because one wants to create the best possible conditions to make the guests feel as comfortable as possible, so they'll perform as well as they can.

Ultimately, I decided to keep it as simple as possible. We would seat them in the order in which they held the office. And we would introduce them with as little fanfare as possible. It was clean, simple, and no one could suggest we were favouring or minimizing anyone's accomplishments.

Happily, all of our concerns about a lack of chemistry among the ex-premiers turned out to be for naught. They engaged beautifully with each other, displayed a self-deprecating sense of humour, and revealed anecdotes and personal concerns they'd never shared publicly before.

It was one of my proudest moments in journalism because I knew only TVO could bring these men together for an hour-long, commercial-free conversation about life "in the arena."

MR. PAIKIN: Good evening, everybody. Thanks for being with us tonight. Joining us now, Ernie Eves, the twenty-third premier of the province of Ontario; Mike Harris, the twenty-second premier of the province of Ontario; Bob Rae, the twenty-first premier of the province of Ontario; and David Peterson, the twentieth premier of the province of Ontario.

We are very happy to have you four here. We want to add, however, that we are so sorry this morning to have gotten a call from Kathy Davis,

Bill Davis' wife, saying that he was really under the weather, wanted to be here, wasn't able to be here. It was not, I think, out of fear of jousting with any of you four, but —

MR. EVES: I'm sure not.

MR. PETERSON: Surely not this kid.

MR. PAIKIN: — but we wish him well obviously, a speedy recovery, and we miss him today.

I want to start with when you all start thinking about getting the job you all had. I think the public is under the impression that perhaps not in the womb, but shortly thereafter, you start thinking about becoming premier.

Is that the case, David Peterson?

MR. PETERSON: Absolutely not. My life is just a case of happy accidents. Just things just happened to me, and there was really no great malice afore-thought or planning. It just kind of happened. I remember when — after I was elected the first time in 1975, the press came to me and said, "Are you going to run for the leadership?" after Bob Nixon resigned. And I said, "Geez, I haven't even found the washroom in Queen's Park. How can I do that?" But I did and almost won [in 1976].

MR. PAIKIN: Bob Rae, you no doubt thought about being premier from the time you were one year old.

MR. RAE: No, not at all. In fact, I didn't really think about being premier until about September the 5th, 1990. I mean, when I went into provincial politics I always thought it was a chance that I'd be premier, but some people said I would never be premier. But I never thought it was a likelihood and I think I've talked on this program a couple of times how, in the spring of 1990, I decided to leave politics. And my brother died the year before and, for a variety of reasons, I thought it was time for me to go. I'm sure a number of other people thought that as well.

So when the election was called, I was thinking to myself, "It's going to be the last election." But there you are. I mean, I think I always felt that it would be a great honour to be premier but you're leader of the third party, as I was when I started, it's not something you necessarily think is your destiny, bound to happen.

MR. PAIKIN: The guy sitting beside you was also leader of the third party when he became premier. Did you, when you were leading a third-place party?

MR. HARRIS: Absolutely not.

MR. PAIKIN: No?

MR. HARRIS: I'm like David. Things happen in your life. Never did I dream that I would be a politician, that I would be an MPP, that I was happy with my little life in North Bay. I was running a golf course. I was running a ski hill. I was chairman of the school board and I thought, "Life doesn't get any better than this." Maybe I was right.

MR. PAIKIN: You actually quit politics. You left.

MR. EVES: I did.

MR. PAIKIN: So did you at that point in your life think that you ever wanted to be premier? I mean, you were gone, after all.

MR. EVES: No. I thought for sure my good friend Michael was going to stay and run at least one more time, and I thought it was a time to do something else in my life. I had contributed almost twenty years of my life to public service.

But public service, I think, is how we probably all got there in the first place. I think that 99.9 percent of the people who get into public life — this may shock the public out there — are actually there for the right reasons.

MR. PAIKIN: We're very interested in that 0.1 percent, though, aren't we?

MR. EVES: And — yeah, you seem to hone in on that 0.1 percent.

My family was fairly apolitical. My grandfather actually was a friend and supporter of Paul Martin's in Windsor, Ontario. So it's a small world and one thing leads to another.

MR. PETERSON: You do have some redeeming qualities.

MR. EVES: You'll be happy to hear that.

MR. PETERSON: You should have told people about this before, Ernie.

MR. PAIKIN: Well, let's show some tape here, shall we? David Peterson, do you want to see what you looked like in 1982?

MR. PETERSON: God, I am embarrassed; it's just like Dorian Gray, is it?

MR. PAIKIN: Here's David Peterson winning the leadership of the Liberal Party of Ontario in 1982. Roll tape.

> *MR. PETERSON: I am optimistic about the future and with this great party, with this team of candidates and with these people in the cabinet, with your help and your talents and your energy and commitment over the next three years, ladies and gentlemen, I am confident that we can form the government. I thank you, very much.*

MR. PETERSON: Do you mind running that again, Steven? I liked that.

MR. PAIKIN: Do you even recognize that guy?

MR. PETERSON: Boy, good looking fellow, eh?

MR. HARRIS: Did you really believe that, David, that you were confident that you were going to actually form the government?

MR. PETERSON: No. Actually, my mother wouldn't have believed we would form the government.

MR. PAIKIN: Leadership conventions — and one of you is going through it again right now [Rae] — leadership conventions can be awfully nasty business. At the end of the day, what's the impression you're left with running for the leadership of a party?

MR. PETERSON: They're tough. It's an internal war, you know, and emotions are felt very strongly. Some parties never recover from that. I think you can argue that the federal Liberal Party didn't recover and it is just going through the process now of recovering from that with a new race and a lot of new people and new energies and new ideas and without the baggage of the past, which is probably a good thing.

MR. PAIKIN: Unless you win big, and you all won your respective leadership conventions, if I can say it, relatively easily.

MR. RAE: No, I still think David's right that I think the hard part about a party convention is that you're asking people that you've known or in some context you've worked with to say, you know, "Why don't you think I should be the person? Why should it be the other one?"

In an election, you've got philosophies, you've got different camps, you're arguing against people and it's easier. There's a kind of a — the sting of partisanship actually allows you to say and do things that, in the context of inside a party, is harder. And I do think there's a sense internally, of people saying, "Well, I remember so-and-so and I didn't get it and I should have gotten it." It is a process to go through and I think you have to work hard as a leader.

I mean, one of the first things that you have to do as a leader when you win a convention is to really work hard with the people who didn't win and say, "How can we create the team here that's going to be bigger than any one of us?"

MR. HARRIS: There's two things that dictate this. There's the people that are running, how they campaigned, how they run, how they handle themselves after the convention for the good of the new leader, for the good of the party. In my case, it was with Dianne Cunningham. She was marvellous and it was very easy.

There is a second thing. There is process. Our party went through a delegated convention, a very bitter one that [Frank] Miller won [in 1985], and then another with Larry Grossman.

MR. PAIKIN: Twice in one year.

MR. HARRIS: Right. And there were great divisions in there, as there were in the Liberal Party with the Martinites and the Chrétienites.

The process helped as well. The one member, one vote ... everybody having a say. No longer were you able to influence delegates, so to speak, and the arm-twisting and the backroom side of it.

MR. PAIKIN: Not quite as interesting to watch though.

MR. HARRIS: It's terrible TV.

MR. PAIKIN: Yes, it is.

MR. HARRIS: But it was good politics from a point of view of selling memberships, of broadening the party, and of having a less bitter race, in my view.

MR. PAIKIN: You, like the others, won relatively easily. I mean, you wouldn't say so today.

MR. EVES: No, I wouldn't say that.

MR. PAIKIN: But it didn't go to five or six ballots or something, right? It was over pretty quickly. Does that help bring things together afterward?

MR. EVES: It does in a way. I agree with Michael's point about the process certainly helped quite a bit. I think when you do have, although it's not as exciting for the media, I understand that. But I think it is a more democratic way of electing a leader and I also think that it helps that you're out there in that process as opposed to trying to lobby ten or twelve or fourteen delegates from each riding.

I also think there's another aspect to this — I think we all in public life understand that there are some nasty things that go on. I think, however, people that work for you in whatever particular leadership campaign sometimes get a little carried away and that certainly builds up animosities that don't need to exist necessarily.

MR. PAIKIN: I want to talk about family, because one of the things we often hear from people who are in public life, they say that members of the general public have no clue what kind of sacrifices have to be made in terms of family life. And we often hear when people leave public life, the first thing they say is, "I'm going to get a chance to spend more time with my family."

I remember Bill Davis once telling me that he sees his grandchildren more than he ever saw his own kids because he was premier when he had little kids and now, of course, after being out of politics, it's easier.

I want to play some tape from Kathy Davis, his wife, and from Neil Davis, his son, on how Mr. Davis, in his day, balanced family life, and then we'll come back and talk. Roll tape, please.

> *MR. PAIKIN: He was, by the standards of today's fathers, not pulling his weight around this house, was he?*
>
> *MRS. DAVIS: No.*
>
> *MR. PAIKIN: I mean, he brags about the fact that he has never changed a diaper in his life.*
>
> *MRS. DAVIS: He was definitely an absentee father.*
>
> *NEIL DAVIS: He was a terrific father but he didn't have the time to devote to us that other fathers had. And he has more time now, so he spends quite a bit of time with his*

grandchildren, I think making up a little bit for the time he missed with us.

MRS. DAVIS: *We did have a rule that the kids would be at the breakfast table and he would appear every morning, and he did. And we had breakfast together because we never had evening meals together. Other families don't eat break-fast together, but have supper together. So we sort of turned that around and that was helpful. There was a period of time every day when they had access to Bill.*

MR. PAIKIN: Mr. Peterson, when you were premier you had three little kids. And I want to ask, in retrospect, was the personal sacrifice worth the public achievements you did in the job?

MR. PETERSON: Don't get the impression this is a horrible, huge sacrifice. You can do all of these things if you have the energy for it. I must say, in my case, my kids were first in my life. I scheduled in their hockey games and their days at school and that kind of thing. There was nothing else in our lives, in Shelley and my lives; it was the kids and work and her work as well.

But I remember Bill Davis. Interesting. Soon after I assumed the leadership of the party, and who knows where it was going to go — he said to me and we were talking about [Davis' predecessor] John Robarts, who he loved and I loved. I was from London, Ontario. But he said, "I'm going to give you some free advice, David. Always go home at night." And I brought Shelley and the kids, and I had two kids then, to Toronto. We had a one-bedroom apartment. One kid had a crib in our bedroom. The other kid slept in a drawer. And we were together as a family.

And every Friday night we would get in the station wagon with the dog, drive back to London, drive back Sunday night. Every single Sunday night that I was in public life, we had Sunday dinner at the McDonald's in Kitchener on the 401. But we were together. And we would talk and play games and all of that kind of stuff.

My kids are pretty terrific and we spent a lot of time with them and Shelley is a fabulous mom.

But I think the kids do suffer somewhat because people criticize them for the mistakes of their father and people can be harsh. But the flip side is it opens a lot of other avenues to these kids. It opens perspectives. They see things they wouldn't in another world.

So I don't think we have any right to feel sorry for ourselves. I think it's our responsibility as family people to make those things work, and I think it can work. And I think I know many, many examples where it has worked extremely well.

MR. PAIKIN: Mr. Rae?

MR. RAE: I think my life's not that different from David's. My kids are a little bit younger than David's, but they were very young when I started in politics. I mean, Judith was born just before I won the convention and then, you know, the kids grew up the whole time I was in politics in Ontario.

We lived in the same house we always lived in, lived in Toronto, which is a big advantage because you didn't have to worry about commuting, which is I think a real problem. When people are living in Thunder Bay or even in North Bay and you're travelling back and forth and you've got that constant two homes going, it's tough.

MR. PAIKIN: Do you think your kids would agree with this analysis?

MR. RAE: Yes, I do. I absolutely do. And, in fact, we've talked about it quite a bit. I mean, they're in school, right? And, who knows what kids say to them about, "What your dad's up to?" and whatever the hell else is going on.

MR. PAIKIN: I think we do know.

MR. RAE: We know a couple of the comments that have been made. But, you know, I remember once we were having a big fight in the House about Christmas recess, right? And I had committed that we were going to go down to Florida for two weeks with the kids, and I went. And some of my caucus colleagues were very upset because we were supposed to stay and fight. And I said, "Look, I'm not in favour of prolonging this thing. Let's get it over with. We've all got families and life."

But we also did things as the House through the eighties that I think did change things. I mean, the sort of image of the hard-drinking, the Mitch Hepburns taking over a floor of the King Eddy Hotel, and that was the life for a period of time in the thirties and forties and that's what you did —

MR. PETERSON: And fifties and sixties.

MR. RAE: And sixties and whatever else.

MR. PETERSON: Not the seventies when we were all there.

MR. RAE: No, no. But I'm just saying when we got rid of night sittings, it was not unusual for me to go home and say, "That's it. I'm done." Home — I'd get home at seven o'clock, 7:30, eight o'clock, and you're done.

MR. PAIKIN: And it must have been harder for Mike Harris, because your home was four hours away.

MR. HARRIS: Listen, I'm more on the side here of David and Bob. Truck drivers had it tougher than I did, on the road for five days. Travelling salesmen, CEOs of worldwide companies.

MR. PAIKIN: That's all true. They don't write about it in the newspaper. They're not accountable to the same number of groups that you are.

MR. HARRIS: Well, that's true. But that's a different issue. There's no secret that education reforms during my term caused my kids a fair bit of grief at school, from a small minority of teachers and a whole bunch of kids. I mean, that's the way kids are.

But I'll tell you, it's a huge net positive. I mean, learning that not everybody loves your dad is a pretty good lesson in life.

MR. PETERSON: Trust my kids; it is the easiest lesson.

MR. HARRIS: Well, that's right. The advantages that you have, and I agree, you make it work. You travel with them. You find those times. But I think it's wrong for anybody to say, "Well, I can't go into politics."

And I used to tell candidates that. They'd say, "I can't go into politics now. I've got young kids." Well, you talk to young lawyers. I mean, you know, with a young family, these guys have got to work eighty, ninety hours in the financial community. It's a public life. That's what different.

MR. EVES: I think the big difference is the last comment Michael just made, and that is, it is a public life. Everything you do is now open to the public. And it takes you a while to adjust to that and to accept that, and that sometimes I think family members find it more difficult to adjust to than the members themselves.

But I agree, it's a double-edged sword. You certainly have more exposure, your children do, to things that they would never be exposed to.

I know Natalie was five and Justin was eight when I was first elected, and Natalie conducted an election in her kindergarten class, which I won quite easily instead of by six votes in a recount; I wish they were all that easy.

MR. PETERSON: As good as it gets.

MR. EVES: But they both did get very involved and interested in the political process. I can remember Justin actually did a few ads for me in the '95 campaign. And they asked some of the questions that you were talking to Neil Davis about. And he said, "Lookit, my dad's always there when he has to be. When there are big things to be done, he makes a point to be there."

MR. PAIKIN: I wonder if any of you would want your kids to go into politics?

MR. RAE: Absolutely.

MR. PAIKIN: You would?

MR. RAE: Without any hesitation. If they wanted to. I mean, only if they wanted to. The one thing you do have to be prepared for is the publicity. If you're not prepared to live at least part of your life in public and manage the kind of criticism and the fish-bowl aspect of it, then that's hard. But everything else, every other part of it — you're doing a public service, the excitement of it, the fact that you're able to make some decisions, you're getting into the great arguments about ideas and about public policy, I mean, it's a fantastic life.

MR. PAIKIN: Well, let me follow up on that because I want to move into a part of our discussion now about actually doing the job, and I've always wondered what it is like. I mean, David Peterson, you took over in the premier's office in 1985. I want to know what that moment is like when you walk into that office that has been occupied by some pretty legendary figures over the years and you actually sit down in that chair and you look at that desk and you think, "I'm one of," in your case, "twenty people who have had this job." What goes through your head?

MR. PETERSON: You're going to accuse me of gross arrogance, but I remember that moment. I remember it very, very well. And I walked in and I sat down and I said to myself, "I feel very, very comfortable." I wasn't filled with trepidation. I had a fabulous team. Even though it wasn't that we had an experienced team. We'd never had anybody that had been on the government side before, but we had very capable people, knew what we were going to do and we started doing it. And I felt very comfortable. I wasn't daunted by it, I wasn't over-awed by it.

And the truth is, politicians are just ordinary people who by chance or circumstance or luck end up where they are because they've taken some risks in their own lives.

MR. PAIKIN: Mr. Rae, you never expected to be in that chair. When you sat in it, what did you think?

MR. RAE: Well, the room was pretty empty when I got there, so ...

MR. PETERSON: You missed all your people, or what?

MR. RAE: No, no, no, no.

MR. PETERSON: They all ran away?

MR. HARRIS: David took everything with him.

MR. RAE: Thank you, David.

MR. HARRIS: He took all the furniture?

MR. RAE: Thank you, David, for asking, but no, that wasn't the problem.

MR. HARRIS: He was so comfortable with that furniture he took it all with him.

MR. RAE: No. I guess for me there was a sense of genuine surprise. The election result itself was a bit of a surprise. I could say it took me a year to feel comfortable in the job. I don't mind saying that.

But I certainly feel a good sense of honour. You say, "Well, you know, here we are. We've done it. Now let's get on with it."

The great thing about living in our democracy is you haven't got very many people around you who are saying, "You know well, sir." You've got the scrum outside and they're waiting to see you and they're going to ask you a question about where did you buy your shoes yesterday and that's what you have to get used to.

MR. PAIKIN: Mr. Harris, if you had a dollar for every time somebody told you you'd never be premier you'd be a very rich man today.

MR. HARRIS: Yes, I'd be wealthy. We'd all be wealthy except for Ernie Eves. He knew when he won the leadership —

MR. PAIKIN: He knew he was going to be premier. When you sat in the chair, do you remember what you thought?

MR. HARRIS: Contrary to David, I was scared. I was nervous. I was scared silly. I thought, "Okay. Here I am. Now what?" And I knew it was a daunting task ahead. It didn't take me long to get into it and, as Bob says, pretty soon you're out there in the scrum. But I was nervous.

MR. PAIKIN: Could you afford to share that view with anybody?

MR. HARRIS: Of course not. Nobody. Perhaps my family. My father, who I used to confide in.

MR. PAIKIN: What did your dad tell you when you told him that?

MR. HARRIS: Well, the same advice that he gave me when I was scared going into the election, and the night before the debate. I had to debate two giant debaters — the first debate that I had. To just be yourself. "You can do it." He always had a great deal of faith and confidence in me and it was reassuring and he helped me through a lot of that part of my career.

MR. PAIKIN: How about you? When you won your leadership convention, you obviously knew you were going to be premier. Does that make it different?

MR. EVES: I had been in the premier's office many times, mostly hauled up on the carpet by my good friend Michael, but I would say there's a great sense of pride and privilege and honour. Very few people get the opportunity to lead a government in our democratic society and I really considered it to be an honour and a privilege.

Michael may recall this when I mention it — he and I having a discussion one night. We had a very difficult agenda when we first started our tenure as government. We did a lot of things that weren't very popular. And I can recall him in the middle of a cabinet meeting — he and I taking a bit of a break and going into his office and his saying, "You know, do you have problems sleeping at night?" because there are some very tough decisions that have to be made.

MR. PAIKIN: Did you have trouble sleeping at night?

MR. EVES: I think we all probably had, if anyone will be direct about it, from time to time. These are not easy decisions. Sure, once you make a decision you go on and you implement it and you do it to the best of your ability. But we are human beings.

MR. PAIKIN: I wonder who premiers take advice from and, in particular, whether they take advice from people who previously had the job. Did you ever call any of your predecessors or did they call you and say … whatever?

MR. PETERSON: On certain issues Bill Davis was — I valued his advice on certain national issues, constitutional issues, or issues of judgments with respect to other personalities you had to deal with across the country.

MR. PAIKIN: How did that work though? Would you call him?

MR. PETERSON: I'd run into him or — it was more informal than formal, but he was pretty wise about dealing with some of these things. He had different approaches and different ways of doing things than I did.

MR. PAIKIN: It didn't bother you that he was in a different party?

MR. PETERSON: No, no, no. You know, Steven, I think one of the things you will find when you get out of the partisan game, partisanship fades away and friendship tends to take over. I mean, you're talking to four former first ministers of Ontario but you could be talking to the same former first ministers right across this nation. We all know each other. We've been engaged in debates, and these are Tories, NDPs, separatists, whatever, and there's a friendship and common purpose that's stronger than the partisanship today. I really believe that.

MR. EVES: Yes, absolutely.

MR. PAIKIN: Mr. Rae, but given the way you came to office, defeating the guy beside you, my hunch is you didn't call him for advice.

MR. RAE: Not a lot at first, but a little bit more later on when we were dealing with the constitutional issues. Definitely. I spent a lot of time talking to Bill Davis, and Bill Davis had been a friend when I got into Parliament, when I got into the Legislature, and he was leader of the government. And we established a very good personal relationship and that's maintained to this day.

And I still think he's got great judgment about issues and people and he was very good about things like — it sounds stupid, but it's the simple stuff, like, "Only do so much in a day," you know, "Take care of yourself a little bit in terms of dealing with crises." The sort of things that Ernie was talking about, sleeping, because there are times when you lose sleep and if you lose sleep, you're not performing well. These are just sort of basic health issues you've got to deal with.

After I got to know them better … the first few months in office, I found talking to other first ministers was very, very helpful. I had friends and Joe Ghiz was a great friend of David's and of mine, and I admired him a lot.

MR. PAIKIN: The premier of PEI.

MR. RAE: The premier of Prince Edward Island. I spent a lot of time with him. I talked a lot with Roy Romanow and Mike Harcourt when they got into office, but certainly Gary Filmon from Manitoba over time became a very good friend. We would spend a lot of time at premiers' meetings just chatting about, "Well, how do you deal with this?" or, "What do you think about that?" or, "How are you going to face up to this problem?"

You know, the issues we have in common in terms of education and health care. Also, issues of people management. "Well, you know, was it a big cabinet? Is it a small cabinet? What do you do with people who are this or that? How do you deal with …"

But there are so many common problems and I think it's learning. As you get more comfortable in the job, you become much more at ease with talking to other people about, "Well, how do you make this decision? What did you do that for? How would you do it that way?" and you start to really admire people.

I think every other premier admired Frank McKenna for the way in which he was able to make decisions and for his ability to focus on some of the key issues facing his province. Given the amount of time that Frank used to spend in Toronto in those days, you would get to see him quite a lot.

MR. PAIKIN: Mr. Harris, what previous premiers would you have called? You never would have called Bob Rae for advice, would you?

MR. HARRIS: Bob and I chat. Again, I would say it would be more later on.

MR. RAE: In the constitutional stuff, at the beginning.

MR. HARRIS: The constitutional stuff.

MR. PAIKIN: How does the bitterness of election losses or victories that one would [have] overcome all of that?

MR. HARRIS: Well, I don't know how much bitterness there is. There's disappointment. When it came to the referendum, which was shortly after my watch, it's the commonality of purpose and of what we all agreed was important. And we were united on that issue, and there's many issues we would have been united on. And that helps overcome any of the disagreements of the past.

MR. PAIKIN: I wonder, Bob Rae, if I'm right in saying that … Mike Harris takes over June 1995. There's a referendum in October of 1995 where the future of the country is at stake. And you've been premier for the previous five years and obviously think you've got a pretty good handle on these issues, and the guy beside you had been premier for five years and had his Meech Lake adventure as well.

Do you not at some point in your inner recesses think, "I could be handling this way better than this guy and unfortunately he's there and I'm not?"

MR. RAE: No. I mean, no. Because it's a futile expenditure of emotion. I went over to Mike's office at his request when I was still in the house and we went over and we talked about the issue. Mike was giving a speech at the Canadian Club and/or the Empire Club, one of those places — and said, "What do you think?" I said, "Well, I'll do whatever you like." He said, "I'd like you to be on the podium with me." I said, "I'll be on the podium with you." He says he wants Ontario to be expressing itself in a clear way. I said, "I think that's very important for that to happen."

MR. HARRIS: He helped write the speech.

MR. RAE: He asked me for advice on, "What should I say?" and I said, "Well, I'll go home and write you some stuff," and some of it was in the speech.

I don't regard that as a strange thing. I mean, to me that's what you would expect your politicians to do at a moment of national crisis.

MR. PAIKIN: Okay. Ernie Eves, can you give me an example of a time you would have called one of your predecessors and what the issue would have been about?

MR. EVES: I have talked to everybody here at one time or another. David gave me advice at a Christmas party at my house and I thought it was very good advice, quite frankly.

MR. PAIKIN: What was it about?

MR. EVES: To look at the broad picture, to not get too caught up in the details. And his comment to me was that if he had to do it all over again he might take more time looking at the broad picture. That was helpful advice.

I talked to Bob many times. I don't know if he remembers this but when we were in opposition and you were the government. [Willowdale MPP] Charlie Harnick and I were members of the constitutional committee that travelled around the country. And he literally would not start a meeting without me being there, and sought out advice and asked me what I thought.

And Michael, of course, had been a great personal friend and provided a lot of advice to me, both when I was finance minister and premier.

I relied upon Premier Davis many, many times. I think that we all agree that we really respect his perspective of public service and he was always somebody you could go to.

MR. HARRIS: I think it is fair to say one thing: We say we're not different. There is something different about being premier. I would say that seeking out other premiers' opinions and those who had had the file probably took place a lot more than just a cabinet-minister level or a caucus member. I mean, the non-partisan nature — and perhaps, David, you alluded to the first ministers' meetings. We had a lot of common cause. Some of them were beating up on the federal government but there were a lot of commonality and we got to know each other pretty well.

And so I think it is a club that is exclusive and it is a club that … if I consulted a former premier, I never once felt that was going to leak into the press or that I would be betrayed in that, whereas I don't think I would have had that same confidence with some ministers or some others. There was just a certain respect there.

MR. PETERSON: Just to illustrate Michael's point, probably the most intense experience of my political life involved the constitutional negotiations. And Bob was there. Bob was leader of the opposition and Bob was invited around, and included in all the briefings. His advice was sought. And so was — Michael, you were there, too.

MR. HARRIS: Yes, I was there too, yes.

MR. PETERSON: And I didn't consider it a partisan issue. I viewed it then, as I still view it, as probably one of the most important issues in the history of the country. But I made friends out of that. You know, the Peter Lougheeds, the Don Gettys, the Gary Filmons, the Frank McKennas. Robert Bourassa was a very dear friend of mine, and the guy that really let everybody, the country, down, was a Liberal — Clyde Wells — in my opinion.

I realize that not everybody shares my view on that, but the point is, it wasn't partisan. There were many, many issues way beyond our partisanship, our political affiliation or our provincial affiliation; it was about this country. And somehow or other, a lot of good people rallied around that flag at a lot of important times in the history of this Canada, of this country. And I include my three friends here in that.

MR. PAIKIN: I know all of you have talked today about the parts of the job that you loved the most. I would like to get a little sense about what the necessary evils are in being premier that you really couldn't stand to do.

Bob Rae, what was something on the job you really didn't like doing?

MR. RAE: Firing people, dealing with personnel problems, dealing with any cabinet change. Sometimes you just make a change because you've got to make a change. That's always very stressful.

You're also responsible for appointing deputies, so do you need to make a change in the deputy minister's people? Do you have to make some difficult decisions with respect to people's personal conduct or something that's happened? I don't think anybody enjoys those experiences.

The premier who is not here [William Davis] told me that he thought it was the worst part of the job, without any question. In fact, the late Eddie Goodman used to tell me that he did it for him. So I don't know whether that's true or not, but I do know that I think that's the toughest. It goes with the territory. You have to do it ...

MR. PAIKIN: Firing Peter Kormos was really hard?

MR. RAE: Well, no. Some of them are easier than others, but I think it's getting used to doing that and knowing how to do it well and then moving on quickly because the one thing about this job is you can't afford too much time for remorse or second thoughts or what if? You can't. You've just got to get on with it and do it. And the day you do, the next day you're up in the house saying it was the greatest thing in the world and it was fine and it was intelligent.

MR. PAIKIN: The hardest part of the job, Mike Harris?

MR. HARRIS: Well, I think Bob has touched on part of it. What is different, I think, from most companies and most CEOs is that we are also the chief spokesman for your party in critiquing the other leaders come election time. So you're the one that's to point out Bob Rae's weaknesses. You're the one that's to point out all the things that he's terrible at.

MR. PAIKIN: You didn't like doing that?

MR. RAE: You never had any trouble doing it.

MR. HARRIS: I don't want to get into how much was there, but that's not fun. You don't see the CEO of Burger King going out running down McDonald's.

MR. PAIKIN: Let's take a look at what — we had a good laugh seeing what David Peterson looked like in 1982.

MR. PETERSON: Laugh?

MR. PAIKIN: How about Ernie Eves in 1995?

MR. PETERSON: I didn't laugh.

MR. HARRIS: We all laughed, though.

MR. PAIKIN: I know, you were a magnificent Adonis. I know.

MR. PETERSON: I am going to laugh …

MR. PAIKIN: Here's Ernie Eves, eleven years ago, when he was Mike Harris' finance minister. And we want to talk about tough parts of the job, you came in and, I think in the first couple of months of the job, you had cut more than two and a half billion dollars worth of spending like that. And not everybody thought it was a great idea.

MR. EVES: That's true.

MR. HARRIS: That's when we weren't sleeping too good.

MR. PAIKIN: Roll tape.

> MR. EVES: *Our government has a renewal plan for Ontario that will restore our financial and social well-being through economic stability and job creation. The plan is based on three building blocks: balancing the budget and squarely facing grave personal and economic costs of high levels of debt.*

MR. PAIKIN: First of all, should I ask you about the hair?

MR. EVES: The hair?

MR. PAIKIN: No, let's move on.

MR. EVES: The hair's changed a bit.

MR. PAIKIN: It has. Everybody assumes that it's hard to do what you did. I know you thought it was necessary to do. When you look back at it, was it as difficult as we thought at the time?

MR. EVES: It was difficult, but the thing that helped us, of course, is we had a very good plan, I felt, that you could follow. I think if you get elected and you don't have a plan I think it may be a lot more difficult. But I really thought that, you know, we did it fairly well, if I do say so myself. Although a lot of decisions were not easy because you're affecting people's lives.

MR. PAIKIN: Was it easier to become premier? None of these three had any experience in government before they became premier; you did. You were a finance minister, which is about as close as you get. Did that making being premier easier?

MR. EVES: In a way, it did. In a way, it did not.
The way it did, because you had been exposed to … and Mike included me in many, many things so I was all part of those discussions and decisions.

However, the part that made it more difficult, I think, is that sometimes you know too much. I mean, you know all the intricacies of finance of all the ministries of the government and you get bogged down in detail as opposed to looking at the broad picture and the broader perspective.

So I would say again it was — there's two sides to the coin.

MR. PAIKIN: Worst part of the job, David Peterson?

MR. PETERSON: I was thinking about that when Michael and Bob were talking and I actually agree with them. But I think the harder part for me was it was just this constant, unbearing scrutiny. You come in, in the morning, and there's guys trying to beat you up. You leave at night and you go into question period and they want to beat you up. And then —

MR. PAIKIN: So it was the media and the opposition?

MR. HARRIS: Mostly media, right?

MR. PETERSON: It was all of that.

MR. HARRIS: It was the media; they were the worst.

MR. PETERSON: Well, it's a combination of all of that. You're always on display and there's a lot of "gotcha" stuff in politics.

MR. PAIKIN: Did you accept that as part of the theatre of the job?

MR. PETERSON: Yes. Absolutely. I'm not whining about this, but I don't miss that part of politics at all, that — that endless scrutiny —

MR. EVES: Absolutely.

MR. PETERSON: — trying to prove you're stupid or jump on you or go after you. And people have to understand this. I use this analogy: When you're the first minister you have all of the responsibility for everything.

And half of the people, by definition, do not like you, would like you out of there, and would like to make you look stupid.

And there's so much violent criticism of each other in this business, it's no wonder people have so little respect for the system ...

MR. PAIKIN: So why don't you all tone it down?

MR. PETERSON: I hate to tell you, Steven, it's been going on for four hundred years. This is nothing new about this, but we just see it all now with television and instantaneous transmission of all this. And we're so hard on ourselves when we're involved in the partisan game, it's no wonder that most people think that politicians are not very nice people or self-serving or stupid or incompetent or crooks.

MR. RAE: Charlie Krauthammer is a friend of mine; he's an American journalist, Canadian-born, who once said to me — and it's really Mike's point about Burger King — but he said, "If Ford and General Motors ran their business the way politicians run their business, nobody would buy cars because Ford would be saying GM is a terrible product and GM would be saying Ford's a terrible product and, by the end of it, everybody rides a bike."

I mean, I think that really is part of what has happened to the culture of politics is simply a product of the adversarial system and that is if you are building yourself up and you are also criticizing the opponent.

But there is the additional element, which David also referred to and that is the media.

I remember Matthew Barrett, who was chairman of the Bank of Montreal, once, after I had been premier for a while, he came to see me. He said, "You guys are having a lot of trouble." I said, "Matthew, okay, you're the president of the Bank of Montreal, right? You go into work in the morning. Imagine you've got a scrum. You go down to your office at King Street. You don't get to go up the private elevator. You've got to go in, through with everybody else, and you've got a scrum of forty reporters every single morning saying, 'Do you know what your guy in the Sault Ste. Marie branch did yesterday? Do you know who he turned down for a loan?' and you go on and on. And you do that every day, every single day." And three times a day. I said, "You cannot compare the level of scrutiny and the fishbowl that we work in in comparison with any other walk of life."

MR. PAIKIN: Did he get it?

MR. RAE: I don't think you ever get it until you've been through it.

MR. EVES: That's true.

MR. PAIKIN: A part of what you all went through were, of course, demonstrations. And I've got to ask you this question, Mr. Harris. You had some of the most lively —

MR. HARRIS: Did I have the biggest?

MR. PAIKIN: I think you did. I'm pretty sure you did.

MR. PETERSON: I had the meanest.

MR. PAIKIN: You all had your share, but I want to know whether any of you changed or altered a decision that you made as premier based on the size or ferocity of a demonstration that you saw on the south lawn of Queen's Park, for example?

MR. HARRIS: Absolutely not. I don't think anybody will say that they did.

However, let me say this: There's two things. One, early on in my mandate we had a fundraiser in Kingston and the OPP that were travelling with me said, "We can't go in. It's going to be too violent. You're at risk." Anyway, we waited an hour and a half and we went in. And after, when we left and we asked about what happened, there was a fire set on the roof, there were all kinds of things.

And basically the report that I got from the people that travel with me is pretty much the same people that were there when Peterson came and when Rae came. And that helped, for me, to put these protests into perspective. It's a way to get on TV; often the issue didn't even matter.

Now, I do want to say the second point of some of these demonstrations. I think it probably helped bring our cabinet together, bring our caucus together, unite us in this cause.

MR. PAIKIN: A sense of being under siege?

MR. HARRIS: Well, yeah, maybe it's a siege mentality a little bit and a resolve. We always viewed we were doing the right thing, so if you had big demonstrations you had a communications problem to some people, or they weren't going to listen anyway.

MR. PAIKIN: Mr. Peterson, did you ever change your decision?

MR. PETERSON: No. I was just thinking of Michael's point in a contemporary context. I've been involved in this Caledonia deal or, at least, I was at the beginning, and I was involved in a huge riot. And people were screaming and yelling. I mean, it was really primitive; it was mankind at its worst.

And there was one particular guy who was yelling at me and dogging me and ragging me, and I finally said, "Where are you from?" He said, "Windsor."

He had seen this thing on television and it was like the devil threw a party and invited all his friends, right? And this guy just showed up to raise hell and to cause trouble, because that's what he liked doing. So I think we all understand that. And those kind of things never particularly bothered me.

MR. PAIKIN: Well, let me ask Bob Rae about this, because you, quite famously, on the first anniversary of your election, changed your position on public auto insurance. And there were a number of demonstrations prior to that which took place. Were they at all influential in your decision?

MR. RAE: No. There were hardly any demonstrations about public auto insurance, one way or the other.

MR. PAIKIN: Well, the industry put a few together.

MR. RAE: Well, you know, they weren't exactly homemade signs. I mean, those things you don't worry about.

I think what you worry about more is something which you actually think is spontaneous, you know, where you sort of say, "Well, what is public opinion really telling me here about something?"

The demonstrations that are highly organized and highly synthetic, you develop a strong resistance to those things because it's like mail-in campaigns. "Are you affected by letters that you receive?" and the answer is I'm not actually affected by mass mailings, which all have the same message and they're all put out by whatever lobby is out there. But occasionally a letter gets through and you see a letter and you say, "Actually, that person's got a point."

MR. PAIKIN: Do you recall an example, off the top of your head?

MR. RAE: No. I can remember feeling on Sunday shopping that we were on the wrong side of history, opinion had shifted and there was absolutely no point in sticking to a position that just didn't have enough public support to sustain itself. I think a lot of people went through that process. David went through it earlier than others.

MR. PETERSON: I think I should have agreed with that from the beginning. See, you guys get smart. They're good people but they're slow, Steven; that was the problem.

MR. PAIKIN: Let me move into our final segment. I want to talk about life after politics. And I want to know, Mr. Eves, you were in politics a long time, right? You were first elected in '81.

MR. EVES: Right.

MR. PAIKIN: And you just got out few years ago. Is there anything that you're doing now that compared to the thrill of being premier of the province?

MR. EVES: No. To use a line of Bill Davis', I think the most exciting day in the private sector is probably a little duller than the dullest day in government. I think that you're making decisions that impact on the lives of many, many millions of people. You're doing the best you can for the public good, but I don't think there's ever anything that compares with that in the private sector.

However, I think that I and everybody else here still contributes somewhat to public service in one way or another. Mr. McGuinty has asked me to help out with investment and trade matters in the province. It's not something that makes me a lot of money, but it's something that I relish doing and I like to do it to improve the lot of the people in the province of Ontario.

MR. PAIKIN: Is it difficult to recapture the purpose in private life that you clearly felt in public life?

MR. PETERSON: Ernie's right. Nothing will duplicate. I remember the thrill, the adrenaline rush, the sense of fun and the big influence you have in public life. But I now live at a much lower intensity level. There's lots of wonderful causes and there's lots of wonderful people that have been in political life.

So I'm involved in a lot of things from the University of Toronto to the hospitals, I lecture and I have a very happy life. Never the same intensity but, actually, I don't want the same intensity again. I've done it and I was proud to be there. I don't want to go back.

MR. PAIKIN: Mr. Harris, is it difficult to recapture the purpose of life now in the private sector that you had before?

MR. HARRIS: Certainly the excitement, the intensity, what was the word you used first?

MR. PAIKIN: Thrill.

MR. HARRIS: Yes, the thrill. Nothing, yes. Although maybe if I were made CEO of a company of a couple of million people sometimes in the private sector, looking for … no. I —

MR. PAIKIN: Do you want to leave your resumé at the door on the way out?

MR. HARRIS: Leave my resumé at the door. No, nothing will compare with that. Having said that, I certainly don't regret it. I think it was the most wonderful experience I had and I've been privileged. I think we would all say that, we've been privileged to have had this opportunity to serve and the learning that went on with it.

The sense of public purpose, you never lose that. I tell you, if a premier anywhere across this country or a prime minister called any one of us and said, "We've got an important thing. This is important for your country. It's important for your province. You know, we need ..." that purpose is there.

David's served. We're all there for that. It's certainly less stressful in many, many ways but I don't want to go back, either. I'm like David. I'm delighted ...

MR. PAIKIN: Look at Bob Rae laughing. Look at Bob Rae laughing.

MR. HARRIS: I don't want to go back. I don't know why anybody on the planet would want to go back.

MR. PETERSON: It's a valid question: "What's the matter with Bob Rae?"

MR. PAIKIN: There was a method to my madness of leaving you for the end here, Bob Rae.

MR. PETERSON: That was quite obvious.

MR. PAIKIN: [*Agenda* director] Michael, roll tape.

> **MR. RAE:** *As I declare today my candidacy for the leadership of the Liberal Party of Canada, I want to assure you that I'm going to devote myself to this task with all the — the energy and all the skill that I can muster.*

MR. PAIKIN: You're back in.

MR. RAE: Absolutely.

MR. PAIKIN: Was it just too thrilling to give up on it, ultimately?

MR. RAE: No. This is not about —

MR. PETERSON: To make more mistakes.

MR. RAE: This is not about adrenaline. I guess it's about service and this happens to be a moment when I feel I can be of service again in politics and public life, and if it happens, it happens. I was just going to say, for me, it's a great opportunity and these things don't happen very often.

And I felt at this particular time, this juncture in my life — I mean, if you had asked me the question five or six months ago, if we had had this panel, I did the Air India review for Mr. [Paul] Martin, I did work for Mr. [Jean] Chrétien on federalism around the world, I did work for Premier McGuinty on higher education. And we've all done very well in terms of an interesting life in a law firm. I had a wonderful time with the Goodmans firm, which is a wonderful place to be; Mike's there as well.

MR. HARRIS: We want you back.

MR. RAE: Yeah. We'll see what happens. Some people do, some people don't. But seriously, I guess at the end I don't regard politics as a bed of nails. I don't regard it as an impossible task. And I do regard it as a kind of a service. And I remember Ernie phoned when he had been out of politics for a while and he was thinking about going back in. And we were chatting about it because you can play golf more often, you can have a more comfortable life. You can make more money, everybody assumes you go into politics to make money. You don't. In Canada, you get out of politics to pay off the debts that you've built up when you were in politics. And that's just a reality of how we live.

But the fact of the matter is, when Ernie phoned me I said, 'Well, you have to ask yourself the question. When you're on the eighteenth tee, are you going to say to yourself, 'Geez, I wish I'd tried for that job. I wish I'd given it a shot,' or would you say 'I didn't really want to do it anyway'?" And it seems to me that's the kind of choice you face.

And I was talking about this with [my wife] Arlene, and she said, "Look, the same question. Is it something you want to try and is it something that if you try and don't make will you feel better than if you never tried at all?"

And for me, I've always said to my kids, there's nothing wrong with not getting something and there's nothing wrong with losing, but not trying if you think you've got something to do — that's something you should do.

MR. PAIKIN: So Mr. Rae left and came back. You [Mr. Eves] left and came back. And you two [Peterson and Harris] have constantly been rumoured to be on the comeback trail. Is this something that you just never get away from? Once you've been in, they always assume you want back in?

MR. HARRIS: Well, not everybody wants us back in, David. We both had successes and we both had experiences, but it's true. I did take a little bit of time to consider federal politics.

MR. PAIKIN: You were very much courted for the [new] Conservative [Party of Canada] leadership.

MR. HARRIS: Yes, I was. And I love the job that [Stephen] Harper's doing and I'm really glad I didn't do it.

MR. PAIKIN: You are?

MR. HARRIS: I'm very happy.

MR. PAIKIN: No regrets about that?

MR. HARRIS: No regrets at all.

MR. PAIKIN: Apropos of Mr. Rae's comments, you're not sorry you didn't try?

MR. HARRIS: No, no, not at all. As Bob says, you've got to ask yourself, "Do you want to win? Do you want to be prime minister of the country," not do you want to be leader of the party.

MR. RAE: No, absolutely.

MR. HARRIS: Do you want to be prime minister? Do I want to spend the next ten years campaigning for and then being the prime minister of the country? And perhaps, if I had not been premier, perhaps if I was twenty years younger, there may have been a lot of perhapses. But I had no difficulty making that decision and I've no regrets.

MR. PAIKIN: Mr. Peterson?

MR. PETERSON: I think it's either in your DNA or it isn't. I also think that there's a time to come and a time to go.

MR. PAIKIN: But you didn't go when you wanted to.

MR. PETERSON: No, I didn't want to go and I hated losing, but I accept it. And I also know you're going to lose or retire one day and you have to sort of build your own personal life to deal with that because everybody has that to deal with at some point or other. Sometimes it's voluntary, sometimes it isn't. I just think at some point we old guys have to fade into the woodwork and say it's time for others.

MR. RAE: What is that nonsense … partisan nonsense!

MR. PAIKIN: I'm going to jump in here and use my moderator's prerogative because we've got about two minutes left and I want to play some tape for Mike Harris still. Here is Mike Harris making history, something that hadn't been done in more than seventy years, going from third place to first place in one election. Roll tape.

> **MR. HARRIS:** *And my fellow Ontarians, having spent five years as leader of my party, meeting people where they live*

and where they work, discussing with them their — their hopes and their dreams for this great province, tonight, I am humbled.

MR. PAIKIN: At the end of the day, was that your best night in politics?

MR. HARRIS: It was the most exciting night in politics, and if exciting is the best, then that was it.

MR. PAIKIN: Okay. I want to read one more thing here, and there's a quote that I'm sure all of you have heard before, but I want to share it with our audience anyway. Here's Teddy Roosevelt.

> *It is not the critic who counts, not the man who points out how the strong man stumbles or where the doer of deeds could have done them better. The credit belongs to the man in the arena whose face is marred by dust and sweat and blood, who strives valiantly, who knows the great enthusiasms, the great devotions, who spends himself on a worthy cause who, at the best, knows in the end of the triumph of high achievement and who at the worst, if he fails, at least fails while daring greatly so that his place shall never be with those cold and timid souls who have never known neither victory nor defeat.*

MR. PETERSON: Hear, hear.

MR. PAIKIN: You say "hear, hear."

MR. PETERSON: I think we all agree with that.

MR. RAE: A great line.

MR. HARRIS: I think a great line, in life — not just politics.

MR. EVES: Absolutely.

MR. PETERSON: Hear, hear.

MR. HARRIS: A great line in life, too.

MR. PAIKIN: I want to thank all four of you for coming in for what was truly an historic broadcast. I know I send good wishes on behalf of the four of you to Bill Davis, who, I suspect, is watching on TV.

MR. PETERSON: Absolutely. He's better than the four of us put together, so get him on his own show.

MR. EVES: That's why you needed four of us.

MR. PAIKIN: We wish you well, Mr. Davis. Please get well soon. Great seeing you again. Much appreciated.

Epilogue

~

It's easy to give a classy election-night speech when you're celebrating a great victory. It's a lot harder to give one when you're licking your wounds from defeat, particularly when that defeat rests mostly on your shoulders as it almost always does when you're the leader.

So, even though it was almost three decades ago, I can still remember Prime Minister John Turner's election night speech on September 4, 1984. Brian Mulroney had just led the Progressive Conservatives to the largest majority government in Canadian history: 211 seats. Turner had just led the Liberals to their worst defeat ever: forty seats. And yet, when the cameras were on and Turner had to take responsibility for the Grits' disastrous performance, he confessed that "the people are never wrong."

Senator Hugh Segal echoed those thoughts after the 1987 Ontario election when his Tories won only sixteen seats, their worst showing ever, telling me in an interview for a TVO documentary, "It's true, the people are never wrong. But they are occasionally excessive."

It may be a cliché to say the people are never wrong, but that's not just a throwaway line politicians use to ingratiate themselves with the electorate for next time. Having seen my share of elections over thirty years in journalism, I can honestly agree with Turner's and Segal's point: the public gets it right. Even though they may not follow the ins and outs of politics as much as its practitioners do, and even though our first-past-the-post system is quite capable of distorting the way the votes break out, we always seem to get a result that is perfectly understandable.

That's not a partisan comment. It's simply an acknowledgement that, through some bit of inexplicable collective wisdom, the people seem to pick the right person for the right times. Or, if on those rare occasions they don't, their choice is at least understandable.

When he stepped down as Ontario's seventeenth premier, John Robarts said, "I am a man of my times, and my time is done." Ernie Eves said it well on the eve of the convention that would make him Ontario's twenty-third premier: "There are different people for different times. I firmly believe that. If you look through the history of anywhere, that seems to be the case."

Partisan people will question to their graves the wisdom of Ontarians' voting for premiers they couldn't stand. But if you watched provincial politics in 1990, you could well understand Bob Rae's getting the most votes, given the other choices of a Liberal premier who made a cynical, early election call for his, but not necessarily the province's, benefit, and a Conservative opponent whose party clearly wasn't ready to govern.

The day after that 1990 election, I called Robert Nixon, whose father, Harry (a former premier), was the longest-serving MPP in Ontario history. Bob Nixon led the Ontario Liberal Party on four different occasions. Nixon waited from his first election in 1962 to 1985 to get to the government side of the House. Then it was over in five years. When I asked him whether he thought people were horrified that they'd elected Ontario's first ever NDP government, he said: "Quite the contrary. I think they think it's kinda neat."

Nixon understood the wisdom of the people and that, given the options, nearly four in ten of us voting for Bob Rae made sense.

Similarly, I have heard the Mike Harris haters for years excoriate Ontarians for electing his government not once but twice. But given the "course correction" many Ontarians thought the province needed after ten years of Liberal and NDP reign, the Harris choice becomes much more understandable. I never thought Ontario suddenly became a haven for the John Birch Society. My sense was, Ontarians wanted to drag their government back toward the middle, which the other two parties had vacated. This is not to endorse any particular policy in the *Common Sense Revolution*. But it is to say, given the choices at that moment in history, Harris' election is completely understandable.

Which leads me to Dalton McGuinty. There is a woman in Oakville named Peggy Tupper who is a frequent visitor to Twitter. She is as "small-c conservative" as they come. She hates intrusive government that wastes our tax dollars and has never hesitated to disparage the McGuinty government whenever she thinks they're doing that, which, in Peggy's view, only happens when the former premier is breathing. I hear from Peggy all the time. She truly despises the McGuinty government. But even Peggy would acknowledge McGuinty didn't get elected three times by brainwashing people. The voters considered the Liberal leader, considered the alternatives, and made their choice. Peggy doesn't agree with their choice. In fact, she hates it. But even she would admit there was a rationale behind McGuinty's three-peat.

Somehow, Ontarians have chosen the person who best reflects their character, values, and priorities of that moment in time. And when the political parties take their eye off the ball and choose someone who makes *them* feel better but isn't the right person for the times (e.g., Frank Miller, Ernie Eves, Lyn McLeod, Howard Hampton), the general public "corrects" the parties' mistakes by inviting others to take over.

What qualities have the last half century of occupants of the premier's office had? I would say, above all else, genuine authenticity. They knew who they were and didn't try to package themselves into something they weren't. While that sounds obvious, it continues to astound me how many party leaders give themselves over to the image-makers and ask them to transform them into something they're not. John Robarts absolutely was the "Chairman of the Board," as his nickname indicated, and people knew it. After a couple of missteps, Bill Davis figured out that the public wanted someone who made them feel comfortable during turbulent times. He was the right man for his times, and the more time passes, the more wisdom people see in his decisions and how he governed. But when Davis' successor, Frank Miller, tried to take his party further to the right and seemed to be more about the past than the future, Ontarians punished the PCs and opted to give a guy they barely knew a shot at it. Six months before that 1985 election, polls showed 10 percent of the public knew who the leader of the Ontario Liberals was. Six months later, everyone knew David Peterson. He was their premier, and an authentic representation of the possibilities that the mid-1980s represented.

People forget, but Bob Rae got elected with 37.6 percent of the total vote in 1990. Three months later the honeymoon with the NDP was still going strong. Rae's approval rating was north of 60 percent. Bob Nixon was right. People did think electing Rae was kinda neat. But not even the skillful Rae could overcome the combination of the worst recession since the Great Depression, Bay Street fear-mongering, union leaders in revolt, and the media, the opposition, the federal government, and almost everyone else telling Ontarians they'd made a mistake.

Interestingly enough, Ontarians don't seem to need their leaders to be cut from the same mould. There could not have been two more different types of leaders than Bill Davis and Mike Harris, in every way. And yet they were members of the same party. The largest plurality of Ontarians seemed just as content with the bland Davis as they were with the fire-breathing Harris. In both cases, the public knew what they were getting: authentic leaders, who may have defined leadership differently, but were highly skilled at demonstrating their version of it.

Davis has been out of politics for almost thirty years now, and yet his intuitive understanding of where the electorate is, is still pretty sharp. "Fundamentals don't change," he says. "Honesty doesn't change. Principle doesn't change."

What a privilege it's been to come to work every day, and in the course of doing that job, try to gain some greater insight into the twenty-five people who've led this province for the past 146 years, since Confederation. And I've been honoured to know the last nine. They don't always get it right, and they'd be the first to tell you that. But John Turner definitely was right: the people never get it wrong. And I can't wait to continue to find out whom the people want to task with the responsibility of leading Ontario even further into the twenty-first century. It's still, for me, one of the great unfolding dramas of our time.

ACKNOWLEDGEMENTS

First and foremost, I owe a debt of gratitude to the nine premiers who have led the province of Ontario through the last half century, and in particular to the eight I've had the privilege of knowing personally. While some were more successful than others at the ballot box, they all brought something unique to politics. And I have very much appreciated, through my perch at TVO, having had the chance to interview them, to find out professionally how they make decisions, and personally what makes them tick.

Covering the White House is supposed to be the most prestigious job in political journalism. However, I'd venture to guess that 99 percent of those who cover the White House never get to ask a single question of the person who is the focus of their daily reporting. That's not for me. So I'm grateful to these premiers for having made time over the years to talk to someone who, for better or worse, has always been fascinated with how and why they do what they do.

I hope the premiers won't mind my singling out William Davis for special mention. Mr. Davis gave me a quote during an interview we did more than a quarter century ago about what his post-political life was like. That quote gave me more insight than any other I've heard in thirty years of covering politics. When I suggested to him that his new job as a corporate lawyer — making much more money, seeing more of his family, having saner hours, and not being hounded by the media — must be the best job he'd ever had, Mr. Davis' response inspired me to write 600 pages and two books (*The Life* and *The Dark Side*) to try to better understand those who go into public life.

"Steven," he said to me, "this job of being a corporate lawyer, on its most fascinating day, can't touch being premier of Ontario on the dullest." Just brilliant.

Ironically, while I've spent three decades watching and analyzing what these premiers have done, the tables have now been turned. On occasion, they now email or call me, sometimes to praise, sometimes to criticize something I've done on TVO. Knowing William Davis may call to chew you out for a bad interview has a way of keeping you on your toes. All I can say is, keep the comments coming. I value the feedback, and the fact that you all still care enough to make sure we get it right honours all of us at TVO.

Let me also recognize the role the often-underappreciated spouse plays. As journalists write the first draft of history, we often neglect to understand that none of these premiers could have got to where they got to without the support and understanding of their spouses. So kudos to Kathleen Davis, Ann Miller, Shelley Peterson, Arlene Perly Rae, Janet Harris, Isabel Bassett, Terri McGuinty, and Jane Rounthwaite, all of whom I've had the pleasure of meeting, some of whom I've got to know well, and one of whom I had the additional pleasure of working for — Isabel Bassett, when she was chair and CEO of TVO.

Let me also thank the trio at Dundurn Press I had the most contact with: former MP Patrick Boyer, also the publisher of Blue Butterfly Books, who initially put the bug in my head to do a book on the premiers; my fellow Hamiltonian, publisher and founder Kirk Howard (who named Dundurn after the castle in Hamilton I visited so many times as a kid); and editor Cheryl Hawley, who was a consummate pro and delight to work with in bringing this book to life. I'm also grateful to Rob Lee and his Late Night Transcripts service. Rob did the painstaking work of transcribing all the interviews with the premiers.

For reasons I've explained in this book, and in my three previous books about it, I think covering politics is different from anything else you can cover in journalism. In my view, there's no other field that combines power, service, accountability, personality, policy, history, personal relationships, and gamesmanship like politics. So I have a lot of time for the people who do it. And I enjoy the company of those who love it as much as I do. So, to that end, I also want to put in a good word for my three travelling political amigos: Arthur Milnes, David Lockhart, and Thomas Harrison. We've had the privilege of travelling near and far to spend time with some of the great legends of the political world, and gents, here's hoping we can keep doing so for many years to come.

I know for partisans, winning is everything in politics. Since I'm not a partisan, I value other things much more. Such as staying power. Or making a wonderful contribution. So I'd like to acknowledge some others I've met along the way who made their mark and taught me much, even if they didn't get to the top of the mountain.

Robert Nixon has the unique distinction of having led the Ontario Liberal Party on *four* separate occasions. His father, Harry, was the last Liberal premier before the forty-two-year-long Tory dynasty, and remains the longest-serving member of the Ontario Legislature ever. His daughter Jane Stewart was a federal cabinet minister. Bob Nixon turned eighty-five years old this past summer. I still love my annual visit to his farm in St. George near Brantford with friends such as Howard Brown or Mark Littell. Mr. Nixon is never short on great political war stories from the past. May he continue to tell them for years to come.

Robert Nixon, beside the final resting place of his father, Harry, who was the last Liberal premier of Ontario before the forty-two-year-long Tory dynasty.

Darcy McKeough, "The Duke of Kent," served with Roy McMurtry in the cabinet of William Davis. They're seen here in June 2010.

Floyd Laughren gave me my honorary degree from Laurentian University in 2012. Then he asked me to be chancellor of Laurentian in 2013. I'm still not over the shock. He's seen here with my daughter, Giulia, during a Christmas visit to Sudbury in 2009.

Darcy McKeough's nickname was "The Duke of Kent" when he was Ontario treasurer on and off (but mostly on) from 1971–78. He had the gumption to run for the PC Party leadership to replace John Robarts at the tender age of thirty-eight and was the kingmaker who crowned William Davis the winner of that 1971 convention. Mr. McKeough and I also get together from time to time to talk about the old days, and I congratulate him on the milestone he will celebrate this year. Fifty years ago, on September 25, The Duke won his first election, and a handful of those still around from the Class of '63 raised a glass earlier in September to mark the occasion. Mr. McKeough turned eighty years young earlier this year.

Floyd Laughren was partially responsible for one of the most shocking events in my life. I've known the man they used to call "Pink Floyd" since his more radical leftist days in the NDP caucus at Queen's Park. A little over a year ago, as chair of the board of governors of Laurentian University, he handed me an honorary degree. A few months ago, he and that university's president, Dominic Giroux, took me out for a beer after a program *The Agenda* shot in Sudbury. After an hour of small talk, getting caught up, the board chair and the president utterly shocked me by asking me to succeed Aline Chrétien as Laurentian's second chancellor. I have never been speechless in my entire life, but I was then. One of the joys of the job will be continuing to see Floyd Laughren on a regular basis. He is one of the most honourable people I've ever met in politics.

To this day, I remember the first politician I ever "interviewed." I put that word in inverted commas because I was sixteen years old at the time, and my parents had purchased (through a charity auction) the right for their two sons to have lunch at the Legislature with the new leader of the Ontario Liberals, Stuart Smith, who represented Hamilton West. Dr. Smith and I still see each other every now and then and joke about that first "interview," which was unforgettable for me and, much to my amazement, is still remembered by him all these years later. Dr. Smith turned seventy-five this year and is now commissioner of the semi-pro Intercounty Baseball League. Now *that's* cool.

It's very unfashionable for journalists to admit they may have heroes in politics. Let me be unfashionable. We lost one of the most significant politicians in Canadian history during the past year. He never became prime minister or premier. In fact, he was only a cabinet minister for about nine months. But Lincoln MacCauley Alexander was a hero of mine. An MP in my native Hamilton for twelve years, Ontario's lieutenant-governor for six, "Linc," as everyone called him, was a trailblazer in so many ways. The Ontario Provincial Police Headquarters in Orillia is named after him, as are four schools in the Greater Toronto Area, a hall at the University of Guelph, and the highway that "links" Hamilton to Highway 403 in the west end and the Queen Elizabeth Way in the east end. Lincoln Alexander was a great man who knew how to bring people together (as his highway now does). I think of him often and the world misses him.

Two of my favourite University of Toronto professors deserve mention for nurturing a love of politics in me. Stefan Dupré, who sadly died this past year, was one of the greats. And Peter Russell taught me the history of the Canadian constitution. Yes, it is still a nerve-wracking experience to have Professor Russell on our program. And I've apparently now been around long enough that I've had his son Alex on *The Agenda* as a guest as well.

Stuart Smith (right) led the Ontario Liberal Party from 1976 until David Peterson succeeded him in 1982. They're seen here at the farewell event to Dalton McGuinty at Maple Leaf Gardens in January 2013.

Lincoln Alexander was a champion to so many people and of so many causes. He's seen here applauding at an event for the Ontario Heritage Trust, of which he was honorary chair.

TVO's dynamic duo: CEO Lisa de Wilde and board chair Peter O'Brian.

I've been lucky enough to have had a number of professional experiences outside TVO — moderating leaders' debates during election campaigns, being appointed chancellor at Laurentian, and writing five books, to name just a few. But I have never forgotten that *none* of those opportunities would have come to me had the foundation of my professional life not been there. So I need to thank all the people who help put *The Agenda* on television five nights a week, and constantly feed our online offerings at *TheAgenda.tvo.org* as well. From our super-supportive chairman of the board, Peter O'Brian, to our dynamic CEO, Lisa de Wilde, to the wonderful gang at TVO I get to work with every day, my deepest thanks to all of you for making the provincial broadcaster the best place I've ever worked.

And finally, the best people in the world that I know: my grandmother Shirley Sibulash, for whom (fingers crossed) we will hold a hundredth birthday party in December; my parents, Marnie and Larry Paikin, without whose love and guidance nothing would have been possible; my brother, Jeff, who is simply the funnest guy I know in this world (I know *funnest* is not a word, but it describes him to perfection); my wife, Francesca Grosso, who puts up with my impossible schedule and somehow makes it all work (and who has her own book coming out this fall on the history of Sunnybrook Hospital — you should buy that one too!); and my kids, Zach, Henry, Teddy, and Giulia, who remain the most fascinating people in my life.

I thank all of you for being in my world.

Index

OF RELATED INTEREST

Two Billion Trees and Counting
The Legacy of Edmund Zavitz
John Bacher
978-1-459701113
$14.99

Edmund Zavitz (1875–1968) rescued Ontario from the ravages of increasingly more powerful floods, erosion, and deadly fires. Wastelands were talking over many hectares of once-flourishing farmlands and towns. Sites like the Oak Ridges Moraine were well on their way to becoming a dust bowl and all because of extensive deforestation. Zavitz held the positions of chief forester of Ontario, deputy minister of forests, and director of reforestation. His first pilot reforestation project was in 1905, and since then Zavitz has educated the public and politicians about the need to protect Ontario forests. By the mid-1940s, conservation authorities, provincial nurseries, forestry stations, and bylaws protecting trees were in place. Land was being restored. Just a month before his death, the one billionth tree was planted by Premier John Robarts. Some two billion more would follow. As a result of Zavitz's work, the Niagara Escarpment, once a wasteland, is now a UNESCO World Biosphere. Recognition of the ongoing need to plant trees to protect our future continues as the legacy of Edmund Zavitz.

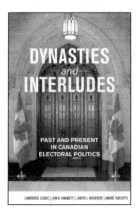

Dynasties and Interludes
Past and Present in Canadian Electoral Politics
Lawrence LeDuc
978-1-554887965
$35.00

Dynasties and Interludes provides a comprehensive and unique overview of elections and voting in Canada from Confederation to the recent spate of minority governments. Its principal argument is that the Canadian political landscape has consisted of long periods of hegemony of a single party and/or leader (dynasties), punctuated by short, sharp disruptions brought about by the sudden rise of new parties, leaders, or social movements (interludes).

Changes in the composition of the electorate and in the technology and professionalization of election campaigns are also examined in this book, both to provide a better understanding of key turning points in Canadian history and a deeper interpretation of present-day electoral politics.

Available at your favourite bookseller

DUNDURN

VISIT US AT
Dundurn.com
@dundurnpress
Facebook.com/dundurnpress
Pinterest.com/dundurnpress